CULTURE CLASH

CULTURE CLASH

THE MAKING OF GAY SENSIBILITY

Michael Bronski

South End Press   **Boston, MA**

Bronski, Michael.
    Culture Clash.
Bibliography: p.
    Includes index.
    1. Homosexuality--United States.   2. Homosexuals--United
States--Psychology.   3. Popular culture.
I. Title.
HQ76.3.U5B69   1984   306.7'66'0973   84—50941
ISBN 0-89608-218-0
ISBN 0-89608-217-2 (pbk.)

cover collage: Walta Borawski
cover design: Ellen Herman and Amy Hoffman
text design, typesetting, and layout done by Ellen Herman, Amy Hoffman, and the South End Press Collective

South End Press/302 Columbus Ave./Boston, MA 02116

Contents

Acknowledgments

This book—or any book—does not materialize in a vacuum. It is the product of more than 15 years of friendship, love relationships, one night stands, and community. Community—from bar life where no one speaks until the charm is suddenly turned on at "last call" and talking begins, to political gatherings where everyone is friendly until the discussion commences and the meeting ends with no one speaking to anyone else. Community—in public cruising grounds where pleasure may be exchanged, wordlessly and passionately: in the tradition of Whitman's image, Edward Carpenter's vision, and both the spirit and letter of good pornography. Without such community, this book would not exist.

And specifically, to my parents, who told me that the most important things in life were to think for oneself and pursue good, deep friendships. I have followed their advice, even if they are surprised at the outcome.

To John Mitzel and Charley Shively for more than ten years of friendship and a never-ending source of intellectual stimulation and respect, both of which are extremely hard to come by. Many of the ideas in this book would not have been articulated without their input and criticism.

To Ellen Herman and Amy Hoffman who have criticized, edited, and nurtured this book (Ellen's idea) to its completion. It would not have happened without them.

To Andrea Loewenstein for being both critic and psalmist, co-worker and playmate, but most of all friend and family.

And finally, for Walta Borawski who has been with me these past nine years and persevered along with, and in spite of, the past year. Words cannot do justice.

Part I

The Making of Gay Sensibility

Friday, June 28, 1969. 1:45 a.m. There was a full moon. Judy Garland had been buried that afternoon. And the queers on Christopher Street had had enough. When the New York City Vice Squad proceeded with a routine raid upon the Stonewall Inn they were attacked by an angry crowd of drags, dykes, and street queens. Supposedly limp-wristed pansies threw broken bottles, cobblestones, and anything else they could get their hands on. The police locked themselves inside the bar until reinforcements arrived. Someone uprooted a parking meter, battered down the door, and tried to set the bar aflame with lighter fluid. The siege lasted 45 minutes. It was reenacted again on Saturday night.[1]

The Stonewall Riots established a homosexual militancy and identity in the public imagination that was startling and deeply threatening. Americans had always been aware of the existence of gay women and men. They were most obvious as hairdressers, chorus boys, girl's gym teachers, and repressed deans of women's colleges. They were the butts of jokes and Joe McCarthy had exposed them all for the pinkos they were. They were also the visible tip of the iceberg of an entire culture's repressed sexual fears and desires. As an early gay liberation slogan declared: "We are your worst fear; we are your best fantasy."

It was almost 1970. America had survived the Depression, fought World War II, plugged through the 1940s, rested in the stolid 50s, and weathered the social upheavals and grassroots discontent of the turbulent 60s. "Culture,"as the word is commonly used, is not a fixed entity and the "American Way of Life" had turned out not to be the enduring life force that *Life* magazine, Norman Rockwell, and the editors of *Readers Digest* sold to an increasingly sophisticated public. Social change occurs and cultural norms move with it. The battle for black civil rights and the second wave of American feminism had begun, and organized opposition to the war in Vietnam had spread across the country.

"The American Way of Life," as portrayed by mass media, was white, middle class, and decidedly heterosexual. In America, there were no people of color, no poor, and most certainly no gay people. This lie of American social life was accepted and reinforced by books, movies, magazines, and television. The real social framework of America had roots in diverse racial, ethnic, socio-economic, gender, and class identified groups, but who is accepted or excluded from the prevailing ideology—and why—is subject to many variables. The interaction of a sub or counter culture with the rest of society is a complex, *political* process.

This book is about the interactions of gay subculture with the patriarchal heterosexuality that is the dominant cultural norm. The overriding presumptions of this dominant culture clearly affect the alternative culture: they limit, restrict, and restrain it. The subculture finds ways to respond to this repression. It hides, recreates itself, takes secret or coded forms, and regroups to survive. The existence of an alternative homosexual culture also affects prevailing cultural norms. Sometimes, as during the past 15 years, change happens because gays make overt demands and, occasionally, those demands are met. A slow social process of assimilation and integration also takes place: values, ideas, social patterns, and styles once identified solely with gay men begin showing up in the dominant heterosexual culture.

After the Stonewall riots, the American press and public could no longer ignore the movement for liberation among lesbians and gay men. They may not have taken it as seriously as other political movements, but they were forced to recognize that it existed. This recognition was reflected in the fairly quick acceptance in popular, though not academic, circles, of the word "gay." It was also adopted by news magazines such as *Time* and *Newsweek* (although *The New York Times* insists to this day on using "homosexual").

There had been a homosexual civil rights movement, both secret and overt, dating back almost 100 years. In the early 1950s, the gay male Mattachine Society and the lesbian Daughters of Bilitis were founded. Both were concerned with promoting a better under-standing of homosexuals to the general public and making some rudimentary challenges to the inequalities of the American legal system. Although both groups had relatively small memberships, they drew public attention to the existence of homosexuals in the society. It was Stonewall and the subsequent formation of vocal, militant gay liberation groups, however, that forced the attention of the country on the demands of gay people not only for civil rights but for an appreciation of their place in American society.[2]

The gay liberation movement provided more visibility than lesbians and gay men had ever had before. The movement cry of "we are everywhere" was reflected in the media attention to the legal and civil liberties demands which gay people were making. This new visibility created an atmosphere which made it more possible for gay people to be open and comfortable about their lives. But it also brought on antagonism from many who had, until then, been able to ignore or dismiss homosexuality as a perversion practiced by a small, socially dangerous group of people. Gay liberation, therefore, brought not only gay people, but also homophobia, out of the closet. Lesbians and gay men were easy targets for hatred. This homophobia was particularly noticeable in the politics and the literature of the new right. By pronouncing homosexuality to be antithetical to traditional sexual values, gender roles, and the family the right was able to use gay visibility and homophobic fears for its own political ends.

In the early 1960s homosexuals were interviewed on television seated behind potted palms to hide their identities. In 1972, Jill Johnston, *Village Voice* dance critic, announced her lesbianism on the *Dick Cavett Show*, flashed a big smile, and waved "Hi Mom!" Since then, the lesbian and gay movement, in all of its manifestations, has proved to be, if not acceptable, then at least good copy. *Time, Rolling Stone, Newsweek, The New York Times*, and a host of other national publications printed features ranging from "Are Homosexuals Sick"*(Newsweek)* to "How to Spot Homosexuality in Children" (*Harpers Bazaar*), to "Gays on the March" *(Time)*. In 1969 *Time* indicated its ambivalence on the topic by beginning an article "The love that once dared not speak its name now can't seem to keep its mouth shut."[3] The American public was intrigued and titillated by the exposure of "new" sex lives and the stories kept coming. The movement itself was mobilizing with new energy and could produce instant demonstrations—"zaps"—against any media coverage it deemed unfair or prejudiced.

Rebellion was not the only aspect of the gay liberation movement that made the headlines. In their war to secure civil rights and equal protection under the law, lesbians and gay men waged battle after battle with the American legal system. The court-martial of Lieutenant Leonard Matlovich in 1975, who fought to keep his position in the United States Air Force, and the custody fight of lesbian mother Mary Jo Risher for her son in 1974, both made national headlines and became subjects of TV docudramas. Every city and state had its own stories: anti-discrimination ordinances, custody cases, injunctions against police harassment, fights to get permits for gay pride marches. What was once a bizarre or off-beat feature story now forced its way into front page news.

As gay communities across the country proliferated and began to exercise power through already established electoral and political processes, they discovered that they could create as well as be featured in the news. They could not, however, control *how* the media covered the news. In 1979, the growth of gay political clout in San Francisco and the backlash against it resulted in the homophobic CBS News documentary, *Gay Power, Gay Politics*. The program was a good example of how the mainstream media continued to control the limits of acceptability. The founders of Mattachine and DOB had realized the importance of creating a gay-controlled media 25 years earlier and both founded magazines for their members: *ONE* and *The Ladder*. Since then, and especially since Stonewall, an expanding network of magazines, newspapers, journals, and book publishers has defined its purpose as interpreting the world from a distinctly gay viewpoint.

While homosexuality has gradually made its appearance in popular culture, there is another, more subtle way that it influences dominant culture: assimilation. Like any subculture, gay culture and all of its artifacts, customs, interests, activities, and aesthetics is gradually rendered acceptable and homogenized into the mainstream. This is a familiar pattern in a culture which has created gourmet soul food restaurants, "You've Come A Long Way Baby" cigarette ads, and "Kiss Me, I'm Italian" bumper stickers.

While people have accepted the notion of subcultures based on class, race, ethnicity, religion, or even gender, there is still some resistance to accepting the notion of a group defined by the shared experience of an outlawed sexuality. In 1970, when liberal educator Benjamin De Mott became president of the experimental New College in Sarasota, Florida, the Gay Student Union lobbied for a course in gay culture. DeMott was said to have quipped, "They'll have to invent it first."

Because all sexuality carries with it such negative connotations in our society, a culture based upon the experience of a particular sexuality seemed unthinkable. Even the most liberal of intellectuals and social philosophers thought of homosexuality as a private choice which had nothing to do with a social or political identity. The politicization of sexuality is the cornerstone of gay liberation. In the early 1950s, Mattachine members believed that homosexuals were "largely unaware" they were "a social minority imprisoned within a dominant culture" and that they were kept ignorant by a "language and culture that did not admit the existence of the Homosexual Minority." Later, during the next decade, gay liberationists took up the feminist slogan "the personal is political" and insisted that such matters as sexual choice, desire, activity, and fantasy had to be viewed within the context of what Christopher Isherwood has called the "heterosexual dictatorship." That is, being gay placed a person at odds with the dominant cultural norms and gay identity thus took on a political dimension. The gay and feminist movements questioned the distinction between the private and the public, the personal and the political, with the goal of fomenting social change.

Change occurs slowly. More than ten years after De Mott's dismissal of gay studies, Midge Decter wrote a long article in *Commentary* (September 1981) which attempted to "explain" gay liberation. Decter admits to having been "more than a little astonished" when the "homosexual rights movement burst upon the scene." She accused gay liberation of defining "homosexuality as nothing more than a casual option among options." She defined gayness as a private choice which results in one's placing oneself at odds with "the tides of ordinary mortal existence," and declared that the moral importance of this "weighty act" of choice had driven homosexuals to self-destruction. "Faced with the accelerating round of drugs, S/M, and suicide, can either the movement or its heterosexual sympathizers imagine they have done anyone a kindness?" Refusing to understand gay liberation as a political movement, Decter conjured up the old stereotypes of gay self-hatred and masochism.[4]

When gay liberation was young, it could be dismissed with a single quip. Ten years later, it took Decter 20 pages of bad prose to prove that the movement was yet another homosexual death trip. DeMott refused to acknowledge a gay community with a culture; Decter, forced to acknowledge it, attempted to discredit it.

A subculture is any group excluded from the dominant culture, either by self-definition or ostracism. The outsider status allows the development of a distinct culture based upon the very characteristics which separate the group from the mainstream. Over time, this culture creates and recreates itself—politically and artistically—along with, as well as in reaction to, the prevailing cultural norms. No counterculture can define itself independently of the dominant culture. By definition it is distinct, yet there is always the urge, if only for survival's sake, to seek acceptance. Concurrent with this urge, the ruling culture, which perceives non-conformity as threatening, attempts to diffuse the conflict by eradicating the fringe culture, by either extinction or assimilation.

The uneasy relationship between the mainstream and the counterculture is symbiotic. The essential characteristics that define the counterculture are politicized precisely because they differ from, criticize, or defy the majority norms. This not only sets up a clear conflict, but also challenges the status quo. By refusing to conform to the gender and sexual arrangements that define and reinforce the patriarchal heterosexual cultural norms, homosexuality—the sexuality itself and any of its cultural manifestations—becomes both a threat and a political issue.

Because sexuality is both a private (psychological) and a public (social) issue, the interaction of homosexual subculture with the dominant (i.e. heterosexual) culture occurs on many levels. Paul Goodman speaks of this social/psychic overlap.

> A "minority" exists because of a psychic boundary, that makes a real or fancied distinction *relevant*, and the anxious clustering and self-identification of the "majority" to keep on the right side. The minority is always a repressed part of the majority. Prejudice is not merely a projection of the repressed *onto* the minority, but indeed, it creates the minority *qua* minority and maintains it in being. Thus, the minority is always right in its demands, for it is moral and psychological wisdom for the majority to accept the repressed part of itself.[5]

Homosexuality, and by implication homosexuals, have been placed outside prevailing social structures as defined by most theological, legal, and medical models. In Western culture, homosexual activity was first categorized as a sin.[6] With the rise of materialism and the decline of religion, it became a transgression against the social, not the moral order: a crime. After Freud, homosexual behavior—under the auspices of medicine and psychology—was "understood" as a sickness, which was physical, psychological, or both, depending on the theory. Although new categories were invented for homosexual behavior, they did not totally replace the old. For many today it remains a sin, a crime, *and* a disease.

Homosexual behavior has existed throughout history. Because of moral and social taboos there is very little written material explicitly discussing the feelings or attitudes of persons engaged in such activity. It is therefore difficult to know if gay people historically experienced their sexuality as a series of isolated acts or if they formed a sense of identity of which their sexuality was an integral part.

The evolution of a homosexual identity is necessary to the development of a homosexual culture. Although this sense of identity may have existed earlier, it was only after the formulation of the medical model, in the later part of the 19th century, that a distinct homosexual identity emerged. Before the 19th century, some have argued, there were homosexual acts, but no homosexuals.[7] The new medical perception of sexuality in relation to the individual and not in relation to the moral or social order was the social change that allowed homosexual identity to "come out." Sexuality was viewed as an intrinsic part of the personality structure. New trends in social thinking promoted the idea of the individual as a social entity as equally or more important than the larger social structures and conditions which shaped society and culture.

Because the religious, social, and legal prohibitions against homosexual acts did not disappear, homosexual identity retained its stigma. However, although identified and defined as outcast, the homosexual counterculture developed a positive gay identity. There are two key characteristics in the early evolution of the gay sensibility. The first was social criticism in reaction to the oppression and ostracism placed upon the homosexual by society. Political theorists like Edward Carpenter, scientists like Havelock Ellis, and writers like John Addington Symonds all criticized prevailing social norms from the perspective of outsiders. In their blatantly polemical works, they challenged existing ideas about sexuality and gender as well as prohibitions against same sex attraction.

Because of social and legal injunctions against homosexuality, many artists and writers could not be public about their sexuality and their work was infused with a plethora of signs and codes that allowed the like-minded to identify one another. This was the second key characteristic. It was conscious, as in some poems by Alfred Douglas, or subconscious, as in the nonsense verse of Edward Lear or the plays of James M. Barrie. Some interpreters believe that Gertrude Stein developed her impressionistic and obscure style of writing in order to write about being a lesbian.

During the 19th and 20th centuries, homosexual writers and artists created a distinct political, artistic, and social identity. This sensibility has a history, an evolving set of definitions, and a future. Since gay liberation has come out of the closet, many of the ideas, creations, and values which originated in gay culture have been avidly incorporated into the mainstream, thus co-opting their radical potential. In the late 1970s, sexual iconography which originated in gay male S/M subculture (the leather man, the construction worker, the cowboy) catapulted the disco group, The Village People, into stardom. Although the images were used as a ticket to commercial success, The Village People offered, to those in the know, gay clues and intimations of homosexuality in their lyrics. Within two years of their formation, they appeared on national television with that most vocal of homophobes, Anita Bryant. What gay men had created as a response to an oppressive stereotype rapidly became assimilated and so totally processed by popular culture that the irony of juxtaposing the group with Bryant seems to have been lost on the show's producers and most of the audience.

Western thought and history is characterized by white, male, heterosexual control. This patriarchy is sustained through a complex network of gender, racial, and sexual arrangements. Erotophobia—the fear of sexuality—is a bulwark of support for these standards. Patriarchy is supported, to a large degree, by sexual repression. Controlling sexuality legally, medically and psychologically is a way for men, who are at the top of the power structure, to retain and strengthen their position. Because sexuality, and the gender arrangements and racial myths which develop in conjunction with it, is such a powerful urge, its control is necessary for establishing and reinforcing a hierarchical structure. Female and male homosexuality confront—head on—the gender and sexual aspects of this control. Because many homosexuals do not conform to strict gender assignments, they are perceived as a threat to normal sexuality. Homosexual activity and passion directly challenges the heterosexual demand that all sexuality be reproductive. It exists in and of itself without any *raison d'etre*, and as such is an affront to the heterosexuality and the sexual repression that remain controlling forces in our culture. This threat to the existing power structure is what makes homosexuality political. Much of gay culture and the gay sensibility, implicitly and explicitly, rests upon this threat.

I am using the term "gay culture" to mean gay *male* culture. Most cultural naming is done by and for a male constituency: the works and words of women are, for the most part, invisible. Lesbian writers, artists, philosophers, and social thinkers are unclaimed either by a mainstream or a gay male tradition. The tradition that contemporary gay culture rests upon is a male tradition. This notion that culture means *male* culture is endemic to patriarchal thinking. It is not surprising that the emerging gay male counterculture— whatever its differences with the patriarchy may be—reflects this basic sexism. As early as 1897, Havelock Ellis included in his pioneering book, *Sexual Inversion*, a list of famous homosexuals to give a history and a degree of respectability to his new, radical theories about sexuality. His list included Christopher Marlowe, Sir Francis Bacon, Oscar Wilde, and Walt Whitman. Sappho was mentioned, but the list was predominantly male. It is common practice for any ostracized group to "claim" as many famous personages as possible. Gay culture has continued Ellis' list, thus establishing itself as essentially male in history and tradition.

By retaining and promoting the works of men, gay culture has provided itself with an acceptability and visibility that has been denied lesbian culture. Consequently, gay culture reflects the misogynist attitudes that are part of patriarchy. It is also true that because homosexual males are not considered "men" by the usual cultural norms, they have, in many instances, expressed an affinity for the images or works of women. This can be seen in the cult of the opera diva or the progressive non-sexist representations of female characters in the works of Henry James or E.M. Forster. However, in many ways gay culture does not reflect a more androgynous vision than the dominant culture.

Homosexuals have created a separate culture that reflects their attitudes, moods, thoughts, and emotions as an oppressed group. However, the gay sensibility also interrelates with the rest of the world. Susan Sontag has written that "every sensibility is self serving to the group that promotes it."[8] Much of gay sensibility (and the whole range of interests it encompasses) aims to gain some entry into, some acceptance by the mainstream culture. In the same way that other groups point to their particular achievements as a way of legitimizing themselves, so do homosexuals. The most common version of this legitimization plea is the argument that gay men excell in the innovation and promotion of the arts. The term is used loosely to mean both "high culture" (opera, "serious" writing, ballet) and "popular culture" (movies, musicals, designing and decorating). Gay input into these fields is generally recognized and we have the stereotype of the tittering interior decorator to prove it. Equally stereotypical is the gay artist, such as E.M. Forster, whose sexuality is excused (or unacknowledged) because of his genius.

In her "Notes on Camp," Susan Sontag has written that "Homosexuals have pinned their integration into society on promoting the aesthetic sense."[9] Sontag maintains that "homosexual aestheticism and irony" is one of the underpinnings of modern sensibility (along with "Jewish moral seriousness"). Because she is writing about the phenomenon of camp, she focuses primarily on the double-edged insight which gay men develop because of their position simultaneously inside and outside of the culture. But she ignores two other gay stances in relation to culture which are equally significant.

The first is an appreciation and involvement with high culture purely as a means of attaining a certain degree of acceptance. Because high culture (opera, classical music) carries with it respectability by definition, many gay men are drawn to it in order to cash in on that respectability. While it is possible to see in an art form such as opera the qualities that Sontag ascribes to camp, it is also possible to understand gay interest in opera as a method of achieving upward mobility. Such an attitude may lead to viewing all culture with a deadly seriousness or an overly fussy preoccupation with correctness. One assumes a position of respectability by association rather than achievement. This attitude is pejoratively called in gay slang "piss elegance." It implies a criticism of gay men who ape rather than reinvent the status quo.

The second mainfestation of gay sensibility not covered in Sontag's analysis is the gay culture that has developed since Stonewall. Gay men *and* lesbians have consciously created a culture that is based upon their own analyses, experiences, and perceptions. Unlike previous gay culture, this work has *not* depended significantly upon reacting to mainstream culture or pressures. While the principles of distinctiveness vs. integration hold true for this new culture, the fact that it is politically motivated places it in a different category. Lesbians and gay men used stereotypes to attack gender roles when they publicly embraced the stereotypes of butch dyke and nelly queen that had been forced upon them; and then again when they decided to play specific gender expectations to the limit with the butch faggot and the femme dyke. The boundaries of sexuality were broadened when gay men spoke openly of their sexual desires and activities. Realizing that they had a history, albeit a hidden one, homosexuals reclaimed the past and used it to reinterpret their lives and create a context for their own feelings and imaginations. This context—gay liberation—became both a political movement and an articulated subculture. The general public may not have liked it, but there was no way to deny that gay liberation, its culture and sensibility, was a fact of life.

Susan Sontag has written: "To snare a sensibility in words, especially one that is alive and powerful, one must be tentative and nimble."[10] The same is true when tracing the social and intellectual history of a sensibility. What follows is a schematic overview in which I will try to make some sense of the historical and social phenomena pertinent to the evolution of gay culture.

Walt Whitman

Walt Whitman could only have been American. The Good Grey Poet, to be called by post-Stonewall gay liberationists, "The Good Gay Poet," broke radically from all earlier poetic forms. His free verse thrilled and distressed the traditional literary community. But it was content as well as form that stirred controversy among Whitman's supporters and detractors.

Born in 1819, Whitman lived through the democratic populism of the rise of industrialization, the Jacksonian era, the Civil War, and the manifest destiny ideology of the Gilded Age. His poetry praised the common people and rested upon an idealized vision of human bonding and equality. Beyond this populism, Whitman saw and described a spiritual bond which united the masses. This metaphysical connectedness was expressed in Whitman's poetry through physical and sexual imagery. Perhaps in reaction to increasing urbanization and industrialization, Whitman's democratic idealism was closely tied, spiritually and physically, to nature. This modified version of transcendentalism, mixed with the obvious sexuality of his verse, moved Whitman to the center of the U.S. literary scene.

Public and critical opinion of Whitman ranged from the ecstatic to the hysterical. "I think him the equal, and in many respects the superior of the much misunderstood Jesus," wrote William Sloane Kennedy, a journalist whose early training included Harvard Divinity School.[11] For every enthusiast there were those who claimed Whitman's poetry to be the devil's work. When what Whitman thought would be the sixth and final edition of *Leaves of Grass* was published, (he was constantly revamping and reediting the poems) the Boston District Attorney wrote to James R. Osgood and Company, Whitman's publishers: "We are of the opinion that this book is such a book as brings it within the provisions of the Public Statutes respecting obscene literature and suggest the propriety of withdrawing the same from circulation and suppressing the editions thereof." Osgood suggested some deletions but Whitman withdrew the book and found a new publisher in Philadelphia.[12]

Not only banned in Boston, *Leaves of Grass* was removed from the library shelves at Harvard and placed in a special case, under lock and key, with other books thought to impair students' morals. Thomas Wentworth Higginson, Boston writer, editor, and public opinion maker, stated that Whitman's mistake was not in writing *Leaves of Grass*, but in not burning it later. Abolitionist and Quaker John Greenleaf Whittier reportedly flung his copy of the poems into the fire. If American public opinion was divided about Whitman, his reputation among Europeans—especially the English socialist intelligentsia—was consistently well established. Celebrities and common people came to the poet's house in Camden, New Jersey to pay him homage. After a visit, Oscar Wilde, his own star on the ascendant, wrote "My Dear, Dear Walt. There is no one in this great wide world of America whom I love and honor so much."[13] Whitman's concepts of the personal, the sexual, the political, and the spiritual took firmer root in England than in his own country.

There had always been a strong undercurrent of homoeroticism in classical American literature.[14] Although the contexts and actions described are particular to the American experience, three themes had roots in European literature. The first is the importance of male bonding in the major relationships of the work. The second is that the setting is usually "natural," (i.e., pre-civilization: a wilderness or a pastoral setting) removed from the social and moral proscriptions of civilization. And finally the male bonding usually occurs between a white man and a "noble savage," the idealized male companion who, because of race or ethnicity, is portrayed as primitive and therefore "natural."

These themes surfaced in the earlier part of the century with the Leatherstocking novels of James Fenimore Cooper. They emerged more explicitly in the works of Herman Melville—a contemporary of Whitman's—and can be seen in the writings of Hawthorne, Twain, and Poe. The most obvious, and well known, examples of this are probably the chapter in *Moby Dick* in which Ishmael and Queequeg bed down together, the relationship between Huck Finn and Jim, and the relationship between Natty Bumpo and Chingachgook in *The Last of the Mohicans*. More obscure examples are Melville's *Redburn* and Poe's *The Narrative of Gordon A. Pym*, a remarkable novel which succinctly discusses questions of race as well as sexuality and gender. Most of these American writers were heterosexual and used these themes as a way to deal with their misogyny and to ease the projected vengeance fears brought on by their racism.

These three components crystallized in early American literature, recurring later as conventions for homosexual writing. The male/male relationships, the flight from a repressive culture, and the equation of less civilized with less repressed all allowed the white, European, homosexual writer to imagine a situation in which he was safe—not sinful—and befriended. These same themes are evident from the homosexual poetry of the late 19th century, called Uranian after the early psychological coinage of "urning" as a word for same-sex lovers, through *Maurice* by E.M. Forster and up to James Barr's 1950s *Quatrefoil.*[15]

It was within this context of unconscious literary homoeroticism that Whitman made his first conscious efforts to glorify male "adhesiveness." Although Whitman's descriptions of male bonding and male/male relationships were not all that different from Melville's, they were generally more explicit and more integral to the conscious effect of his work as a whole. Whitman's concept of homoeroticism, and sexuality in general, played a major role in his larger political and philosophical framework. Robert K. Martin succinctly encapsulates this underlying structure in all of Whitman's work:

> ...Whitman displays the development of a political consciousness which bases its call for social reorganization upon a major change in sexuality. Whitman, like his contemporaries Engels and Lewis Morgan, appears to have seen the connection between the organization of society (concentration of capital and power) and the organization of sexuality (marriage and the subordination of women). Whitman's democratic society...would require the suppression of the aggressive forces which lead to capitalism, imperial power, and the domination of women by men, and their replacement by the loving forces which lead to an economic system of sharing, a political system of universal participation, and a sexual system that allows for a full expression of sexual energy in ways that are neither aggressive nor directed towards use. In other words, Whitman's ideal society requires socialism, democracy, and homosexuality.[16]

Although Whitman used the term "adhesiveness" to denote the affection and sexuality that exists among men, the imagery in many of his poems makes it quite clear that he was speaking of homosexual activity. Even though, late in life, he denied the homosexuality of his poems, his vision of sexuality, especially homosexuality, and its place in the social structure was analytic rather than just descriptive.

Thus, most of Whitman's writings can be called "gay" in the modern sense because they make a conscious effort to place homosexuality in a larger social scheme.

"Song of Myself," the first poem in *Leaves of Grass*, is the poet's discovery of the goodness intrinsic to his being a homosexual. It begins with the realization of the nurturing tie that exists between his body and soul. "Undisguised and naked" in the woods, Whitman invites his soul to lie on the grass with him. Both body and soul then engage in what is clearly an autoerotic union:

> I mind how we lay in June, such a transparent summer
>   morning,
> You settled your head athwart my hips and gently turned
>   over on me,
> And parted the shirt from my bosom-bone, and plunged
>   your tongue to my bearstript heart,
> And reached till you felt my beard, and reached till you
>   held my feet.[17]

The poet, masturbating, has invoked his soul and the calm that follows his orgasm unites him to God, man, and nature.

> · Swiftly arose and spread around me the peace and joy and
>   knowledge that pass all the art and argument of the
>   earth;
> And I know that the hand of God is the elderhand of my
>   own,
> And I know that the spirit of God is the eldest brother of my
>   own,
> And that all the men ever born are also my brothers...

This is how the poet accepts his sexuality in an erotophobic world. From this acceptance he goes on to revel in his homosexual fantasies. In the persona of a lonely young woman, he sees "twenty-eight young men, and all so friendly"; "An unseen hand also passes over their bodies./ It descends trembling from their temples and ribs." This fantasy is so exciting that the poet masturbates again to it: "They do not know who puffs and declines with pendent and bending arch./ They do not think whom they souse with spray."

It is a quick step from the fantasy of the erotic encounter to the encounter itself.

Is this then a touch?...quivering me to a new identity,
Flames and ether making a rush for my veins,
Treacherous tip of me reaching and crowding to help
   them,
My flesh and blood playing out lightening, to strike what
   is hardly different from myself...

Behaving licentious towards me, taking no denial,
Depriving me of the best as for a purpose,
Unbuttoning my clothes and holding me by the bare waist,
Deluding my confusion with a calm of the sunlight and
   pasture fields...

I talk wildly...I have lost my wits...I and nobody else am the
   greatest traitor,
I went myself first to the headlands...my own hands carried
   me there.

After his orgasm, he again feels the peace and union he experienced with other men, God, and nature.

Swift wind! My soul! Now I know it is true what I
   guessed at,
What I guessed when I loafed on the grass,
What I guessed while I lay alone in my bed...
   and again as I walked the beach under the paling stars of
   the morning.

Whitman found nourishment in his sexuality, and because he did not support the accepted structures of monogamy he was able to reach out with unfocused sexual energy to encompass all other men in the intensity of the moment. Whitman's sexual vision is very close to the promiscuous lifestyle led by many modern gay men. This promiscuity is not simply a by-product of the sexual revolution of the 1960s but is a way for gay men to reaffirm their social, political, and sexual identities: the personal and the political inextricably bound together.[18] The union of the social and the sexual that many gay liberationists speak about today can be seen in Whitman. "What is it I interchange so suddenly with strangers?/ What with some driver as I ride on the seat by his side?" All of this fills him with a spontaneous feeling of love: "The young fellow drives the express wagon...I love him though I do not know him."

Whitman's ideas about sexuality were advanced for his time but many of his ideas about gender were culture-bound, and his view of women's place in his democratic ideal is ambiguous. The work of women artists was a source of inspiration and ideas for his own work. He read and praised the works of such feminists as Margaret Fuller and Frances Wright. He claimed that the novels of George Sand—especially *Consuelo*—first inspired him to write poetry. He was also a fan of the opera and stated that the work of some sopranos—particularly Marietta Alboni—gave him the foundation for his break from the conventional, metered, rhymed poetic line. Whitman's enchantment with and emotional connection to the female voice does not seem all that different from modern gay male attitudes towards some women singers: both are motivated by a desire to break through social barriers and find a new means of emotional expression.[19]

Although a proponent of sexual freedom, Whitman's image of women's sexuality was tied to the prescribed roles of mother and nurturer. In the "Children of Adam" section of *Leaves of Grass*, which he saw as a companion to the more frankly homoerotic "Calamus" poems, he tried to reunite the body and soul in hopes of achieving a natural sexuality that was the cornerstone of his philosophical and political thinking. And while he could sympathize with the oppressed prostitute, or proclaim the glories of female sexuality, it is clear that women did not interest him as much as men. Caught in the middle of a rapidly evolving society, Whitman clung to the idea of the natural, native America (which for him and many other male writers was totally male) in the wake of the gradual "feminization" of the culture. Since women were seen as the perpetrators of repressive gentility, they were at odds with Whitman's basic notions of sexuality and freedom. "That only when sex is properly treated, talked, avowed, accepted, will the woman be equal with the man, and pass where the man passes, and meet his words with her words, and his rights with her rights."[20] Although Whitman saw sexual repression as the primary cause of social inequality, Whitman, and others, identified this repression with women.[21]

This stance associated Whitman closely with the tradition of Cooper and other American male writers in their flight from civilization. With Whitman, however, it was not so much fleeing from women, *per se*, as it was finding a safe place to express his sexuality. If Whitman the sexual liberationist has informed a great deal of contemporary gay male culture, so has his cultural "gender gap." The explicit presentation and celebration of male sexuality has been a source of tension not only to the straight world, but to many feminists and lesbians since the public proliferation of gay culture since Stonewall.

Whitman's importance, for both poetry and gay culture, is that he understood the relationship between the personal and the political; he acknowledged the importance of sexuality and found in it the possibility for progressive social change. His vision of ideal democracy comes directly from his experience as a homosexual.

In *Democratic Vistas*, Whitman wrote:

It is the development, identification, and general prevalence of that fervid comradship, (the adhesive love, at last rivaling the amative love hitherto posing imaginative literature, if not going beyond it,) that I look for the counterbalance and offset of our materialistic and vulgar American democracy...I say democracy infers such loving comradeship as its inevitable twin or counterpart, without which it will be incomplete, in vain, and incapable of perpetuating itself.[22]

The acceptance the poet finds for his sexuality in "Song of Myself" forms the basis of his egalitarianism, and the social and political tranquility of the society he envisions is mirrored in this sexuality. Whitman may have been the first to celebrate consciously his homosexuality and place it in a broad context. In the "Calamus" poems, the homoeroticism is undeniable.

For the one I love most lay sleeping by me under the same
    cover in the cool night,
In the stillness of the autumn moonbeams his face was
    inclined towards me,

And his arms lay lightly around my breast—
and that night I was happy.[23]

Although he would later use the word "adhesiveness" to describe "love for comrades," Whitman was at a disadvantage in speaking of his sexual nature. To declare it openly, rather than indicate it, would have opened him to charges of both sin and crime. Going further than anyone else had, Whitman took the precaution of choosing a word—adhesiveness—that might carry more meanings than the strictly sexual. Pioneer though he was, Whitman was unable to make the leap from a consciously identified to a "named" sexuality. At the end of "Song of Myself," he wrote:

> There is that in me...I do not know what it is...but I know it is in me. Wrenched and sweaty...calm and cool then my body becomes, I sleep...I sleep long. I do not know it...it is without a name...it is a word unsaid, It is not in any dictionary or utterance or symbol.[24]

"It" was the love that dare not speak its name.

While Whitman was writing in America, more scientific writing was being done in Europe. First, and most important among these writers was Karl Heinrich Ulrichs, a lawyer who, from 1862 to his death 35 years later, published many books and pamphlets defending and attempting to understand homosexuality. According to Ulrichs, homosexuality occurred when there was an abnormal development in the human embryo. While the genitals that developed were male, the same change did not occur in the part of the brain which regulates the sex drive. Thus, the male homosexual is an *anima muliebrus virile corpore inclusa*—a female soul in a male body. Ulrichs was unhappy with the connotations of the words "sodomite" and "pederast" and turned to Plato's *Symposium*, where those who worship Aphrodite Urania (Heavenly Love) "are attracted towards the male sex, and value it as being naturally the stronger and more intelligent...their intention is to form a lasting attachment and partnership for life."[25] Ulrichs Germanized the word to *urning*, but the English "Uranian" was widely used in both scientific and literary circles. (In 1869, a Hungarian doctor, Karoly Marie Benkert, coined the word "homosexual," which was to have a more lasting use.)

Ulrichs' theory, which was more metaphysical than scientific, had several effects. By making homosexuality a congenital rather than an acquired trait, it was possible to argue that legal and moral proscriptions against same-sex activities were wrong and inhumane; the Uranian was born, not made. Ulrichs proposed that the condition made people different, not sick or inferior. His assumption that homosexuals constituted a "third sex"—or "intermediate sex" as it would later be called— reinforced traditional gender roles, thus perpetrating the notion that homosexual men were effeminate and that lesbians were mannish. This image has had a lasting effect upon the way that dominant culture portrays homosexuals. Ulrich's reference to Plato's *Symposium* tended to legitimate same-sex affection and actions, and the implication that it was "stronger and more intelligent" than Aphrodite Pandeumia (Common Love) was a necessary defensive reaction to the opprobrium that had always been associated with homosexuality.

Ulrichs' reconceptualization of same-sex attractions profoundly affected the social history of homosexuality. By arguing that it was congenital it was possible to conceive of a homosexual identity, to see that identity interacting with the rest of the social pattern, and to formulate a history and a culture around that identity. The basic philosophical, political, and literary aspects of this emerging identity were to be explored and charted over the next 50 years by three Englishmen: Edward Carpenter, John Addington Symonds, and Havlock Ellis.

Edward Carpenter

Edward Carpenter was born in 1844 into an upper middle class Victorian family. He went to the university and, planning a career in the ministry, was ordained in 1870 while functioning as a curate at Cambridge. While there, he read one of the first British editions of Whitman's verse. Within two years, he fled Cambridge and his church duties to tour Florence. His passion for Greek and Renaissance sculpture—the glorified male form—surfaced his own homoerotic desires and he returned to England determined to renew and restructure his life.

The surviving Greek statuary of Florence not only ignited Carpenter's sexuality; it presented an alternative to what he perceived as the increasingly oppressive constraints of Victorian morality and materialism. As did many gay men after him, Carpenter idealized Hellenic culture, and to some degree the Italy which had preserved it, finding in it the political and philosophical roots of a new democratic vision. In 1877, Carpenter visited Walt Whitman and began forming a philosophy which would embrace his political principles, his spirituality, and his sexual desires. In 1881, he wrote *Towards Democracy*, a long Whitmanesque poem which attempted to reunite nature, sexuality, and the human body outside of the boundaries of "civilization."

English socialist and radical groups in the late 19th century attracted many people and dealt with varied concerns. Industrialization had not only caused a sharpening of class lines, but prompted a general cultural retreat that expressed itself in an aesthetic based on the thinking and teaching of such theorists as William Morris and John Ruskin. In what was the beginning of the "art for art's sake" movement, this aesthetic generally endorsed crafts over industry, the rural over the urban, and a return to a simpler mode of living over the rigidity and narrowing of contemporary life. This new aesthetic concept eventually led to the idea of totally divorcing the utilitarian aspects of art (especially in the service of a moral or political end) from its creation or meaning. This new aesthetic was to have its most extreme advocate in Oscar Wilde who championed the perfection of the creation over any meaning which might be construed from its content.[26] While some socialists were involved in trade unionism, others endorsed suffrage as a way of dealing with women's oppression, and still others involved themselves with questions of culture and ethics: the relationship between people and nature, personal relationships between men and women, and the problems of leading a fuller, more complete life in an overly organized world.

Carpenter's life had changed radically from his Cambridge days. In 1883 he moved to Sheffield where he made a small living out of gardening and sandle-making. In 1886, he helped found the Sheffield Socialist Society and in time, through his writings, became a well known figure in socialist circles. Many of the people involved in Sheffield and other socialist centers such as Leeds and Bristol attempted to consolidate their personal lives and political thought. For them, the vision of equality included thinking and acting on such issues as feminism and sexuality.[27]

During this time, Carpenter himself was exploring the relationship between sexuality and civilization. In 1891, he embarked on what became a life-long relationship with George Merrill and in the early part of the decade wrote three essays—"Women," "Marriage," and "Sex Love"—which were published by the Manchester Labour Press. In 1895, he completed *Love's Coming of Age*, an exploration of sex and society that included his essay "The Intermediate Sex." Carpenters' publisher, T. Fisher Unwin, refused to publish the book because of the repercussions of the Wilde trial but Carpenter was able to secure publication with the Manchester Labour Press again. The main contention of *Love's Coming of Age* was the obsession of Western culture with "the arbitrary notion that the function of love is limited to childbearing, and that any love not concerned with the propagation of the race must necessarily be of dubious character." While arguing that love was both social and emotional, Carpenter insisted that the fact of sexual pleasure never be denied.

Insisting on the importance of sexual pleasure in and of itself was perhaps Carpenter's most radical philosophical concept. Sexuality, in the Western tradition, had been viewed solely as a means of procreation. This utilitarian notion was strengthened by the onset of industrialization and the materialist philosophy of the necessity of production. Even today, one of the criticisms most frequently leveled at gay people is that they do not reproduce, i.e., are not productive. (These critics do not distinguish between the non-procreative character of gay sex and the fact that many gay people have children.) Because women have been viewed as essentially non-sexual in our culture, it has been gay men, and not lesbians, who have personified the concept of a non-reproduction-oriented sexuality. This new vision of sexuality, along with the growth of organized feminism, the increasing availability and use of birth control technology, and the general breakdown of the traditional family unit have all resulted in the formation of a unique modern sensibility in which an unrepressed and acknowledged sexuality plays a major role. Because of their identification with eroticism, gay men are on the cutting edge of this sensibility. Male homosexuality, as liberation from and threat to the existing cultural norm, is therefore worthy of both assimilation and attack.

Carpenter attempted to place same-sex love in a historical context. In 1902, he published *Iolaus: An Anthology of Friendship*, a survey of male/male relationships in literature from the ancient Greeks to Whitman. In 1908, he collected and reworked his essays on homoeroticism in one volume entitled *The Intermediate Type*, which argued that this intermediate or third sex contained the best elements of the other two. While many Uranian writers extolled the primacy of male qualities and upheld the Greeks as an ideal, Carpenter's ideas of feminist and socialist egalitarianism allowed him to take a more critical approach.

> Nothing is more surprising to the modern than to find Plato speaking, page after page, of Love, as the safeguard of the states and the tutoress of philosophy, and then to discover that what we call love, *i.e.* the love between man and woman, is not meant at all—scarcely comes within his consideration—but only the love between men—what we should call romantic friendship. His ideal of this latter love is aesthetic; it is an absorbing passion, but it is held in strong control. The other love—the love of women—is for him a mere sensuality...But it is evident in this fact—in the fact that among the Greeks the love of women was considered for the most part sensual, while the *romance* of love went to the account of friendship, we have the strength and weakness of Greek civilization. Strength because by the recognition everywhere of romantic comradeship, public and private life was filled by a kind of divine fire; weakness, because of the non-recognition of women's equal part in such comradeship, her saving, healing, and redeeming influence was lost, and the Greek culture doomed to be that extent one-sided. It will, we may hope, be the great

triumph of modern love (when it becomes more of a true comradeship between men and women than it yet is) to give both to society and to the individual the grandest inspirations, and perhaps in conjunction with the other attachment, to lift the modern nations to a higher level of political and artistic advancement than even the Greeks attained.[28]

Because homosexual acts were still illegal in Great Britain, Carpenter had to be very careful of how he worded his writings on same-sex male relationships. It was not unusual for him to refer to them as "friendship" or to borrow Whitman's phrase, "the love of comrades." Since explicit discourse about sexuality was impossible or unsafe during much of history, many writers coded their literary productions with ambiguous phrases and images and it is difficult to know if they are speaking of actual sexual or emotional/affectional experiences.[29]

The actual physical experience was probably less important than the sentiments involved in much of Carpenter's writing, although, as is clear from the following verses, Carpenter feels a strong erotic attachment to the images in his material.

> You, proud-curved lipped youth, with brown sensitive
>   face,
> Why, suddenly, as you sat there on the grass, did you turn
>   full upon me with those twin black eyes of yours,
> With gaze so absorbing so intense, I a strong man stumbled
>   and was faint?...
>
> Solemn and dewy-passionate, yet burning clear and
>   steadfast at the last,
> Through the long night those eyes of yours, dear, remain
>   to me—
> And I remain gazing into them.[30]

The Mediterranean appearance of his subject reflects Carpenter's own experience of self-discovery in Florence and the English fascination with the non-Anglo—and therefore more "primitive" and "natural"—cultures. This labeling of non-anglo cultures, seen in a positive, pro-sex light by these men, was also based in and inseparable from deeply rooted standards of white British racism and political and cultural imperialism. The same impulse can be found in the photographs of Sicillian youth by the German gay photographer, Baron von Gloeden, the artistic studies of boys in the work of Boston photographer F. Holland Day, and in novelist Charles Warren Stoddard's *South Sea Idyll.* While the lure of the "primitive" clearly has a sexual subtext, it also represents a longing to recapture a past free of social constraints and prohibitions.

Carpenter and other like-minded Europeans began using Whitman's code words "comradeship" and "adhesiveness" when discussing same-sex physical activity and relationships. Outside of his poetry, Whitman himself never admitted (and in one famous instance denied) his homosexual life. The difference between the public (writing and speaking) and the private (how one actually lived one's life) was to some extent maintained. It is ironic that Carpenter spent a great deal of his adult life openly living with a male companion, yet was cautious in his prose. While other writers found confirmation of their sexuality in the past, Carpenter looked to the future. In a dream vision he sees:

> The love of men for each other—so tender, heroic,
>   constant;
> That has come all down the ages, in every clime, in every
>   nation,
> Always so true, so well assured of itself, overleaping
>   barriers of age, or rank, or distance.
> Flag of the camp of Freedom;
> The love of women for each other—so rapt, intense, so
>   confiding, so close, so burning passionate,
> To unheard deeds of sacrifice, of daring and devotion,
>   prompting;
> And (not less) the love of men for women, and of women
>   for men—
> On a newer greater scale than it has hitherto been
>   conceived.
> Grand, free and equal—gracious yet never
>   incommensurable—
> The soul of of Comradeship glides on.[31]

The gay sensibility, which helped other writers to reinvent the past, allowed Carpenter to imagine a new future where homosexuality and same-sex affection (as well as all other sexuality) could exist securely and grow.

John Addington Symonds

John Addington Symonds was a cultural historian, critic, and a contemporary of both Carpenter and Wilde. Born in 1840, he realized his homosexual nature late in adolescence. Nevertheless, he married at the age of 24 and eventually fathered three daughters. Discovering Whitman's poems a year after his marriage, Symonds began his life's work of understanding the sexual and cultural aspects of same-sex love in general and its meaning in the writings of Walt Whitman in particular. Besides his numerous essays, biographies, and translations from the ancient Greek Symonds also wrote poetry. In 1871, he sent Whitman "Love and Death," a celebration of male/male friendship and loyalty. By way of introduction, he included a fawning letter humbly explaining Whitman's influence upon his work.

As I have put pen to paper I cannot refrain from saying that since the time I first took up *Leaves of Grass* in a friend's room at Trinity College, Cambridge six years ago till now, your poems have been my constant companions...I have found in them pure air and health—the free breath of the world—when often cramped by illness and the cares of life.[32]

This letter began a long correspondence between the American poet and his English apostle.

I have pored for continuous hours over the pages of Calamus, as I used to pore over the pages of Plato, longing to hear you speak, *burning* for a a revelation of your more developed meaning, panting to ask—is this what you would indicate?—Are then the free men of your lands really so pure & loving & noble & generous & sincere? Most of all did I desire to hear from your own lips—or from your pen—some story of athletic friendship from which to learn the truth."[33]

As late as 1889, Symonds was still asking the same questions of Whitman; the quest for assurance had become a little more personal.

I shall ask you about things which have perplexed me here—to which I think you alone could have given me an acceptable answer. All such matters will probably sink into their proper place in the infinite perspective and when we meet, a comrade's hand-touch and kiss will satisfy me, and a look into your eyes.

A year later, after much evasion on both sides, Symonds finally came to the point.

I want next to ask you a question about a very important portion of your teaching, which has puzzled a great many of your disciples and admirers. To tell the truth, I have always felt unable to deal, as I wish to do, comprehensively with your philosophy of life, because I do not even yet understand the whole drift of "Calamus"...In your conception of Comradeship, do you contemplate the possible intrusion of those semi-sexual emotions and actions which no doubt occur between men? I do not ask whether you approve of them, or regard them as a necessary part of the relation? But I should much like to know whether *you are prepared to leave them to the inclinations and conscience of the individuals concerned?*...I agree with the objectors I have mentioned that, human nature being what it is, and some men having a strong natural bias towards persons of their own sex, the enthusiasm of "Calamus" is calculated to encourage ardent and *physical* intimacies.

Symonds ended his letter with an obsequious, calculatedly off-hand reference to his own interests.

> It is perhaps strange that a man within 2 months of completing his 50th year should care at all about this ethical bearing of Calamus. Of course I do not care much about it, except that ignorance on the subject prevents me from forming a complete view of your life-philosophy.[34]

Whitman finally answered the question with such a flurry of disclaimers that the letter verges on parody. (The original has been lost but Whitman's original draft remains.)

> Y're of Aug. 3ed just rec'd and glad to hear f'm you as always...Ab't the questions on Calamus pieces &c: they quite daze me. L. of G. is only to be rightly construed by and within its own atmosphere and essential character... that the Calamus part has even allowed the possibility of such construction as mentioned is terrible—I am fain to hope the pages themselves are not to be even mention'd for such gratuitous and quite at the time entirely undream'd & unreck'd possibility of morbid inferences—wh're disavow'd by me & seem damnable. Tho' always unmarried I have had six children—two are dead—one living southern grandchild, fine boy, who writes me occasionally. Circumstances connected with their benefit and fortune have separated me from intimate relations. I see I have written with haste & too great effusion—but let it stand.[35]

Most traditional Whitman scholars have seized upon this as proof of Whitman's heterosexuality. They have found the letter to be filled with "consternation and anger"[36] and have noted that "the anger fairly burns from his scalding reply."[37] They ignore Whitman's years of friendly correspondence avoiding this very question. More recent Whitman scholarship examines the poet's life and work from a post-Stonewall perspective. Robert K. Martin and Jonathan Katz in particular see the letter as "comic" and a joke in the tradition of gay sensibility: an outrageous denial of the perfectly obvious. Whatever the letter's subtext, it is most probable that Whitman was unable to answer truthfully because to do so would have amounted to an admission of criminal activity and might have placed him in danger of legal prosecution. Even if chances of this were slim, the possibility of general public criticism might have been enough for Whitman to fear risking his popularity. Symonds, however, was rather put out by the poet's response; he did, after all, know the true answer. He wrote to a friend: "That is clear enough; & I am extremely glad to have the statement—though I confess to being surprised at the vehemence of the language."[38] Never one to give up, Symonds later wrote: "Whitman never suggests that comradeship may occasion the development of physical desires. On the other hand he does not in set terms condemn, deny or warn his disciples against their perils."[39]

The "comedy of eros" that sustained and finally defeated the Whitman/Symonds correspondence has a deeper meaning than a humorous historical misunderstanding. Symonds, Carpenter, and other Victorian same-sex lovers looked to the Greece of antiquity for a sane, workable model of sexuality in everyday life. Alongside of this classical model they also had hopes pinned on the newly forged, apparently more egalitarian American social structures. They found the specifics of their search in Whitman: a meeting of the sexual and social. Urged on by the popularized notion of the "noble savage," (which appears in literature like Aphra Behn's *Oroonoko* (1678) and was given philosphical underpinnings by Rousseau) English social thinkers had turned to the new world for a loosening of what they perceived as the stifling restraints of English culture. The social freedoms of America as the Europeans imagined them included more social mobility and the possibility of extended and meaningful social (and sexual) relationships for men.

Symonds' prolonged insistence that Whitman verbalize the true meaning of his "Calamus" poems was a desperate attempt to satisfy his own longings for a new, reliable structure on which to base his sexuality. He did not understand that his ideals of American freedom did not correspond to the reality. "Perhaps, after all," wrote Oscar Wilde in *The Picture of Dorian Gray*, "America never has been discovered. I myself would say that it has merely been detected."[40] Whitman was important to British intellectuals because his poetry confirmed and defined their ideals of a non-European, egalitarian social structure. They believed that while the British class system was based upon birthright, America's depended on money. The truth was that ethnic, racial, and economic constraints strongly defined and protected the American class system. Symonds and others viewed the New World as holding new freedoms; they viewed these freedoms in a metaphysical rather than a historical context. The gay sensibility, as it was evolving through Symonds, depended upon the notion of acceptance and an upward mobility within the social system rather than upon Carpenter's utopian socialist vision of entirely restructuring social and economic networks.

While Carpenter looked to the future, Symonds appealed to the past for insight and inspiration. At the age of 33, just after beginning his correspondence with Whitman, Symonds marshalled his knowledge of Greek culture and wrote *A Problem in Greek Ethics*. Although not published for another ten years, (1883) and then only in a private edition of ten copies to be distributed among friends, *A Problem in Greek Ethics* was probably the first positive examination of homosexuality to appear in English. Symonds' analysis of Greek culture was overly simplistic and romantic. He presented the Greeks as "an example of a great and highly developed race not only tolerating homosexual passions but deeming them of spiritual value and attempting to utilise them for the benefit of society."[41] Symonds used his analysis of Greece to integrate his own sexual feelings into a socially acceptable framework. He shared none of Carpenter's criticisms of gender arrangements or of slavery in the social and economic structure of Athenian society.

Although not as critical as Carpenter of the British class system, Symonds' poetry makes clear his romantic judgment about the importance of personal vs. social loyalty.

> I come to save thee, Ithocles, or die:
> Better is death than shame or loveless life.
> I love thee as I love this land we tread,
> This dear land of our fathers and our gods:
> I love thee as I love the light of heaven
> Or the sweet life that nourisheth my soul;
> Nay, better than all these I love thee, friend;
> And wouldst thou have me die, dishonoured die,
> In the fair blossom of my April days,
> Disconsolate and disinherited,
> With all my hopes and happiness undone?

"What will men say, Lysander, if we love?"
"Let men say what they will. Let us be pure
And faithful to each other to the end."[42]

The tone and language of the poem are emblematic of themes that were to occur later in both Symonds' work and the writings of other homosexuals: the desire for and inclination towards the beautiful, the idealization of male friendship, and the transcendence of personal feelings and experiences over social expectations.

A Problem in Greek Ethics took a circuitous route towards Symonds' true concern, but, eight years later, he began to write *A Problem in Modern Ethics*, one of the first attempts to discuss homosexual love in the light of science, psychology, medicine, and legal reform. The book could also be seen as a closely reasoned explication of Whitman's "Calamus" poems and his essays in *Democratic Vistas*. Symonds wrote to his daughter, Margaret, who knew of her father's non-public life, that it was a painful book: "I am glad to have got through the fierce tension of this piece of production even though I am left with a gnawing pain in my stomach—stomach or heart, I know not which..."[43]

Symonds attempted to correct what he saw as the wrongheadedness of much previous writing on homosexuality, and, taking a cue from the progressive stance of Karl Ulrichs, proposed a primarily psychological rather than physiological theory of the etiology of homosexuality. Rejecting the notion that heterosexuality was "natural" because it could result in procreation, he felt that "the first thing is to force people to see that their passions in question have their justification in nature."[44] He proposed an analysis in which sexuality was "a rhythm of subtly graduated differences extending from the extremity of sexual inversion up to the most positive type of sexual instinct."[45] Symonds also had the practical aim of legal reform in mind. Early in 1891 he wrote to his close friend Henry Dakyns:

I am glad to hear you have got my Essay. If you would do me a kindness, please scribble over its blank pages etc. something of your thoughts, & send the printed thing back to me. If you like, I will return it to you. But, as you know, it is only sent forth to stimulate discussion. I thought that the best way to do this would be to give it in the form of a Ms in print, which I have done. Enough of that. Though I must say that I am eager about the subject from its social and juristic aspects. You know how vitally it has in the past interested me as a man, & how I am therefore in duty bound to work for an elucidation of the legal problem.[46]

Quoting Edward Gibbon, Symonds traced the history of anti-homosexual legislation from the court of Constantine, where laws were based on the Old Testament. A woman accused of adultery was only:

...condemned to solitude and penance, and at the end of two years she might be recalled to the arms of a forgiving husband. But the same Emperor declared himself the implacable enemy of unmanly lust, and the cruelty of his persecution can scarcely be excused by the purity of his motives. In defiance of every principle of justice he stretched to past as well as future offenses the operations of his edicts, with the previous allowance of a short respite for confession and pardon. A painful death was inflicted by the amputation of the sinful instrument, or the insertion of sharp reeds into the pores and tubes of the most exquisite sensibility."[47]

After showing how these laws were adopted by different countries and cultures and then used (by false witness) against unpopular groups and sects, Symonds stated his main theory: these early laws presupposed that the invert (as Symonds now preferred to call the same-sex lover, finding the term non-perjorative) had turned *from* women to men. This, he argued, was rarely true: in "by far the larger proportion of cases...such instincts were inborn, and [in] a considerable percentage...they are also incontrovertible. Medical jurists and physicians have recently agreed to accept this as a fact."[48] He then challenged the popular belief in homosexual degeneracy by quoting Greek classics, Walt Whitman, and other literary sources to show that male/male friendships could be morally and spiritually fulfilling and even be a "saving and enobling aspiration."[49]

Symonds ended his book with "Suggestions on the Subject of Sexual Inversion in Relation to Law and Education." In 14 points, he argued morally: Justinian's interpretation of scripture was incorrect; logically: these sexual acts do no harm and there is no way to properly enforce them; legally: the laws of both France and Italy have been changed so they did not persecute the invert with no harm to the social fabric; and ironically: the laws created an atmosphere where blackmail was not only common but, many times, inevitable, thus causing rather than curing crime. He pointed out the further irony that the intensive study of Greek classics in English education not only promoted but exposed youth to the very feelings and actions which the laws were designed to eradicate.

Symonds was careful to keep his argument tight and appeal to the intellect rather than to the emotions. His ideas were radical for 1891 and he was careful never to endorse or promote actual sexual activities.

In mid-1892, Symonds approached social scientist Havelock Ellis through a friend and inquired whether Ellis would be interested in a book on "Sexual Inversion" for a science series he was editing. Symonds felt that a "historical study of Greece is absolutely essential to the psychological treatment of the subject now. It is being fearfully mishandled by pathologists and psychiatric professors, who know nothing whatsoever of its real nature."[50]

Henry Ellis—who chose and cultivated the name Havelock after beginning his literary career—was the father of modern sexology. He was the first to analyze sexuality scientifically. His pioneering, six volume *Studies in the Psychology of Sex,* (published between 1896 and 1910) though limited to some degree by class and culture, is still referred to today. While Symonds was concerned mainly with homosexuality, Ellis was attempting to modernize the entire construct of sexuality.

Against the Victorians, the modernists hold that sexual experience was neither a threat to moral character nor a drain on vital energies. On the contrary, they considered it an entirely worthwhile, though often precarious, human activity, whose proper management was essential to individual and social well being. Put bluntly...the modernists were sexual enthusiasts.[51]

Along with promoting a view of sex as healthy, Ellis also wanted to legitimize various types of sexual activity, questioning the presumption that the necessary underpinnings of Western civilization were marriage and the family.

Symonds and Ellis were not writing in a cultural vacuum. In 1885, Henry du Pre Labouchere, a member of the House of Commons, introduced a law making an act of "gross indecency" in public or *in private* punishable by two years of hard labor. The Labouchere Amendment was a clause in the Criminal Law Amendment Act of 1885 whose original purpose was to halt purported trafficking in young women and raise the age of consent from 12 to 16. Sensationalist journalism, especially of the *Pall Mall Gazette* and *Truth*, caused such an uproar that Labouchere had no trouble including his anti-homosexual amendment.[52]

The new law was the most stringent in all of Europe; it not only recommended two years of hard labor for "gross indecency" but also defined any connection *"per anum"* as a felony which required life imprisonment. The Amendment's wording was vague enough to include any number of sexual activities. Labouchere's witch hunt mentality is apparent in his proposal to the committee considering the Amendment.

> In doing so they recognized that the offense was on the increase, and they expressed their desire that it should be stamped out; and, presumably, it was intended that the law should be used equally against high and low.[53]

Labouchere's public statements, as well as the vague language and harsh sentences required by the Amendment, made it clear that he was mounting a campaign against the increasing visibility of same-sex lovers.

Both John Addington Symonds and Havelock Ellis realized that they needed one another as collaborators. Symonds had done a great deal of writing and thinking about his sexual nature and Ellis had the ambition to work that knowledge into a respectable and impressive structure. Ellis was, at first, afraid that Symonds' own homosexuality, and certain more emotional passages in *A Problem of Modern Ethics*, would damage the purely scientific scope of the work. But they managed to reach agreement on both methodology and content and the first volume of *Studies in the Psychology of Sex* was to be called *Sexual Inversion*.

Sexual Inversion makes three main arguments: homosexuality is congenital and therefore not a vice and beyond legal or moral proscriptions; homosexual behavior is natural because it is found in the animal kingdom (an argument used by Kinsey more than 50 years later); and such behavior was viewed with indifference by many non-western cultures. By removing homosexuality from moral and legal classifications, and by using the new sciences of biology and anthropology to analyze it, Ellis and Symonds gave the world a new way of understanding "inversion."

To avoid any pejorative language, they settled upon "abnormality," in the statistical rather than the pathological sense, to describe homosexuality. They suggested a comparison to "color hearing" (the ability to associate certain sounds with certain colors) thus removing homosexuality from the realm of a deficiency and implying that it could be a special gift. To avoid the connotation of degeneracy, they associated this "abnormality" with cultural figures of "exceptional ability" ranging from the philosopher Erasmus to Verlaine, from Sappho to archaeologist Johann Winckelmann.

The most persuasive arguments in *Sexual Inversion* were its 33 case histories. Written mainly by American and English intellectuals—mostly friends of Symonds—they collectively presented a portrait of the homosexual as a creative, sensitive, thoughtful man who was not effeminate, enjoyed the company of women, and was in general good health. Perhaps most importantly, the case histories insisted again and again upon homosexuals' deep emotional attachments to their partners. As social science, the book was a fine job in a field that had just been invented; as polemic it was masterful.

The major gap in *Sexual Inversion* was that neither Ellis nor Symonds showed much interest in lesbianism. The study contains only one chapter about women and only six case histories. They made little attempt to challenge the popular image of the lesbian as "mannish." Symonds was primarily interested in the male experience and Ellis, because of his 25 year marriage to feminist, writer, and lesbian Edith Lees, may have been less than eager to explore the topic with his usual intellectual vigor. *Sexual Inversion* suffers from the fact that it was culture bound in refusing to take women's sexuality as seriously as men's. Neither Symonds nor Ellis had the psychological and political insights of an Edward Carpenter. Although they may have supported some feminist ideas, they still relegated women to a minor status in their social and psychological scheme.

Although Symonds was closely connected with the writing of *Sexual Inversion*, he died before it was published. Ellis secured the permission of Symonds' family to use his material and the book was published in Germany to great acclaim. A British edition was impossible because of the backlash of the Oscar Wilde trials in 1895. (To this day, the book has not been published in England.) An American edition appeared in 1897 and Symonds' material was scattered throughout the book in acknowledged footnotes; his name was dropped in the second edition because of family pressure and Ellis' fear that Symonds' homosexuality would undercut the book's credibility. In 1898, the book was seized by the British police and, although no prosecution followed, the bookseller was reprimanded and the book attained the dubious status of an obscene publication. Symonds was also writing his *Memoirs* at the time of his death—a candid, sexual evaluation of his life and thought—but they were suppressed by his literary executor and remain, open only to a few, in the British Museum.

The writings of Edward Carpenter, John Addington Symonds, and Havelock Ellis radicalized intellectual discourse on sexuality. They provided a new foundation, scientific rather than moral, for understanding sexuality within the broad range of human activity. Sexuality, and especially same-sex love, was moving quickly from the unspoken to the analyzed. Against this social background, the gay sensibility was evolving. It was the gradual appearance of literary works by self-consciously homosexual men, in conjunction with the writings of sexologists such as Kraft-Ebbing, Ellis, and Freud that was to cause a further evolution of the gay sensibility, a bitter backlash, and then another period of evolution.

From its earliest beginnings, the gay sensibility has consistently encompassed two distinct points of view. As a means of expression for a suppressed voice, its social criticism has covertly and overtly argued for political analysis and social change. This impulse can be seen in the writings of Carpenter. On the other hand, the gay sensibility has also conveyed the desire to be accepted by the prevailing culture. Though radical for his time, Symonds' writing was basically a plea for acceptance. These two approaches—criticism vs. acceptance—are evident even today. The gay movement since 1969 has fluctuated between a radical analysis which demanded broad social and cultural changes and the more reform-oriented, acceptance-seeking approach.

Birth of a Sensibility

The poetry of Walt Whitman, the political philosophy of Edward Carpenter, and the historical and scientific writings of Symonds and Ellis all set the stage for the blossoming of a gay sensibility. All four of these men were products of a progressive movement in the last half of the 19th century, a movement that was to endorse a notion of a private self as distinct from the wider social world. Whitman's break with accepted conventions of verse, Carpenter's move to the country to make a living growing vegetables and selling hand-made sandals, and Symonds' and Ellis' expanding ideas of sexuality are all examples of a new sense of selfhood.

The lives and actions of these men were a manifestation of profound changes which were occurring in social structures. The industrial revolution had caused a major dislocation in social arrangements. The idea of "class" developed in the late 18th century. A more ambiguous term than "rank," it was indicative of a change in the economic organization of society and implied, among other things, the possibility of upward mobility.

Industrialization brought about the development of the idea of "art." Previously used to signify a skill or a craft, the word took on the more limited meaning of an imaginative creation. As factories grew and supplanted cottage industries, personalized skills became associated with a particular type of person: the artist. *Aesthetics* was used to judge the work of artists and there was even a term to describe a person involved in making those judgments: the aesthete. The arts were distinguished from other crafts and skills, and fulfilled a special function in the new social order. They fell within the general classification of "Culture," a word that came to mean "a whole way of life, material, intellectual, and spiritual."[54]

These new concepts of "class," "art," and "culture," in conjunction with the emerging notion of a private "self," became basic assumptions of industrial society. Perhaps the most important aspect of this tangle of ideas to the development of gay sensibility is the meaning of the "imagination." The imagination, unique to every person, was seen as the root of both art and the self. The writings of Carpenter, Symonds, and Ellis gave some social permission for speaking openly about homosexuality. Homosexual artists began to look for new ways to express themselves creatively in response to oppressive social conditions.

Modern gay sensibility developed through a historical process that both prohibited its growth and made it possible. At the same time that homosexuals were able to use the arts as a means of upward mobility between loosening class lines, things like the Labouchere Amendment were a direct attack on personal freedom and privacy. In the following five sections, I define five characteristics important to the history of the gay sensibility.

The Cult of the Imagination

In *Prancing Novelist*, her biography of Ronald Firbank, Brigid Brophy defends an art form which she feels has fallen into disrepute: fiction. A novel emerges from the imagination of the novelist like an elaborate daydream. Brophy argues that novel writing (and most creative writing) is like daydreaming: essentially masturbatory and thus socially unacceptable. It is a public exhibition of the most private (i.e. sexual) self.

Nineteenth century naturalism was an attempt to remove the stigma from novel writing. "By the naturalistic convention, the events of a novel succeed one another in the reader's experience as if they were events in real life."[55] While the naturalistic novel was a creation of the imagination, it tried to persuade the reader it was a reflection of real life. Early prohibitions against novel reading were all based on the fear of expanding the imagination, letting the reader escape into "fictions." Novels were condemned because they were not productive. The novel circumvented some of these proscriptions by becoming more utilitarian; it taught morals so it would not be thought frivolous. (It is no accident that the first acceptable English novel, *Pamela*, is subtitled *Virtue Rewarded*.)

Naturalism and morality enlisted fiction in the service of prevailing social conventions, thus depriving it of its radical potential. Just as daydreaming (because of its sexual subtext) was frowned upon, so too was using the imagination to create fictions. Virginia Woolf and Samuel Taylor Coleridge both portrayed the imagination as androgynous.[56] Imagination is especially threatening to a culture that repressively and rigidly defines gender roles. Brophy argues that the unlimited imagination is subversive, not only because it is primarily sexual in origin, but because it can provide an alternative vision to the "real" world. It promises the possibility of reinventing social structures.

Modern gay activists have pointed out that unfettered sexuality and imagination are threats to a world that is ruled by patriarchal, heterosexual gender and sexual arrangements. To unleash either would be to undermine the "heterosexual dictatorship."[57]

> Whereas straight people have a vested interest in being dull, literalist, and unimaginative to keep their world going, gay people are, I have learned, in the truest sense of the word *fabulous*. More than any other people in the macroscopic society, we've broken down the rules that are used for validating the difference between real/true and unreal/false. The controlling agents of the status quo may know the *power* of lies; dissident subcultures, however, are closer to knowing their *value*.[58]

The difference between "power" and "value" is important. Because gay sensibility was an expression of powerless people, its creators tried to find new ways to present and understand the culture in which they lived, making it represent and respond to their lives. Refusing to accept the oppressive world as it is, gay sensibility has often imagined it as it could be. This visionary tradition has become known, through a host of manifestations, as "camp."

The word "camp" and what it denotes have become so over-popularized that it has lost some of its specific meaning and history. Susan Sontag has written that:

> ...the essence of Camp is its love of the unnatural: of artifice and exaggeration...something of a private code, a badge of identity...Camp is a certain mode of aestheticism. It is *one* way of seeing the world as an aesthetic phenomenon...not in terms of beauty, but in terms of the degree of artifice, of stylization.[59]

Camp is the re-imagining of the material world into ways and forms which transform and comment upon the original. It changes the "natural" and "normal" into style and artifice.

Ultimately, camp changes the real, hostile world into a new one which is controllable and safe. The beginnings of camp can be found in the novels of Ronald Firbank, with their wildly exotic settings and characters with bizarre, unreal names, or in the photos of Von Gloedon where the photographer poses attractive teenage boys in "classical" settings. Firbank meant to be funny, but his works are also serious; Von Gloedon meant to be serious, but his studied style and obvious sexual intentions lend humor to his artistic endeavors. In both cases, the work is a transfiguration of the real and the commonplace.

Camp was and is a way for gay men to re-imagine the world around them. It exaggerates and therefore diffuses real threats. If proscribed gender roles leave no room for homosexuals, they can easily be ridiculed: the homosexual fondness for such sexual/gender stereotypes as Mae West, Hedy Lamarr, or Victor Mature come from the fact that they are parodies (in West's case intentional) of what is thought to be normal. The hysterics of Susan Hayward in *Back Street,* the archness of Bette Davis in *All about Eve,* and the high flown theatrics of Maria Callas in *Lucia de Lammermoor* are all loved because they are expressions of emotions usually kept under wraps. By exaggerating, stylizing, and remaking what is usually thought to be average or normal, camp creates a world in which the real becomes unreal, the threatening, unthreatening.

By making things not what they are, camp can also be camouflage to provide an outlet or protection. To dress as the opposite sex, especially in a theatrical way, is a form of camp. Drag allows the wearer to make a comment upon usual gender assignments, to perhaps act out his own feelings (which may not be acceptable for a biological man), or to act in a flamboyant manner acceptable for a drag queen but not for a "real" man or a woman. What is sometimes referred to as "camp talk"—especially gay men referring to one another with women's names or pronouns—evolved as a coded, protected way of speaking about one's personal or sexual life. If one man were to be overheard at a public dinner table saying to another: "You'll never guess what Mary said on our date last night," nothing would be thought of it.

Camp is a product of the imagination. On some level, it is a way to obtain power in one's own life. On a deeper level, it is the ability to see beyond what is clearly evident; to grasp a reality beneath or totally separate from what is taught. Although her essay on camp is perhaps the best thing written on the topic, Sontag makes a grave error. "It goes without saying that the Camp sensibility is disengaged, depoliticized—or at least apolitical."[60] Because it has been used by gay people as a means of communication and survival, camp is political. And because it contains the possibility of structuring and encouraging limitless imagination—to literally create a new reality—it is not only political, but progressive.

Gay men could use camp to protect themselves, but another, more aggressive strategy was needed to fight homosexual oppression: wit. In its earliest meanings, "wit" referred to the capacity for thought, intellectual ability. In the mid-16th century, it took on its contemporary connotation of "quickness of intellect or liveliness of fancy; talent for saying brilliant or sparkling things, especially in an amusing way."[61] Oscar Wilde added wit to what would become the gay sensibility. Wilde's wit encompassed both the older and the more contemporary meanings of the term. Not only was what he said funny, it was also incisive and truthful. And, most importantly, it was a means of criticizing social mores and structures while shielding himself from retribution. Little has changed today: "I have expressed myself, as much and as often as I can, through epigrams and wit. I

Walt Whitman, studio portrait, 1883

SOCIETY'S HOPES AND FEARS.

Oscar Wilde, cartoon in *Society*, 1882

Even before his downfall, Oscar Wilde was perceived as both a
threat and a promise. This cartoon captures the ambivalence
which the public associated with his self-promoted image.
Whitman also knew the joys of self-promotion and this studio
photograph plays heavily on his image as a natural and free spirit.
As with all advertisement, the point is stretched: the butterfly is
dead and wired to his finger.

There are constants in history. The iconography of von
Gloeden's posed Ganymede is not unlike the photos found in
today's soft core porn. Thomas Eakins' photo of boys bathing—
perhaps the boys in Whitman's poem—conveys the same search for
the pastoral and for idealized beauty as the still from Artie
Bressan's "Frobidden Letters." The recent change in acceptable
gay imagery has allowed an older, mature man to accompany
"youth" into this bower of freedom.'

Richard Locke and Robert Adams in Artie Bressan's *Forbidden Letters*, 1980

"Students at a Swimming Hole" by Thomas Eakins, 1883

nude boy by Baron von Gloeden

have come to view wit as an integral and *essential* part of gay male living. Wit and irony provide the only reasonable modus operandi in the American Literalist Terror of Straight Reality."[62]

Gays have hidden themselves from oppressive straight society through circumlocution—camp—and defended themselves through wit. In gay life nothing is what it seems to be. By pulling the rug out from under the usual gender expectations—is it a boy or a girl?—or sexual arrangements—what *do* they do in bed?—homosexual life and culture undermine patriarchal and heterosexist social assumptions.

The Cult of Beauty

The inclination towards and glorification of the beautiful is a theme that runs through almost all of the imaginative and theoretical literature of Victorian homosexuals. It was Greek statuary that first stirred Edward Carpenter's repressed sexual feelings; John Addington Symonds' interests were the same. In *A Problem in Greek Ethics*, he was very concerned about explaining that the Greek notion of *paiderastia* (the love of the older man for the younger) was inextricably bound up with the classical Greek conception of beauty.

This search for the beautiful was, on the most obvious level, an excuse for homosexuals to indulge in a forbidden admiration for male pulchritude. Until a decade ago, a plaster reproduction of Michaelangelo's *David* was a fixture in gay male households: besides being beautiful, it was respectable enough to be safe. Gay male porno from the 1920s on through *Physique* magazine of the 1960s presented the male body posed in the style of Greek statuary. The classical theme is found even today in such books as *An Asian Minor*, Felice Picano's retelling of the Zeus/Ganymede story from a smiley, boy-love perspective.

The idolization of beauty grew from the Victorian fascination with classical Greece and the Renaissance. The writings and aesthetics of Walter Pater, John Ruskin, and the Pre-Raphaelite Brotherhood, begun with Dante Gabriel Rossetti and revived by William Morris and Edward Burne-Jones, led directly into what was to become known as the "art for art's sake" movement. The anti-utilitarian aesthetic declared that beauty need fulfill no other function than its own existence.

Beauty as a separate entity within a repressive culture paralleled the role of the same-sex lover as an outcast: like the isolated beauty he was set apart from his surroundings. This status was viewed as elevated but at the same time, piteous. Their feelings of self-pity signified for many writers their uniqueness. If they suffered because they were not accepted, this suffering ennobled them, even while it placed them further outside the bounds of ordinariness.

Images of beauty occur often in the writings of 19th century homosexuals. Oscar Wilde was able to use the convention and take it, in a letter to his lover Alfred Douglas, almost to the verge of parody while never losing his hold upon it.

> Your sonnet is quite lovely, and it is a marvel that those red rose-leaf lips of yours should be made no less for the madness of music and song than for the madness of kissing. Your slim-gilt soul walks between passion and poetry. I am sure Hyacinthus whom Apollo loved so madly was you in the Greek days. Why are you alone in London, and when do you go to Salisbury? To go there and cool your hands in the grey twilight of Gothic things. Come here whenever you like. It is a lovely place and lacks only you. Do go to Salisbury first. Always with undying love. Yours, Oscar.[63]

The use of hyperbole to reinforce the physical exquisiteness and moral sensitivity of persons and situations was both a literary technique and a statement of social difference. In an England which was becoming increasingly industrialized and considerably less beautiful, (or even habitable, in many of the factory cities) this insistence on refinement was a small revolt against the byproducts of empire-building.

The image of piteous beauty was potent for 19th century homosexual writers and readers. In 1894, Lord Alfred Douglas published "In Praise of Shame" in the Oxford magazine, *The Chameleon*:

Last night unto my bed methought there came
Our lady of strange dreams, and from an urn
She poured a live fire, so that mine eyes did burn
At sight of it. Anon the floating flame
Took many shapes, and one cried: I am Shame
That walks with Love, I am most wise to turn
Cold lips and limbs to fire; therefore discern

And see my loveliness, and praise my name.
And afterwards, in radiant garments dressed
With sound of flutes and laughing of glad lips,
A pomp of all the passions passed along
All the night through; till the white phantom ships
Of dawn sailed in. Whereat I said this song,
'Of all sweet passions Shame is the loveliest.'[64]

The sonnet turns on the irony of praising "shame," but as with some undergraduate writing, Douglas also aims to shock, to dare a new response from the reader. In the same issue of *The Chameleon*, Douglas also published a longer poem entitled "Two Loves." The poet dreams he is in an Idyllic glade where he meets a youth.

...one hand he raised
To shield him from the sun, his wind-tossed hair
Was twined with flowers, and in his hair he bore
A purple bunch of bursting grapes, his eyes
Were clear as crystal, naked all was he,
White as the snow on pathless mountains frore,
Red were his lips as red wine-spilth that dyes
A marble floor, his brow chalcedony.
And he came near me, with his lips uncurled
And kind, and caught my hand and kissed my mouth,
And gave me grapes to eat, and said, 'Sweet friend,
Come I will show thee shadows of the world
And images of life.'

Two more youths materialize.

...The one did joyous seem
And fair and blooming, and a sweet refrain

> Came from his lips; he sang of pretty maids
> And joyous love of comely girl and boy,
> His eyes were bright, and 'mid the dancing blades
> Of golden grass his feet did trip for joy;...
> But he that was his comrade walked aside;
> He was full sad and sweet, and his large eyes
> Were strange with wondrous brightness, staring wide
> With gazing; and he sighed with many sighs
> That moved me, and his cheeks were wan and white
> Like pallid lilies, and his lips were red
> Like poppies, and his hands he clenched tight,
> And yet again unclenched, and his head
> Was wreathed with moon-flowers pale as lips of death.

The poet asks his name, and why he is so sad in so pleasant a setting.

> 'What is thy name?' He said, 'My name is Love'
> Then straight the first did turn himself to me
> and cried, 'He lieth, for his name is Shame,
> But I am Love, and I was wont to be
> Alone in this fair garden, till he came
> Unmasked by night; I am true Love, I fill
> The hearts of boy and girl with mutual flame,'
> Then sighing, said the other, 'Have thy will,
> I am the love that dare not speak its name!'[65]

"In Praise of Shame" confronted its reader with a moral argument, and "Two Loves" uses some of the same language but is more explicitly sexual. The youths are described in glorified physical detail. The kiss upon the mouth hints—much more than other poems of this period—at a sexual intimacy that goes beyond "comradeship" or "adhesiveness." In his personal letter to Douglas, (which was not written for publication, whereas Douglas' poem was) Wilde mentions "the madness of kissing" but within its context it is a form of extravagant praise. Although relying on classical allusion and the prevailing taste for preciousness in attitude and detail, "Two Loves" goes further than other works of its time to say what it means.

Ironically, it is the very refusal to speak which relays the poem's meaning.

Singing the praises of beauty soon became somewhat suspicious to the average reader and critic, especially if the beauty being praised was that of young boys. Both of Douglas' poems and Wilde's letter were introduced as evidence during Wilde's trial. Although defended on literary grounds, with their overly ripe language, they became, to some, symptomatic of a homosexual style of writing. Until the advent of recent feminist criticism, the stigmatization of writing according to gender (he writes like a woman; she writes like a man) was used to attack and dismiss male homosexual writing as well as all writing by women. Literary analysts felt this kind of "effeminate" writing was a betrayal of gender, adding to the impression that homosexuality was a gender disturbance rather than a sexual preference.

The Cult of Male Friendship

In Victorian culture, emotional and social expectations based upon gender created a wide chasm between men and women. Although industrialization and the shifting of family responsibilities affected the working class and the rising middle class in very different ways, both experienced ever-more-separate spheres of masculine and feminine behavior and action. Thus separated, it was not surprising that people formed firm bonds with others of their own sex. This was further encouraged, for men, by the unquestioned assumption of male superiority. The cult of male friendship—many times not even implicitly sexual—is evident in much Victorian writing.

Alfred Lord Tennyson published "In Memoriam," a testament to his deceased friend Arthur Hallam, in 1850.

> Ah yet, ev'n yet, if this might be,
>   I, falling on his faithful heart,
>   Would breathing thro' his lips impart
> The life that almost dies in me;

That dies not, but endures with pain,
  And slowly forms the firmer mind,
  Treasuring the look it cannot find,
The words that are not heard again...

What art thou then? I cannot guess;
  But tho' I seem in star and flower
  To feel thee some diffusive power,
I do not therefore love thee less;

My love involves the love before;
  My love is vaster passion now;
  Tho' mix'd with God and Nature thou,
I seem to love thee more and more.

Far off thou art, but ever nigh:
  I have thee still, and I rejoice;
  I prosper, circled with thy voice;
I shall not lose thee tho' I die.[66]

In 1896, A. E. Housman produced *A Shropshire Lad* containing "Look Not in my Eyes."

Look not in my eyes, for fear They mirror true the sight I
  see,
And there you find your face too clear And love it and be
  lost like me.
One the long nights through must lie Spent in star-
  defeated sighs,
But why should you as well as I Perish? gaze not in my
  eyes...
A Grecian lad, as I hear tell, One that many loved in vain,
Looked into a forest well And never looked away again.
There, when the turf in springtime flowers, With down-
  ward eye and gazes sad,
Stands amid the glancing showers A jonquil, not a
  Grecian lad.[67]

Even Benjamin Disraeli, certainly beyond social reproach, was able to write in his 1832 novel *Contarini Fleming*:

His face was quite oval, his eyes deep blue: his rich brown
curls clustered...upon...his downy cheek...I behold him: I
loved him. My friendship was a passion...Oh! Days of pure
felicity, when Masaeus and myself, with our arms around
each other's neck, wandered together.[68]

Even though he uses the Grecian motif and the Narcissus myth,
(an image commonly used by other homosexual poets) Housman
escaped criticism and was accepted as a major poet. Disraeli's high-
flown prose was also seen as unexceptionable. The sentiments
expressed in these three pieces were so ingrained in Victorian culture
that they provoked no moral or social censure although all three seem
to us today unmistakably homoerotic. How are these different from
the writings of Carpenter, Symonds, and the Uranian poets of the
early 20th century?

The first difference is one of intent. Although the homoeroticism of Tennyson and Disraeli may seem clear to the modern reader,
the authors probably did not intend their imagery to be sexual. The
cult of male friendship was so dominant that the extravagant praise
of a male friend, even his physical attributes, was not regarded as
unusual. Although novels, and all literary forms, clearly have
psychological (and sexual) subtexts, a framework had not yet been
invented to analyze them. Passages which seem overtly sexual to us to
the Victorians fell into the catch-all category of "sentiment." Depicting heterosexuality would be considered highly improper; depicting homosexuality would have been unspeakable. The social
ignorance about all sexuality prevented the reading public from
interpreting these descriptions as sexual: the unspeakable was
unimaginable.

The second dissimilarity between Carpenter, Symonds, and the
other writers is that they were, to varying degrees, consciously
addressing the issue of homosexuality. To the degree that they were
becoming known as same-sex apologists, their literary endeavors
became suspect. Carpenter rewrote *Love's Coming of Age* many
times to "guard against misunderstandings."[69] Anything approach-
ing an explicit discussion of homosexuality would have been socially
taboo and probably illegal.

Finally, literature must be viewed in a historical context.

Disraeli wrote *Contarini Fleming* in 1832, a much more naive time than 50 years later. Tennyson's poem might not have been as lovingly expressive if he had written it 40 years later. As the scientific and intellectual discourse about sexuality became more open and public, even the most innocent of homoerotic literary expressions became suspect. Although the end of the 19th century saw a great deal of homosexual writing, much of it was heavily coded or produced in such a way as to limit readership. It was impossible to sustain the concept of "just friends."

Because the literary tradition depicting male friendship was so strong, gay writers had no trouble using the genre to mask their real concerns. Average readers did not have the psychological sophistication to see through the artifice of literary construction, of if they did, they did not have the desire to pursue the implications. After the Wilde scandal, the situation was completely reversed. By playing it too close to the line, and by not being very discreet in his private life, Wilde's literary subtext became all too apparent to the general reading public. (This was perhaps the first time in modern literature where it was generally recognized that a literary work had a meaning other than its face value.) Because such a strong connection was made between Wilde's life, philosophy, and literary output, it became virtually impossible for gay writers to hide behind the facade of "male friendship." They had to find other ways of expressing their real meanings and desires.

The Cult of Dispossession

It should be no surprise that gay men, finding that they are not welcome in this world, invent in their imaginations safer, more congenial places. One of the most common themes in gay writing is the creation of edenic situations free from the world's hostility.

As early as Virgil's *Second Eclogue*, the verdant forest, far from urban strife, was portrayed as a refuge for the same-sex lover. The pastoral retreat figures prominently in much late 19th century homosexual literature. John Le Gay Brereton, in Australia, wrote in 1896:

Under a sloping roof
Of twining branches, as I thought, I lay
And read, and in among the perfect green
Of new-burst leaves the sunlight pierced and threw
Round splashes of lilac colour on the book.[70]

Pastoral images often dovetailed with the idealization of classical Greece. Symonds writes in 1896 of the lovers Eudiades and Pheidias who have just finished a friendly wrestling match in view of their comrades.

Nor, though the eyes of many lovers burned
Upon them, from their forward course they turned;
But modestly, with calm clear brows, whereon
The light of innocence and honour shone,
Sunbright, they passed; then in the water wan
From their pure stainless forms the trace of toil
Purging, they rubbed their breasts with fragrant oil.[71]

This poem uses the paradigms of male friendship, love of beauty, and an idyllic setting to create a homosexual fantasy.

Idyllic as such settings usually are, their creators frequently connect pain to this flight from civilization. Douglas described "the love who dare not speak his name" in "Two Loves" as "sighing," having cheeks which "were wan and white," and wearing a garland made of flowers "pale as lips of death." The "sloping roof/Of twining branches" in "Rouge et Noir" is the setting for the poet's dream of the funeral of his lover, which in turn prompts his own dream suicide from which he wakens just before death when he hears his lover call his name. The flight from civilized repression often occurs because of the pain of homosexual oppression, bringing melancholy to even the most idyllic setting.

Perhaps the best example of a homosexual author's writing which uses the flight from civilization to escape from enforced heterosexuality and stifled freedom is James M. Barrie's *Peter Pan*. This 1904 drama is usually thought of as a children's story, and while it certainly has functioned well as such, it is also a deeply disturbing meditation on the impossible desire for flight. Peter, as an infant, leaves the real world because he hears his parents talking about his future: growing up, going to school, getting a job, having a family. He goes to Never Land (the second, more final "never" came when Barrie novelized the play several years later) where he lives in a pastoral world populated by fairies, (especially the jealous Tinkerbell who carries on like a miffed lover for most of the play) the same pirates and Indians who inhabit the all-male worlds of Melville and Cooper, and a band of "lost boys." The boys, we are told, are young male children who have "fallen out of their prams when the nurse is looking the other way. If they are not claimed in seven days they are sent far away to Never Land."[72]

But *Peter Pan* is not so much a fantasy of escape as it is a clear-eyed exposure of escape's impossibility. Barrie sadly mocks the stock images and themes of the gay literary tradition. The pastoral setting is frankly termed "Never Never Land." Peter Pan's very name alludes to the impish, young Greek god of forests and creation, but instead of the idealized lover, he is shown to be a selfish, cruel boy who is unable to care for anyone. Only in Never Land can gender become meaningless: Barrie specified that Peter be played by a woman, and notes that in Never Land the boy fairies are mauve, the girls white, and some fairies don't know what sex they are. The use of "mauve" was shocking in Barrie's time since the color had become associated with Wilde's aesthetics and with homosexuality in general during Wilde's trial ten years previously.

Peter Pan is also about "not growing up." Barrie's own confused sexuality excluded him from the adult world. The sadness that permeates some of the other homosexual poetry of the time is present in *Peter Pan*, but not as melancholy for lost love, rather as regret for lost life. At the end of the play, Peter is left alone and Barrie adds in a stage direction: "It has something to do with the riddle of his being. If he could get the hang of the thing his cry might become 'To live would be an awfully big adventure!' but he can never quite get the hang of it, and so no one is as gay as he."[73] While other writers of the period glorified their social and emotional dispossession, Barrie delineates it with pained cynicism.

The escapist longings in early gay writings turn up again in the 1950s in such books as Gore Vidal's *The City and the Pillar* and James Barr's less well known *Quatrefoil*. James Fenimore Cooper's novels are lightly spoofed in the 1966 gay porno classic *Song of the Loon* by Richard Amory. In it, frontiersmen romp and frolic among tall phallic trees and blithely enjoy an unrestrained sexuality.

Perhaps the most well-known expression of the longing to leave a hostile environment that has been adopted by gay culture is the song, "Over the Rainbow." Closely identified with Judy Garland, the song, with its unaffected longing for a haven, contributed to her devoted gay male following. When lesbian feminist singer Holly Near performed at the 1979 lesbian and gay march on Washington, she ended her set with this song and dubbed it "the gay national anthem."

The Cult of the Dandy

Oscar Wilde was accused by the Marquess of Queensberry of "posing as a somdomite (sic)." The charge leveled was one of sexual impropriety but the word "posing" raises the complex question of the exact nature of Wilde's outrages against the social order. Quite unintentionally, the Marquess hit succinctly upon the relationship between gay life and mainstream society. Since homosexuality was forbidden, gay people were always in the position of "posing" as something else. It is ironic that Wilde should try to make a name for himself by presenting himself with a flamboyance which suggested such a strong social deviance. The irony is doubled by the fact that the Marquess accused him of "posing" rather than of *being* a "somdomite," suggesting that the crime was "posing" and not sodomy. Social strucuctures are predicated on everyone having, and staying within, his or her place. If people "pose" (i.e. be other than who they are supposed to be) the structures of society are threatened. Wilde used his pose as a form of self-advertisement, to sell himself in the overcrowded literary and social world. However, the pose he used was not something self-invented. His dandy image had a social history in British culture which fit in very neatly with Wilde's homosexual identity.

The concept of the dandy developed early in the century and was most closely identifed with George Bryan "Beau" Brummell. Brummell managed through sheer will power and a great sense of self-importance to move from being a civil servant into the highest social circles. In the social strictures of Regency England this was close to a miracle. By simply declaring himself the arbiter of taste Brummell was able to lead and control social trends. He represented a triumph of style and imagination over class structures and social restrictions.

Brummell cultivated refinement to con the upper classes into accepting him. This was also a large part of Wilde's public posturing, as well as his aesthetic theory. Although from a wealthy and influential family Wilde was Irish, and would have difficulty entering the English social circles he desired.[74]

The dandy catered to the autocratic sensibility: all style and no content. Dandyism was an exercise in perfecting the externals and giving the impression that anything beneath the surface was incidental. Taste was life's most important attainment: any politics, emotions, or ethics that conflicted with this goal were to be discarded. As the 19th century progressed, the rise of the middle class, the growth of industrialization, the decline of monarchy, an increasingly strident demand for social equality, and the growth of a utilitarian work ethic rendered the dandy an anachronism. He ignored the responsibilities of heterosexual family life and the new capitalist imperative to produce.

Because it had to remain hidden, gay sensibility has expressed itself by implying rather than stating, by indicating with appearance what it was not allowed to express with content. The circumvention which was part and parcel of the philosophy of the dandy dovetailed perfectly with the needs of gay men. Not only could one express oneself through style rather than statement, but dandyism also offered the distinct possibility of social advancement. This has been true of gay culture and society since the time of Wilde. Sontag has noted that modern gay men achieve their "integration into society [by] promoting the aesthetic sense."

Wilde attempted to scale the class walls using Brummell's methods of self-promotion and trendsetting. By arguing that art needed no reason beyond itself to exist, he was making a radical statement: art, form, style, and "posing" all existed outside of accepted social and moral codes. Their value was intrinsic, their power was that they represented an alternative and a threat to those codes.

Wilde's aesthetic theories were ultimately rejected by the general public because they were non-utilitarian, threatening, and subversive. While he succeeded in attaining social position and in making an indelible mark upon the culture, he ultimately fell because he misjudged the extent to which he could transcend the prevailing social and moral climate.

Oscar Wilde

Oscar Wilde is perhaps the most important figure in the history of gay sensibility. He exemplified in his work and his life a fusion of the separate strains of the gay sensibility that had been developing over the last 30 years of the 19th century. He drew from some of the same traditions as Edward Carpenter in his social criticism, but used the inverted wit of epigram when presenting these criticisms to the public. He followed the example of Brummell to rise in society. He declared the value of the private sphere and the worth of the individual in a culture which preached the importance of the public and demanded conformity. He was destroyed, by society, for his revolutionary ideas.

Wilde was born in 1854 in Dublin to upper middle class parents. He attended private schools and excelled in his studies at Magdalen College, Oxford in 1878. He married in 1884 and soon began a literary career which consisted as much in promoting himself as a personality and wit as producing a body of work. In 1889 he became the editor of the enormously popular magazine *The Woman's World* and a year later received more publicity, and a certain degree of notoriety with the publication of his novel *The Picture of Dorian Gray.*

Wilde espoused an "art for art's sake" aestheticism and spent a successful year, 1882, in America lecturing on the topic. It is ironic that his lecture tour was sponsored by Richard D'Oyly Carte, to accompany the U.S. production of Gilbert and Sullivan's newest operetta, *Patience*, a satire on the aesthetic movement. Wilde apparently had no qualms about publicizing a theater piece which ridiculed his artistic principles as long as a it provided him with a chance to promote himself. Gilbert's libretto for *Patience* was subtly homophobic: it is clear that as early as 1880 the aesthetic movement was closely identified with and stigmatized by its association with homosexuality.

Wilde was endlessly quoted, invited to the best dinner parties, and looked to as the vanguard of the chic and fashionable, and his literary career took off. Between 1892 and 1895 he wrote and had produced four enormously successful plays: *Lady Windermere's Fan, A Woman of No Importance, An Ideal Husband* and his most popular piece, *The Importance of Being Earnest.* Then, in 1895, at the height of his career, Wilde was brought to court and after a series of trials, sentenced to two years hard labor under the Labouchere Amendment. After serving out the full sentence—the judge had been appalled by the case and claimed the sentence was "totally inadequate"—Wilde lived out his last three years in Paris, sick and destroyed as both an artist and a man.

The emergence in the public eye of Wilde's private homosexual life was the catalyst that led to the legal proceedings and Wilde's abrupt fall. But Wilde's crime was not so much the acts of "gross indecency" of which he was accused as cultural and moral subversion. Underneath his frivolous patina, Wilde was a serious social critic.

To the Victorians art and literature were inseparable from morality. In *The Picture of Dorian Gray* one character remarks: "There is no such thing as a moral or an immoral book. Books are either well written or badly written. That is all." This quote was to figure prominently during Wilde's trial, and quite rightly. It was evidence that not only was Wilde imprudent enough to challenge the moral utilitarianism of literature but he was also prepared to expose moralist hypocrisy: "The books that the world calls immoral books are books that show the world its own shame."

Those in power are serious; those who are not make jokes. Oscar

Wilde, and the gay men who came after him, learned to use wit and imagination to diffuse and deflate the attacks of serious society. Wilde relied upon his wit during his trial and it caused his conviction. Wit alone was not enough; those in power ultimately got the last laugh, even if it was a vulgar queer joke. The tradition of wit and humor is an important and necessary aspect of gay self-defense against repressive political power. Although it is important to understand and cultivate these aspects of the gay sensibility, it is just as important, as Stonewall proved, to be assertive rather than defensive, to gain political and cultural power in a forthright and conscious manner. Wilde was not convicted *because* of his wit, but in spite of it. His conviction occurred because there was no political movement to protect him against sexual, social, and political repression.

Wilde provoked further controversy with the publication of overt political writing. In February of 1891 he published *The Soul of Man Under Socialism* in the popular *Fortnightly Review*. Witty and thought provoking, the long piece explained the political basis of Wilde's aesthetic theories. Socialism was more acceptable in England than in America at this time. Eminents such as William Morris, George Bernard Shaw, and Beatrice and Sidney Webb felt no conflict between their secure bourgeois lifestyles and their political beliefs. Even the radical Edward Carpenter found a tolerant and sympathetic audience. Wilde's political ideas fit comfortably into this setting. His main concern was the connection between individualism and art.

> Socialism, Communism, or whatever one chooses to call it, by converting private property into public wealth, and substituting cooperation for competition, will restore society to its proper condition of a thoroughly healthy organism and insure the material well-being of each member of the community. It will, in fact, give Life its proper basis and proper environment. But, for the full development of Life to its highest mode of perfection, something more is needed. What is needed is Individualism.
>
> Disobedience in the eyes of anyone who has read history

is man's original virtue. It is through disobedience that progress has been made, through disobedience and through rebellion.

Yes, there are suggestive things in Individualism. Socialism annihilates family life, for instance. With the abolition of private property, marriage in its present form will disappear...

Man has sought to live intensely, fully, perfectly. When he can do so without exercising restraint on others, or suffering it ever, and his activities are all pleasurable to him, he will be saner, healthier, more civilised, more himself. Pleasure is nature's test, her sign of approval. When man is happy, he is in harmony with himself and his environment. The new individualism, for whose service Socialism, whether it wills it or not, is working, will be perfect harmony. It will be what the Greeks sought for, but could not, except in Thought, realise completely, because they had slaves, and fed them; it will be what the Renaissance sought for, but could not realise completely, except in Art, because they had slaves, and starved them. It will be complete, and through it each man will attain to his perfection. The new Individualism is the new Hellenism.[75]

Wilde, famous for his exquisite taste in wallpaper or blue and white china for his house, could not credibly advocate the overthrow of the government. Yet his essay met with severe criticism. The *Spectator* editorialized:

All these literary bullets are shot out in defense of the thesis that men should be themselves, in contempt, it would seem, not merely of the public, but of all law which restricts their individualism. The article, if serious, would be thoroughly unhealthy, but it leaves on us the impression of being written merely to startle and excite talk.[76]

Wilde's essay was consistent with the rest of his views. He saw the the individual in conflict with the state; the imagination against the literal; the beautiful against the mundane. The piece synthesizes Whitman's individualism, Symonds' longing for the ideal Grecian state, and Carpenter's political quest for a less repressive future. Wilde used these images and theories to reinforce and defend his own personality and temperament.

"If one tells the truth, one is sure, sooner or later to be found out" wrote Wilde. "Thoroughly unhealthy" was the phrase used to describe *The Soul of Man Under Socialism*, but it was also a phrase that appeared in many reviews of *Dorian Gray*. Wilde had been found out.

Although married—the marriage was clearly a social arrangement for both husband and wife—and the father of two children, Wilde lead an actively homosexual life since his earliest days at Oxford. He met Lord Alfred Douglas in 1891 and the two became fast friends and probably lovers for a while. Wilde was Douglas' entree into artistic circles and Wilde was enchanted with the prestige of courting a nobleman. The two travelled together and made no secret of their friendship. Wilde was also becoming more public (or less careful, depending upon your point of view) with his other sexual activities. He was seen dining in public with men not his social equals. He frequented houses of assignation and had the habit of giving expensive gifts to the young working class men he met.

Douglas' father, the eighth Marquess of Queensberry, was noted for his outrageous social behavior, his boxing, and his bad temper. He demanded that Douglass and Wilde discontinue their relationship. Douglas refused and provoked several public incidents culminating with Queensbury's leaving a scribbled note at Wilde's club: "To Oscar Wilde, posing as a somdomite." (Some ascribe Queensbury's misspelling to his anger, others to sheer ignorance.) Wilde had had enough and sued the Marquess for libel. It is difficult to understand why Wilde brought this suit against an accusation that might well be proven. Usually ascribed to (homosexual) self-destruction the truth is probably that Wilde misjudged the level of his social prestige. He was overly assured of his ability to make society conform to his rules and overestimated the power of wit against the power of the state.

There followed a series of three trials. Queensberry was found "not guilty" at the first, establishing the fact that Wilde was a "somdomite." The state then brought charges against Wilde for "gross indecency" and the second trial ended with a hung jury. At the re-trial Wilde was found guilty of the charges and sentenced to two years of hard labor.

It was not only Wilde's private life which was on trial but his literary work and ideas as well. The prosecutor continually quoted passages from Wilde's writing as evidence of his immorality. The public ultimately rejected the style and sensibility Wilde had cultivated so cleverly and to such an extreme. They rejected the notion that art was separate from morality. And they rejected most vehemently the idea that the individual had the right, if not the duty, to flaunt social standards.

The *Evening News* placed the matter in moral terms.

England has tolerated the man Wilde and others of his kind too long. Before he broke the law of his country and outraged human decency he was a social pest, a center of intellectual corruption. He was one of the high priests of a school which attacks all the wholesome, manly, simple ideals of English life, and sets up false gods of decadent culture and intellectual debauchery.[77]

The *Daily Telegraph* found in Wilde's trial a warning.

Young men at the universities, silly women who lend an ear to any chatter which is petulant and vicious, novelists who have sought to imitate the style of paradox and unreality, poets who have lisped the language of nerveless and effeminate libertinage—these are the persons who should ponder with themselves the doctrines and career of the man who has now to undergo the righteous sentence of the law.[78]

The media hysteria that surrounded the Wilde trials reinforced their moral. How tolerant society would be of individualism and especially *sexual* individualism was made explicit. The Labouchere Amendment—probably in response to the growing public discussion of sexuality—made criminal "private acts"; a stringent and novel prohibition.

The hostility generated by the Wilde trials put a damper on any progressive writing about sexuality. Several of Edward Carpenter's pamphlets were withdrawn from circulation by his publisher. People were suspicious of any literature or art that was connected with Wilde or the aesthetic movement. A backlash developed, insisting upon conformity, strict gender roles, class divisions, and traditional values.

After Wilde

Wilde's trials hindered but did not put a complete stop to gay writing. Homosexuals were certainly more circumspect in their public lives and the general reading public showed a distaste for writing that seemed similar to Wilde's. But writing continued that fell into the already established traditions of gay sensibility and which was directly descended from the patterns set by Wilde.

Frederick Rolfe, in an extreme form of Wildeian self-invention, claimed to have been given the title "Baron Corvo," which he retained as a pen name. His writing is filled with overwrought prose and sprinkled with epigrams. His histories, such as *Chronicles of the House of Borgia* (1901), tell us more about his paranoid imagination than they do about Italian history. His most famous novel, *Hadrian the Seventh* (1904), in which a rather obscure English writer becomes Pope, is a mixture of wish fulfillment and revenge upon those whom he felt prevented him from taking Holy Orders.

Clearly a child of the 1890s aesthetics, Ronald Firbank's style and sensibility would have an important effect upon future gay writers. Evelyn Waugh credited Firbank with being the first modern writer to "solve the problem of fiction" by releasing it from the strictures of 19th century naturalism. Firbank had little connection with his contemporaries—most of his books were privately printed and he did not have a literary reputation. He seems to have sprung, fully formed, from the head of Oscar Wilde.

A thin person, Firbank always encouraged the impression of frailty and ill health, languishing upon chairs or divans whenever he entertained. He claimed to eat nothing but fruit and flowers and drink nothing but champagne. He also demanded that his home always be filled with exotic blooms. At a time when a small bowl of roses was considered serviceable, Firbank's tables, decked with exotic orchids, were quite alarming. He wrote only with purple ink, and then only on large blue postcards, some of which he sent to friends and others upon which, claims Osbert Sitwell, he wrote all of his novels. Wilde's pose became Firbank's lifestyle.

Although Wilde praised style over content, he always had something to say. Firbank declared that style *was* content. His novels are elaborate fantasies filled with invented languages and characters whose names bear no relationship to common English nomenclature.

Where Wilde was a satirist and a moralist, Firbank was an impressionist. His books are a series of images which create visual or emotional effects. His use of italics and capital letters ("I adore italics, don't you?", he once wrote to Siegfried Sassoon) transcends affectation and creates a visible pattern upon the printed page. Dispensing with plot and suggesting rather than defining characters, Firbank created a dream world on paper. "What made Firbank 'modern' was his setting the author and reader at a distance from the material without making him emotionally remote from it."[79]

Firbank was nine years old when Wilde was convicted but the moral of the trial—"don't be so obvious"—was not lost upon him. Firbank created a unique lifestyle (they can't arrest you for filling your house with flowers) but he apparently had no sexual relationships. Nevertheless, his writings are prime examples of a gay sensibility. By inventing a new reality he could create situations where he could show emotion safely. By turning from the literal to the suggestive, Firbank created a style that examined the psychological in a manner that pre-dates both Virginia Woolf and James Joyce.

Firbank's literary effects were achieved by exaggeration and non sequitur: " 'Men are my raging disgust,' a florid girl of stupendous beauty declared, saturating with a flacon of *Parfum cruel* her prematurely formed silhouette."[80] "Neither her Gaudiness the Mistress of the Robes nor her Dreaminess the Queen were feeling quite themselves. In the Palace all was speculation"[81] "Those demons, imps, fiends, and fairies with horns like stalactites and indigent, scurrying angels and virgins trampling horrors beneath their firm, mysterious feet..."[82]

Firbank creates a barrage of impressions. The use of unusual words, (flacon rather than flask) the overwrought adjectives, ("*stupendous* beauty") and odd juxtapositions (virgins with firm, mysterious feet) create a strong impression of concreteness along with a sense of the unreal. Firbank's imaginary world has few points of reference outside of itself. Every now and then some obviousness creeps in. *Concerning the Eccentricities of Cardinal Pirelli* is clearly about homosexual passion and Firbank's play, *The Princess Zoubaroff*, has a strong lesbian subtext. However, the frustrated reader sometimes wonders whether Firbank wanted anyone to know what he was writing about.

Gay writers have frequently been unable to speak plainly because of social and legal repercussions. Gay men developed unique manners and speech as a means of self-protection. Many gay writers have conveyed their sense of isolation and alienation through codes, either conscious or unconscious. The humorist Edward Lear, writing at the end of the 19th century, used specific code words in his diary to note masturbatory episodes and homosexual attractions. Sexual overtones, usually concerning loss or anxiety, are less consciously used in his limericks.[83] H.H. Munro (Saki) referred in his writing to bathhouses and restaurants that others in the know understood to be "that way."[84] Firbank invented a style that allowed his imagination to be freed from the usual literary restrictions and structures. He used elusiveness as much to convey psychological states as to cover for openly homosexual content.

Bloomsbury and the Fathers

Mrs. Henry Wood's 1861 novel, *East Lynne*, a melodramatic affirmation of home and mother love, was England's most popular literary work for over 50 years. Books that extolled Empire and aggressive manhood were widely read. This was particularly true of adventure stories, written for boys. H. Rider Haggard's *King Solomon's Mines* was published in 1885 and sold 31,000 copies in twelve months. He wrote 57 other books of a similar nature. George Alfred Henty produced over 80 adventure books which pitted brave Englishman against the dangers of Africa and India. Kipling's 1899 poem, with the non-facetious title "The White Man's Burden" gave the world a phrase that aptly described English manhood. Henty and Haggard taught the soldiers of WWI the language of patriotic duty.[85] The impact of the first World War was devastating. Poets like Siegfried Sassoon, Wilfred Owen, and Rupert Brooke blasted pre-war ideals of British manhood as they brought home the horror of the trenches.

Change had begun even before the war. The Bloomsbury Group started to coalesce around 1906. Only ten years after the Wilde trials, sexual and gender arrangements were already loosening in some social circles. Homosexuality and bisexuality were accepted with little hesitation by the Bloomsbury circle. Although most of the members of the group were from the upper class or the intellectual aristocracy, they were skeptical of British imperialism, and mocked its seriousness. In 1910, Virginia Woolf and several friends, masquerading as the Abyssinian ambassador and his entourage, toured the British Navy's most secret and modern man 'o war, the H.M.S Dreadnought. The hoodwinked officers and the proper British public were outraged.

Although in revolt against Victorian decorum, few Bloomsbury writers wrote in the tradition of Wilde and Firbank. Woolf, and others, spoke of "androgynous minds,"[86] and their ideas about art transcending gender harked back to the writings of Carpenter and Symonds. However, they lacked the inverted wit that characterized Wilde. Perhaps the acceptability of their class and social status made such defenses less necessary.

The two exceptions to this were Lytton Strachey and E.M. Forster. In 1918, Strachey's *Eminent Victorians* revolutionized the art of biography. Until then, the standard biography was a three volume, panegyric compilation of virtues. Strachey introduced humanity and malice. Rather than record a life, he interpreted it; where earlier biographers defended reputations, Strachey deflated them. Seeking and lampooning foibles, like Wilde, Strachey attempted to pierce Victorian pomposity with humor and critical intelligence.

Forster was always on the fringes of Bloomsbury, and enjoyed a long career as a novelist, short story writer, and essayist. It was not, however, Bloomsbury which had the greatest effect on Forster, but Edward Carpenter. Forster and Carpenter shared an interest in Eastern mysticism and the interactions between personal evolution and utopian socialism. Although aware of his homosexual feelings, Forster, unlike Carpenter and the Bloomsbury men, kept them private. In 1915, already a successful novelist, he visited Carpenter and his lover, George Merrill. Merrill touched Forster "gently and just above the buttocks. The sensation was unusual and I still remember it...It seemed to go straight through the small of my back and into my ideas, without involving my thoughts."[87]

As a result of his friendship with Carpenter, Forster began writing an explicitly homoerotic novel, *Maurice*, which was published only after his death in 1970. Like his other novels, *Maurice* charts the voyage of a middle class man learning to "connect" with others. In the novel's first half, Maurice has a three year, platonic affair with Clive, who appreciates the Greek ideal of friendship but not its physical expression. After Clive leaves him to marry, Maurice meets and beds Alec, a working class gamekeeper. After some problems the two live happily ever after. *Maurice* compares Symonds' ideal of platonic love to the spiritual *and* physical relationship advocated by Carpenter.

Forster, despite his own problems in dealing with his sexuality, was able to present a clear portrait of it in his writing. He was aware of a tradition of homosexual writing (in 1907 his reading list included: Sturge Moore, A.E. Housman, Symonds, Pater, Shakespeare, Beddoes, Whitman, Carpenter, Butler, Fitzgerald, and Marlowe).[88] However, Forster did not follow in the elliptical tradition of the aesthetes, but told his story of homosexual attraction in a novel of social manners. For Forster, as in Symonds' poem "Ithocles," personal connections take precedence over social obligations. Although Forster used sentiment where Wilde used flippancy, and did not, like Firbank, invent a fantasy world, Forster did imagine a world that allowed homoerotic passions to exist and grow. Unlike other gay writers, Forster did not write in code; however, because of his book's happy ending, he didn't publish it at all during his lifetime.

Children of the Sun

In 1922, a poem written by Brian Howard and published in *The Eton Candle* when he was 17, spoke to a whole generation.

> You were a great Young Generation...
> And then you went out and got murdered—magnificently
> Went out and got murdered...because a parcel of damned
>   old men
> Wanted some fun or some power or something.[89]

A whole generation of young men, born between 1901 and 1911, rejected everything that pre-war England, and their fathers, stood for. Many of them attended Eton and Oxford where they established a revival of dandyism and aestheticism. Many were homosexual: Brian Howard, Harold Acton, W.H. Auden, Christopher Isherwood, John Lehmann, and Tom Driberg. Others, like Evelyn Waugh and Stephen Spender, were ambivalent during college, but spent their adult lives apparently heterosexual.

In an odd juggling of cultures, the post-war dandies mixed a longing for Victoriana with the latest imports from the New World: jazz and cocktails. The death of Victoria and the war had shaken up social restrictions. Their private sexual activity was likely to remain so. They wore outlandish outfits and professed tastes for such out-of-date and childish works as *Alice in Wonderland*, the poems of Edward Lear, and Beatrix Potter's *The Tale of Peter Rabbit*. But they also considered themselves the "smart set" and saw themselves in revolt against conventionality. (The opposing set, called the "hearties," of which Geroge Orwell and D.H. Lawrence were the most famous members, maintained values which, although politically to the left, were solidly heterosexual.

Perhaps the epitomal figure of the post-war smart set was Noel

Coward. A precocious child, he established himself in theater at an early age and became a spokesperson for the "bright young things." In 1924 he scored a hit writing and starring in *The Vortex*. With such daring themes as drug addiction, homosexuality, and mother fixation, the play had a psychological insight that was new to the stage. A child of Wilde, Coward wrote a string of sophisticated comedies that used Wilde's epigrammatic style but replaced his sense of underlying seriousness with flippant cynicism. The second act of *Private Lives* (1930) sums up Coward's philosophy:

> **Elyot:** Death's very laughable, such a cunning little mystery. All done with mirrors.
> **Amanda:** Darling. I do believe you're talking nonsense.
> **Elyot:** So is everybody else in the long run. Let's be superficial and pity the poor philosophers. Let's blow trumpets and squeakers, and enjoy the party as much as we can, like very small, quite idiotic school children. Let's savor the delight of the moment. Come kiss me darling, before your body rots and worms pop in and out of your eye sockets.[90]

Many of Coward's plays, *Blithe Spirit,* for instance, are more believable as homosexual than heterosexual situations. His flippancy suited his times and there were few social prohibitions curtailing his public behavior. But while Coward's style never changed, his social attitudes did. As World War II drew close he discarded his rejection of pre-war England and became a staunch supporter of English imperialism. By the late 1940s he wrote in his diary: "Gandhi has been assassinated. In my humble opinion, a bloody good thing but far too late."[91] Coward's career floundered during the last 30 years of his life because although he maintained the pose of the dandy, he repudiated its rebellious history; for him it had become an empty posture.

As political turmoil erupted in Europe in the 1930s many of the Oxford dandies retained their mistrust of the established political structures and joined progressive forces. They spoke out for the cause in Spain and Auden and Isherwood traveled to China to report on the war there. They had established themselves as anti-English, anti-establishment; for many, this was bound up with their sexual identities and the fact that their queerness separated them from the world of their fathers. As Isherwood writes about himself (in the third person): "his strongest negative motivation is ancestor hatred. He vowed to disappoint, disgrace, and disown his ancestors."[92] The dandy pose was no longer tenable in England. The real world was closing in, and, unless you were going to capitulate and support the old regime like Coward and photographer Cecil Beaton, the only option left was flight. In 1939, Isherwood, Britten, Britten's lover, (the singer Peter Pears) and W.H. Auden left for America.

America

Homosexual culture and writing had progressed very differently in the U.S. than it had in England. The development of a gay sensibility in England was intimately connected with the gradual breakdown of the British class system and a change in economics which allowed for social advancement based upon factors other than class or money. Although American culture was based more upon populist than elitist presumptions, the U.S. was hardly the land of freedom imagined by many English people, even if its class lines were defined economically rather than by ancestry. If Wilde's cultivated elitism gave him some social mobility in Britain, then Horatio Alger's more than 120 "pull yourself up by the bootstraps" books were purely American fantasies. Alger had been removed from the Unitarian Church in Brewster Massachusetts in 1866 for having sexual relationships with several boys. The novels—a mainstay of American children's literature—are clearly homoerotic and suggest that the best way to get ahead is to work hard and make friends with an older man who will help you along.

Besides Whitman, 19th century America saw little of the early scientific work or more blatant homoerotic fiction that was prevalent in England and Germany. Poets Fitz-Greene Halleck, Bayard Taylor, and George Santayana gained reputations in literary circles but made no lasting impression upon the national literature.[93]

Although there was an active American gay subculture little of it was reflected in popular literature.[94] There were, however, some distinctly American cultural phenomena. Novelists Thorn Smith and James Branch Cabell wrote popular novels which toyed with ambisexual experiences and revealed a more open attitude towards sexuality than was acceptable to a wide reading public. Novelist Carl Van Vechten was also exceedingly popular. His novels, with their artificial attitudes and precious writing, were examples of a specifically gay sensibility.[95] Novels such as *Parties* and *The Blind Bow-Boy* (1923) explored the open morality and sexual looseness of the jazz age. They afforded readers a glimpse into the hidden lives of gay people of a certain upper class and artistic set. Van Vechten's most popular novel, however, was *Nigger Heaven*. A melodrama set in Harlem, (the title refers to the upper balconies of movie theaters to which people of color were restricted) *Nigger Heaven* was extraordinarily popular. It was the product of Van Vechten's intense fascination with American blacks and black culture, then gaining some recognition as part of the Harlem Renaissance.

The first world war had caused major social and economic upheavals, including a major shifting of population centers. As early as 1905, Harlem, a white, middle class neighborhood above Central Park North, was beginning to house the majority of Manhattan's black population. By the early 1920s, it was a vital center of black American culture. During this period there was a new wave in black nationalism and an intense interest on the part of many black Americans in reclaiming and consciously creating an autonomous national culture. Politicians, writers, musicians, performers, painters, and sculptors formed a constellation of creative energy which reflected both a pride in an African heritage and their consciousness of being black in white America.

The importance of the Harlem Renaissance to the development of a gay sensibility is twofold. While it was generally difficult to discern signs of either gay life or gay sensibility in white American culture at this time, there was a more evident manifestation of it in black culture. Additionally, many white people, like Carl Van Vechten, who were occupied with gay cultural concerns, were strongly attracted to the creative impulses of the Harlem Renaissance. Not only a center of black culture, Harlem became the gathering spot for the avant garde and bohemian fringes of black and white society, garnering for itself a reputation as the Afro-American Paris.[96]

Because of the lack of scholarship in both black and gay studies, it is difficult to ascertain the impact which homosexuals, and a specific black gay sensibility, had upon the Harlem Renaissance. Some of the outstanding leaders and writers of the period were homosexuals. Alain Locke, whose anthology *The New Negro* is generally considered to have brought the movement to the public, was known to be gay. Poets Langston Hughes and Countee Cullen were also openly gay and this is reflected in their work. Richard Bruce Nugent, a writer, painter, and dancer, published "Smoke, Lilies and Jade" in *Fire!*, a black literary journal, which spoke explicitly of homosexual desire.

Lesbians and gay men also exerted a huge influence upon the non-literary side of the Renaissance and on Harlem life and black culture in general. Homosexuality was tolerated in the parts of the black community connected with the entertainment business. Charles Anderson and "Gloria Swanson" were noted drag queens and such lesbian or bisexual women as Mabel Hampton, Bessie Smith, Ma Rainey, and Gladys Bentley found show business perfectly compatible with their sexual enthusiasms.[97]

It was this aspect of black culture which many white people, especially fringe groups like bohemians and homosexuals, found exotic. The perception of social freedom, the wider leeway in artistic and sexual expression, and the racist notion that blacks were more "primitive," and therefore more sexual all fueled whites' fascination with black culture. (This appeal was similar to what Victorians like Symonds, Von Gloedon, and Stoddard felt about other "primitive" cultures.) Black performers were also idolized in Europe; Josephine Baker, a bisexual, spent most of her life entertaining at the *Follies Bergere* in Paris and many other black entertainers began their careers in Europe because they could not find acceptance in their own country.

Black culture was destined to make its mark with music. Jazz, a purely black phenomenon with a free, open sound mixed with frank sexual lyrics, appealed to white audiences who experienced the general sexual repression fostered by social and cultural norms. Dr. E. Elliot Rawlings, described by his contemporaries as a "noted New York physician," wrote:

> Jazz releases stronger animal passions, affects the brain through the senses of hearing, giving the same results as whisky and other alcoholic drinks taken into the system by way of the stomach. It has the same effect as a drug, and one may become addicted to its use. The more you hear it, the more you desire its stimulation.[98]

Non-traditional sexualities were often the topic of early jazz lyrics: "Sissy Man Blues," "Fairy Blues," "Two Old Maids in a Folding Bed" and "B.D. Woman's Blues" (B.D. stood for bull diker or bulldaggers) were popular tunes, sung by accepted performers. It is interesting that all of these songs were written before the beginning of organized jazz criticism. They have, for the most part, been written out of jazz history and, like much of gay culture, hidden from popular knowledge.

The Harlem Renaissance gave black culture a strong history and reinforced its cultural identity. Blues and jazz, especially performed by female vocalists, played a large part in the formation of white gay male sensibility. Alberta Hunter, still performing at 90, has said: "We sing the blues because our hearts have been hurt, our souls have been destroyed. But when you sing the blues, let it be classy." Over the years, blues and jazz singers have been favorites with gay male listeners. Hunter's statement explains the dual nature of their appeal: pain accompanies ostracism and prejudice, but its expression has style and conveys integrity, self-worth, and a determination that transforms self-pity into personal strength.

The image that jazz and other black musicians manifested during the 1930s was one of elegance. Lester Young, Duke Ellington, Count Basie, Sarah Vaughan, Mabel Mercer, and especially Billie Holiday worked on creating an alternative to bumbling, bug-eyed, foolish minstrel images which had long been a staple of white American culture. Their dignity and sophistication appealed to the imaginations and aspirations of their audiences. Like gay men, they recreated themselves as people they chose to be, not people they were told they had to be.

Because so much of popular culture is concerned with unrequited love, lost love, or just plain fouled up love, jazz singers with a background in blues hit upon a powerful combination. A black woman singing about unhappiness in love with the consciousness that she was outcast because of her race, was sure to attract the attention and empathy of gay men. The effect that Billie Holiday and other black women singers have had upon American music is immeasurable. They brought heart, soul, and an immediacy of emotion and sexuality to music which had just not existed before. Their influence is inescapable whether you are talking about Frank Sinatra, Barbra Streisand, The Rolling Stones, or Judy Garland.

Although black musicians have had the major influence on American music, their contribution has not protected them from the realities of race hatred. While at the height of her career, Billie Holiday was singing in an elegant jazz club on New York's 52nd Street when a drunken sailor called her a "nigger." She smashed a beer bottle on a table top and the man was quickly removed. Several days later, a friend stopped her on the street and asked, "How are you doing, Lady Day?" She replied, "Well, you know, I'm still a nigger." The cold-blooded irony of her retort is a sobering message and lesson for any oppressed group that imagines acceptability and equality come quickly, easily, or without struggle.

Van Vechten and other white intellectuals and artists were drawn to black culture, adopting aspects of it which later became part of a white gay sensibility. Whites appreciated and absorbed those apects of black culture which they could relate to, neglecting to acknowledge their origins. Not surprisingly, this was perceived as nothing less than voyeurism and exploitation by blacks. Van Vechten's novel *Nigger Heaven*, for example, although admired by some black writers, was treated by most of the black community as a traitorous act. Middle class blacks did not approve of the social or entertainment aspects of black culture that white cultural radicals were so enamoured of. This distaste continued through the 60s, when black nationalists demanded that Harlem's Apollo Theater cease its presentation of drag shows because "it glorified the homosexual...and was a threat to black life and the black family."[99]

The tremendous impact which lesbians and gay men had upon black culture and the Harlem Renaissance was buried for many decades because they were both black and gay. Even recent scholarship reclaiming the importance of the Renaissance ignores the sexual orientation and practices of many of the most important people involved.[100] The racism of white gays has meant that the contribution of black culture to the development of gay sensibility has been ignored, while the homophobia of black scholarship has made invisible the contribution of lesbians and gay men to black culture.

The flourishing gay culture of England in the 1920s and 1930s, which seems to be missing from white American culture, can be seen in the black culture of the Harlem Renaissance, the popular culture of jazz, and show business. Although hidden in each for different reasons, this juncture is an important milestone in the history of gay sensibility and black culture, giving a tradition and history to contemporary black writers from James Baldwin to Alice Walker.

The second World War caused other major upheavals in American society. While American men were off fighting the war, the country was changing: the standard family unit was disintegrating; women were encouraged to work in factories; and the strict distinctions between urban and rural were beginning to crumble. When the war was over the society began to reorganize itself back into pre-war structures. Gender expectations—at least for the white middle class— were once again firmly defined: women at home, men at work. Evicting women from the workplace avoided drastic economic changes and reinforced patriarchal standards of sex and gender. The nuclear family unit was more heavily propagandized than ever before. America after the war was a country longing for conformity and gay women and men had little place in it.

However, the growth of urban life after the war had also brought gay women and men into contact with one another more than ever before. San Francisco and New York became havens for gay men and lesbians returning from overseas as well as for any homosexual looking for others with similar passions. As these communities grew, so did their visibility. Kansas City, Denver, and San Jose all had gay bars in the 1940s.[101] America was trying to patch up the cracks in the social framework that opened up during the war, but try as it might, the damage was already done. The changing economy and social values now allowed some women to live and work independently, enabling lesbians to come out; life outside the nuclear family became a possibility.

While the gay community was beginning to form a distinct identity, America was shocked by the 1948 publication of Alfred Kinsey's *Sexual Behavior in the Human Male*. Kinsey gave empirical evidence that homosexuality was pervasive in all strata of American society and that homosexuals could not be identified by stereotypes. The *Kinsey Report* told homosexuals what they already knew: they were everywhere. Kinsey also reinforced many heterosexuals' most basic fear: the invisible, undetectable enemy *was* everywhere.

Although gay people were becoming more visible to one another, they were for the same reason more subject to harassment. The federal government reinforced the idea that "sexual perversion" was a threat to American life and in June of 1950 authorized a committee to investigate moral perversion in the government. The few gay literary works that had been published just after the war— Gore Vidal's *City and the Pillar*, John Horne Burns' *The Gallery*, and Charles Jackson's *The Fall of Valor*—were severely criticized and new standards were set up to safeguard the American literary scene.

After discovering the basic social structure—the family unit— was not as secure as believed, and then confronted with a scientific analysis of sexuality that attacked romantic notions of sexual behavior and gender arrangements, the general public felt pushed against the wall.

Spurred on by the Army-McCarthy hearings, the American public went out for queer-baiting as well as red-baiting. The implication that both of these groups, sometimes in tandem, had influenced the government led to purges at all levels of government and the military. These witch hunts had actually begun earlier. The national mobilization for the war effort brought many gay men and lesbians into the military. Many women and men, once isolated in traditional families and non-urban settings, discovered their homosexuality and support for it in the military. There was no desire to create an official policy for dealing with homosexual behavior in the military until Junuary 1943. A year later, regulations were devised to deal with military personnel who displayed "tendencies."[102] Soon the military was making an all-out effort to screen homosexuals out at the induction level and purge them if they managed to sneak by. Military officials threatened homosexuals to get them to reveal their own sexual lives and to implicate others. Almost everyone so discovered was given a dishonorable discharge and was stigmatized as deviant in his or her civilian life.

At times the purges reached fantastic proportions. Gay writer and activist Pat Bond remembers being in the WACS.

> Once they got you in, they decided they wanted you out. Nobody could understand that, since most of our officers were gay—and kind of openly. They started an incredible witch hunt in Tokyo. Unbelievable! Sending 500 women home for dishonorable discharges. Practically every woman I knew who was in the army has a dishonorable discharge. Every day there were court martials and trials. You were there testifying against your friends, or they were testifying against you—yes, they had seen you necking with a woman, or they had seen you dancing with a woman too close, or whatever—until they got you afraid to look your neighbor in the eye. Afraid of everything.[103]

The purges that began in the military continued over the years. Suspected homosexuals were ferreted out of government. Intellectuals, always somewhat suspect in American life, were also viewed with suspicion and many colleges and universities were particularly zealous in ridding themselves of un-American elements. Tragedies occurred. Harvard professor and literary critic F.O. Matthiessen, who was both a homosexual and a leftist, committed suicide in 1950 because of the pressures on his professional and personal life.[104] Matthiessen's story is known because of his preeminence as a writer and critic. It is impossible to say how many other deaths were the result of McCarthyite homophobic and anti-communist backlash.

These issues of sexual preference and political leaning were so charged with hysteria that it was nearly impossible to combat them legally. Attempts were made by some service people to fight the

dishonorable discharges, but there was little publicity or organization about the issue. It was not until 1960 that Frank Kameny, who
had been fired from a government job three years earlier because of
suspected homosexuality, challenged his dismissal in court. Writing
his own brief, Kameny stated:

> ...the Civil Service Commission's policy on homosexuality
> is improperly discriminatory, in that it discriminates
> against an entire group, not considered as individuals, in a
> manner in which other similar groups are not discrimi-
> nated against, and in that this discrimination has no basis
> in reason, is inconsistent with other policy and practice,
> and thus is plainly arbitrary and capricious.[105]

Kameny lost on all court levels and his case was declined review by
the Supreme Court. Although some progress has been made, the
fight for legal protection still goes on today.

Birth of the Gay Movement

The 1950s was the decade of the "organization man." This was
as true for homosexuals as for heterosexuals. By organizing and
defining themselves, homosexuals reassured straight people terrified
by the *Kinsey Report*: they were visible. Clearly recognizable
homosexuals implicitly guaranteed the boundaries of heterosexuality.[106] Homosexuality was pitiable, disgusting, and titillating.
Much of the anti-gay hysteria which had characterized the 1950s was
a result of these conflicting emotions. Homosexuals were not simple
scapegoats used as a political football, but a minority whose very
identity raised such fear and confused desire in the hearts and minds
of American people that they bore the brunt of personal bigotry and a
deep hatred. This was a result of the confusion that their presence
caused in the sexual and gender arrangements of a national identity.

1950s gay stereotypes—the fluff sweaters and poodles, the butch
dyke with a crew cut and her ultra-femme girlfriend—enabled some
homosexuals to create an identity; they also reassured the hetero-

sexuals who desperately needed gay men and lesbians to be identifiable. Although most homosexuals could choose to "pass," the majority of homosexuals who formed this visible subculture were effeminate men, butch women, obvious queens, and the drags who gained a positive identity, but who were also the targets of disdain from mainstream culture and often from closeted homosexuals who were interested in keeping their cover or maintaining a "good image." While the world seemed to be divided between real people and "obvious" homosexuals, a new movement was beginning. Breaking away from stereotypes, gay women and men began to organize themselves politically and socially.

There were some gay male organizations right after World War II: the Veterans' Benevolent Association was founded in New York in 1945, Knights of the Clock, a racially integrated gay male group formed in 1949, and liberal "bachelors" banded together to work for presidential candidate Henry Wallace in 1948, calling themselves, rather surreptitiously, Bachelors for Wallace. It was this group, once disbanded, whose members founded the Mattachine Foundation in 1950. The repression of McCarthyism had already begun and this group was more cautious than its original formation. Although the group only lasted two years, other homosexual rights groups—or homophile, as they called themselves—emerged. More importantly, members of the Mattachine Foundation got together and founded, in October of 1952, *ONE*, the first continuously published gay magazine to appear in the U.S. In 1953, other members of the Mattachine Foundation formed the Mattachine Society and began publishing the *Mattachine Review*. In 1955, four lesbians formed the Daughters of Bilitis and began publishing their own magazine, *The Ladder*, for lesbians, who, though granted token status on *ONE* and *Mattachine Review*, were not generally represented as having special concerns.

Although the membership of these organizations was quite small—it did not exceed a few hundred for any of them at any given time—the publications surveyed the entire country. In 1956, *ONE* had subscribers in every state, was sold at a number of newsstands, and had readers in Europe, Asia, Australia, and South America. While the readership was probably much larger than the circulation figure, (these were magazines that were passed around a lot) in 1960

ONE's circulation was 5000, *Mattachine Review's* 2,500, and *The Ladder's* 750. These publications made an enormous impact on the scattered American gay subculture. Gay women and men identified with them and used them as a centering force for their thoughts and experiences. Although culture-bound, *ONE, Mattachine Review,* and *The Ladder* represented the beginnings of the gay press and of a mass gay culture.[107]

Both *ONE* and *Mattachine Review* assumed positions of political neutrality. Although *ONE* claimed to represent "the homosexual viewpoint," it was quick to point out that homosexuals were entitled to their own opinions. As late as 1960, they were detaching themselves from any specific goal-oriented commitment; their intention was to improve the status of homosexuals by making people think. The notion of an activist politic was anathema to them.

> Let no one rashly assume that the Magazine is now going into politics. Nothing could be further from its intentions. It has its field: the homosexual and homosexuality.[108]

Mattachine Review was even more adamant in disassociating itself from any blemish of activism or illegality. Its position is made clear by a cathechism of information on the back cover of their first issue.

> WHAT IS MATTACHINE INC.?
> It is an incorporated organization of persons who are interested in the problems of the sex variant—especially the homosexual—and its solution.
> IS IT AN ORGANIZATION OF HOMOSEXUALS?
> Emphatically *NO.* All persons—men and women alike—who are over 21 years of age and interested in the problem and its solution are invited to give cooperation and support. This is *NOT* an organization attempting to create a "homosexual society" but rather an organization seeking the integration of the homosexual as responsible and acceptable citizen in the community. The Society will not tolerate use of itself or its name for any subversive political activity or reprehensible conduct.[109]

Both *ONE* and *Mattachine Review* found themselves in a fairly schizophrenic situation. On the one hand, they urged discussions about "the homosexual" and his or her position in society. They referred to the "problem" and the "solution," using language which would not antagonize non-homosexual readers and officials. Yet on the other hand, (and this is especially true of *ONE*, which was consistently pro-homosexual in its "neutrality") they could not ignore the grave injustices being done to gay people across the country. In its "Tangents" column, *ONE* ran news stories about police harassment of bars and cruising places, as well as media abuse ranging from *Time* magazine to a small daily in the Midwest. Both *ONE* and *Mattachine Review* insisted on respectability and counter- ing the negative images of gay people, while at the same time pointing out that all those perfectly nice, law-abiding citizens were being systematically persecuted. The split consciousness surfaced again and again. In the May 1963 issue, *ONE* published a cover story entitled "The New Nazism." After detailing specific local police harassment in New York, Miami, and other cities, the author speculated that the FBI was behind a nation-wide crackdown on homosexuals. He compared the American equation of anti-com- munism with homosexuality to the Third Reich's anti-Bolshevism and anti-semitism.

> In the United States the average person is not aware of the
> creeping Nazification of American thought...in this nation
> homosexuals are finding themselves in much the same
> position as that of the Jews in the beginning of the Nazi era
> in Germany.

The article then proceeds to lambast homosexuals for not taking a more active role in fighting for their rights and attacks the New York Mattachine Society for not organizing a boycott of the YMCA when police were brought in by the executive staff.

> Homosexuals were numerous enough to have forced their
> will had they so desired. But how many would have been
> willing to have made the simple sacrifice? Not many, I
> wager.

The article ended with the warning: "If the homosexual continues to acquiesce as he has done in the past, his future in this nation will be grim indeed."

The article violates the usual tone of *ONE* with its analysis and its aggressive attitude. One month later, as if to compensate, *ONE* ran an editorial.

> The law in our land does not only persecute. It protects...
> I am proud of being an American. I'd be proud of it if I were heterosexual. But being homosexual, I am *especially* proud, and just plain glad I am an American.
>
> Because I know I am lucky to be living in a land whose laws permit me to speak, write, and organize as a homosexual, and whose laws permit me to propagandize for the repeal of those I believe to be inhumane and archaic.

Because *ONE* tended to be a little more open in its espousal of a homosexual lifestyle, the contrasts are more evident in it than in *Mattachine Review*. But both tread a fine line between offense and defense with caution and tact. As careful as both magazines were, there was always a lively interplay of ideas and opinions in their pages. In October 1964, *Mattachine Review* ran a short story—"The Cowboy and the Swastika"—which presented the same idea as "The New Nazism" and ended with stormtrooper-like police machine-gunning everyone in a gay bar. (It is curious that neither piece mentions the Nazi persecution of homosexuals.) As early as 1958, when *ONE* tended to be more conventional than it was later, it published an article by a lesbian that caused much furor: "Homosexuals Without Masks," was a spirited defense of the dreaded stereotypical image.

> I think the queen and dyke are, in a sense, emancipated. They are doing that which many of us would like to do— proclaiming their feelings and desires to the world. They are not bound to the facade of normality which most of us erect to make it easier to live and get along in this world. They have virtually said: "Here I am. Take me for what I am or not at all."

Even the detached, analytical image of the magazines came under attack from some readers.

Your articles are very nice, very ethical, and very informative, but they are as cold as hell! You speak with great authority, from great heights...and of course we read and nod our old grey heads in agreement...but what about the frustrated, lonely teenager, or twenty-ager? The kids want warmth, and *ONE* hasn't got it. *ONE* has facts.

You are advancing our "cause" as nothing else has ever been able to do. You are showing us that we are not alone, and that others have the same problems. However, your magazine is aimed at people who think, not at people who feel.[110]

In a way, Miss W, the author of the above letter, identified the core problem of both *ONE* and *Mattachine Review*: although both promoted a sense of gay identity and attempted to find ways in which gay people could manage to live in a hostile world, they did not have the resources to promote a self-generating, positive gay lifestyle. *Mattachine Review* focused mainly on legal issues and relations between the homosexual and society. *ONE* looked at relationships within the gay community; it published articles on "The Homophile Marriage" and "Secrets of a Gay Novel" by lesbian pulp writer Ann Bannon. Although it occasionally admitted that there was a world of bars, social clubs, and baths, it usually downplayed that aspect of gay life. It would take the publication of *The Advocate* in 1967 to begin making broadly based social connections between the secure gay identity that *Mattachine Review* and *ONE* established and the concrete social identity that many gay people were discovering.

What *Mattachine Review* and *ONE* did encourage, however, was a greater sense of gay community and cultural continuity through reading. Understanding that many gay people were hungry for *any* information on homosexuals, both *ONE* and *Mattachine Review* had active book review and book chat columns. *Mattachine Review* published a comprehensive gay bibliography of over 1000 titles and both magazines ran profiles of famous homosexual writers such as Jean Genet, Radcliffe Hall, Walt Whitman, and Edward Carpenter. In many ways these book reviews and columns were the most vital part of the magazines. They also brought to the attention of readers mainstream books such as those of Mary Renault, whose homoerotic themes might not be mentioned in the average newspaper or magazine review. Even denunciations of gay subculture opened up possibilities for homosexuals. If *Life* magazine did a photo essay on homosexuals in Greenwich Village, this enabled homosexuals to find out about the Village. The explosion of television and other media in the 1950s helped break through the isolation of the average homosexual. Although homosexuality was hardly acceptable during the 1950s, it was written about more and more each year.

It is a truism to say that the 1950s were sexually repressive. The flip side of this is that the 1950s were also obsessed with sexuality. The family was sacrosanct, yet Jayne Mansfield was on the cover of magazines everywhere. Sex and gender roles were so rigid that they became parodies: Marilyn Monroe and Victor Mature. In the face of the solid corporate society which America had become since the war, the beats showed that you could just drop out, not deal with it at all. Derided by television and magazines, the beats posed a tantalizing alternative to conformity. *Playboy* magazine and its "lifestyle" also posed an alternative to men who were tired of the pressures of business, husband, and family roles.[111]

Suddenly America's youth was dissatisfied and the whole country—or at least the movie screens—was filled with motorcycle gangs and juvenile delinquents. If men could turn to *Playboy* for an alternative, women found new insights in Betty Freidan's *The Feminine Mystique*. People of color demanded their civil rights and there was a growing movement—to be called the new left—which was generating progressive ideas. Not that any of these groups were particularly open to homosexuals—they generally hated them as much as the general population did—but they all represented a broader range of options, of ideas, than had previously been available to the American public.

As the 1950s progressed into the 1960s, the disintegration of the old social structures began to evolve into social movements. At first ridiculed by the popular media and the general public, the second wave of American feminism soon took root and its ideas—mainstream and radical—became common currency throughout the country. Questioning the role of women in the culture, women's liberation quickly began to affect the lives of college women, housewives, and working women. Because it dealt with such issues as gender and sexuality and declared that personal life was also political, the women's movement catalyzed a new discourse in American intellectual life and in the minds of average people, thus paving the way for the explosive discussions of gay liberation which came later.

The movement for black civil rights which became visible early in the decade was growing and affecting the lives of all people of color. What began as a civil rights battle became a movement for the emergence of a national identity based upon the cultural heritage of black people in the U.S. As with the women's movement, the many groups which promoted black liberation were concerned with challenging negative stereotypes and replacing them with new images based not only on a new found pride, but also on reclaiming a historic legacy which had been consciously obscured and misrepresented by the dominant culture.

The dissatisfaction of youth in the 1950s, which manifested itself in the cult of the rebel and a fascination with outlaw images, had changed.[112] Instead of becoming Marlon Brando types who stewed in their own anger, or beats who rejected social norms but who had no concrete analysis or future vision, the new youth movement offered middle class youth the option of dropping out and into a whole new youth culture. This counterculture promised release from the angry world and preached love; it promised new sexual arrangements which did not include the stifling institutions of marriage, monogamy, or suburban living; it even promised an alternative drug-induced view of reality. Because many of the young people involved were products of the 1950s baby boom, the youth movement was a major cultural phenomenon. It also presented an enviable alternative to the everyday lives of many people. Although the whole country did not become hippies, people were more than willing to read about them with a combination of vicarious enjoyment and hesitant condemnation.

The political stirrings which became the new left found a rallying point in opposing U.S. policies in Southeast Asia. Organizing against the war in Vietnam provided a focal point for the new left, and it was quick to relate the war to problems at home such as black civil rights, unemployment, and capitalist exploitation.

Although many social movements were working and growing simultaneously, there were tensions among them. It would take the women's movement a long time to deal with racism and the questions of class and culture which other movements were formulating. The movement for black liberation had trouble examining sexism, and often viewed the 1960s counterculture as a perverse expression of white privilege. The new left talked a good line on equality, but it was years before feminist concerns and cultural insights were taken seriously. The pleasure-seeking which was a principle of the counterculture was antithetical to the goals, ideology, and tradition of the new left. Even the youth movement, which in theory supported personal freedoms for everyone, was often too spaced out to figure out how to achieve that goal. It did not question the role of women within the cutlure, or attempt to understand why racism and the economic status of black people did not allow them to "tune in, turn on, and drop out." Although they believed in peace and love, cultural radicals were not organized enough to battle U.S. policies, domestic or foreign, successfully. There were alliances made, to be sure, between diverse movement organizers, but these often left activists disappointed and embittered by the lack of basic understanding and shared goals.

Despite the many differences and lack of communication, these groups brought about a massive cultural change in the late 1960s and 1970s. They also set the stage, each in its own way, for the emergence of a radical gay movement which occurred in 1969 at the Stonewall Riots. This defiant, innately political act changed the status quo between "queers" and "straights." The gay liberation movement had learned lessons from all the other groups, reformulating and integrating their strategies and analyses.

Although none of the other groups were particularly receptive to homosexuals, there were of course many homosexual men and women working in them. Allen Young has written about being a closeted gay man working with Liberation News Service, experiencing the frustration of having to hide his sexuality in order to escape the homophobia of the left.[113] Many lesbians discovered their sexuality after having worked in the women's movement, and some radical feminists even stated that lesbianism was the logical extension of a feminist political commitment. Lesbians and gay men of color founded the Third World Gay Revolution in several cities and wrote manifestos which reflected upon their oppression as both homosexuals and people of color. The youth movement, especially on the West coast, provided a huge impetus to gay liberation. Carl Whitman, an activist in the new left and in the San Francisco counterculture, wrote *A Gay Manifesto* months before the Stonewall Riots occurred.[114] His political analysis of sexuality, culture, and repression reflected his New Left experience, but his gay sensibility brought something new to his writing: a consciousness of the interactions of sex, politics, and culture.

Gay liberation brought sex and style to radical politics. It also brought an explicit political vision to a culture and sensibility which had existed for almost 100 years. By politicizing and bringing gay sensibility into the open, it forced the popular imagination and the mainstream culture to deal with homosexuality in a way it had never done before. Any dynamic which now occurred between the two would be on a new plane. Gay sensibility, which had functioned covertly for so many years, was public. It was the worst fear; it was the best fantasy. Anything was possible.

Part II

"Toto, I don't think we're in Kansas anymore."

Movies
Hollywood Homo-sense

Hollywood manufactures icons to excite the adoration of the American public, and gay men have been particularly enthralled by the glamour and the thrill of stars, especially women stars. Before gentrification, disco, and the 70s looks of hyper-masculinity and high-tech elegance, eight-by-ten signed glossies of movie stars were standard bar decor.

Screen images, perhaps more than any other medium, have shaped popular consciousness in the U.S. Gay men in American culture occupy a peculiar position in relation to this consciousness. The popular view of homosexuality is that it is a flight from something. Psychoanalysts have insisted that (for men) it is a flight, variously, from women, from masculinity, from the "responsibilities" of heterosexuality, (i.e., wife, children, and a house in the suburbs) from male competition, or from the "self": a futile attempt to find the "self" in another man. And while these theories of the etiology of male homosexual behavior are both psychological

nonsense and deeply homophobic, it is true that in the face of the
hostility from the heterosexual world a great deal of gay life—and
thus gay culture—is indeed a flight—from constant fear of being
discovered and disowned, of being terrorized psychologically and/or
physically, of being placed in a position where the basic necessities of
life are beyond reach.

These fears are based soundly in gay experience. Mainstream
culture offers very few places to which gay men can safely escape. If a
large portion of gay life is a flight from terrifying realities, it is also a
flight *to* an alternative world that offers solace and understanding.
For gay men who can spend their lives passing as presumed
heterosexuals, it is the emotional and sexual side of homosexual life
that remains hidden, a psychological, but not a social, reality. One of
the major charges against movie going—similar to criticisms of
novel-reading when novels first developed in the mid-1700s—is that
movies are pure escapism: that they have no redeeming moral, social,
or psychological benefits and that watching them is a debilitating
indulgence. This is, of course, why movies are so popular. They do
cater to fantasy, exploiting the emotional and the sexual. For many
gay men, the movies became a place to experience strong feelings and
sexuality with others in a socially acceptable environment. Gay men
could feel part of a world from which they usually felt excluded.
Movies provided an emotionally safe place where the imagination
could flourish. In the movies, it was possible to go "over the
rainbow."

In *The Glass Menagerie*, Tennessee Williams' alter ego, Tom,
flees his stifling home life every chance he gets.

> **Amanda:**   But, why, *why*, Tom, are you always so *rest-
> less*? Where do you *go* to, nights?
> **Tom:**   I...go to the movies.
> **Amanda:**   Why do you go to the movies so much, Tom?
> **Tom:**   I go to the movies because...I like adventure.
> Adventure is something that I don't have much of at work,
> so I go to the movies.
> **Amanda:**   But, Tom, you go to the movies *entirely* too
> *much*!
> **Tom:**   I like a lot of adventure.

The "adventure" Tom found in movies may have been more than vicarious. Having few places to congregate and socialize, gay men have been meeting in movie houses since movie houses have existed. In gay life, the movies provide not only a psychological escape but a comparatively safe and secure place to meet gay friends and sex partners.

Movies make everything, quite literally, bigger than life. The depiction of a once private sexuality, exposed and enlarged, both shocked and titillated the first moviegoers. When *The Kiss* was screened in 1896, the four second sequence of the eponymous act provoked near riots which were quelled by police in the theaters. Audiences grew accustomed to such images very quickly, however, and sexuality became a movie plot staple. Filmmakers were also discovering—no surprise—that sex was a sure-fire sell. By 1913 films depicted sexuality by masquerading as "social documents": *Traffic in Souls* and *Inside the White Slave Traffic* (both 1913) gave the public what it wanted without making it feel guilty.

In 1915 William Fox produced *A Fool There Was*, a story of female sexuality and destruction, featuring Theda Bara as "the Vamp." The exotic "Theda Bara" was in reality Theodosia Goodman, daughter of a Cincinnati tailor, who went from being a $5.00/week bit player to a household word. Complete with a glamourous past, a fabulous name, and a marketable image, Bara was the first person totally created by a public relations department. "I read so many lies about myself," she once said, "that I hardly know what the truth is anymore." Hollywood became an industry whose product was unreality, whose sales pitch was vicarious emotional or sexual stimulation, and whose major attraction was female personalities.

Although many gay men have appreciated and been sexually turned on by the beauty of gay actors like Romon Novarro, Douglas Fairbanks, or Rudolph Valentino, they certainly never received textual reinforcement of those feelings. In fact, because sex role stereotypes so strongly secured the films' plots, many of the male stars projected wooden, lifeless images. When Valentino *did* show emotion in his acting—and how could you be a great lover without being emotional?—that, mixed with his dandified manners in real life, destroyed his career. He was accused of being a "powder-puff." Gay men responded emotionally to films and to the men in films through identification with women stars. In film semiotics, women are the vehicle of emotion and sexual passion.

There are hosts of female actors, singers, and personalities with whom gay men have strongly identified. Some have been practically deified: Judy Garland and Barbra Streisand. Others have been admired for their distinctiveness or idiosyncrasies: Carmen Miranda, Eartha Kitt, Tallulah Bankhead, Maria Montez. There are gay men who have been drawn to such diverse women as Rochelle Hudson, Jane Withers, Elizabeth Taylor, Hedy Lamarr, Marilyn Monroe, and Eve Arden. Manias for women stars are well entrenched in gay male life.

Although the images of women in films are always changing—reflecting the position of women in the society—there are solid psychological reasons why many gay men feel an affinity for the personae of screen actresses. Society has created a gender dichotomy in which men "act" and women "feel." Because of the social meaning of their sexuality, gay men are denied many of the privileges that society affords "real" men, but they also more freely experience the qualities usually associated with women. Many gay men are in close touch with their sexual feelings and emotions. While there are certainly male sex symbols in Hollywood movies, and many gay men lust after them as sexual objects, they identify with the women as emotional subjects.

George Mansour, a gay film booker who has worked in the film business for more than 30 years, recalled his teenage years at the movies.

> I can remember Susan Hayward and Dana Andrews in *My Foolish Heart* and it is always tied up with the fact that I was sitting next to a sailor at the Trans-Lux. He was groping me and I was groping him and I was watching Susan Hayward pregnant in *My Foolish Heart*. That is part of my whole sexual experience.
>
> I'm sitting there, identifying with Susan Hayward, of course, and she is in love with Dana Andrews and suffering these trials, and the song is "My Love, My Foolish Heart"

and here I am with a stiff cock in my hand. I mean, that's just heaven![1]

By identifying with the female star gay men were able to find an outlet for their sexual feelings. When interviewed about his childhood, playwright Harvey Fierstein, who won two Tony Awards for *Torch Song Trilogy*, talked about seeing *Gone With The Wind*: "There I was falling in love with Clark Gable as Rhett Butler. I mean if I was in love with Clark Gable, then I must be Vivien Leigh. Right."

Since the gender arrangements in movie romance demand that women represent sexuality, this gives them power within the dramatic situation, and over the male characters. Of course, if a woman character uses her sexual power independent of patriarchal rules and laws, she is almost always punished for her transgressions. Even so, for the average gay male who knows that his sexuality will get him in trouble, the idea that it might also give him some power, albeit limited and precarious, can be exhilarating.

Carla, a character in gay playwright Robert Patrick's *Kennedy's Children*, talks about her desire to become a sex goddess after she hears of Marilyn Monroe's death.

> ...I knew then what I wanted to do with my life. I wanted to
> be the next one. I wanted to be the next one to stand radiant
> and perfected before the race of man, to shed the luminosity
> of my beloved countenance over the struggles and aspira-
> tions of my pitiful subjects. I wanted to *give* meaning to my
> own time, to be the unattainable luring love that drives
> men on, the angel of light, the golden flower, the best of
> the universe made womankind, the living sacrifice, the
> end![2]

Playwright Patrick captures perfectly the false sense of power that comes with being desired in a world in which sexuality is valued as a commodity whose distribution is controlled by a patriarchal hierarchy. However, gay men's identification with women stars is a celebration of their own sexual feelings and a means of experiencing them in an exalted context.

From its beginnings, Hollywood divided female stars into the "sacred" and the "profane." It was the profane women, glamourous, exotic, sexual, who captured the imaginations of gay men: Greta Garbo, Marlene Dietrich, Mae West. Although they are all distinctly different from one another, Garbo, Dietrich, and West share two common factors—they exude sexuality and are, at the same time, strikingly androgynous.

> The androgyne is certainly one of the great images of Camp sensibility. Here, Camp taste draws on a mostly unacknowledged truth of taste: The most refined form of sexual attractiveness (as well as the most refined form of sexual pleasure) consists of going against the grain of one's sex. What is most beautiful in virile men is something feminine; what is most beautiful in feminine women is something masculine...[3]

It is not surprising that in a society which places so much emphasis on gender roles gay men should be drawn to personalities that blur such distinctions. In the cases of Dietrich and West, they were not only appreciated by gay men, but their gay followings helped shape their images.

Film critic Molly Haskell has said of Garbo that "she understood the trick of being actively passive, of being all things to all people." She is the embodiment of pure and passionate love which transcends social circumstances. The titles of her earliest films set the tone for her future image: *The Temptress, Flesh and the Devil, Love, The Mysterious Lady, The Divine Woman, The Kiss, A Woman of Affairs*. Garbo presented passion so purely that she transcended gender. In *Queen Christina* she is dressed as a man for a good part of the film, but appears neither distinctively feminine nor a masculine parody. Garbo's "actively passive" acting allows the audience to project any and all emotions onto her characters. Garbo's characters were always punished for their moral transgressions, many times left either dead or loverless. However, the tragic endings merely reinforced how brightly the passion had burned.

While Garbo was love eternal, Marlene Dietrich was love incarnate: mysterious and sexual. While Garbo's trademark was her full-faced, fragile beauty, Dietrich's was her knowingly arched eyebrow, her cynicism when accepting protestations of love. Her characters accepted their sexuality and expected to be respected for it: "It took more than one man to make me Shanghai Lily," she tells stuffy Clive Brook in *Shanghai Express*. If Garbo was "actively passive," Dietrich was "actively active." In both *Morocco* and *Blonde Venus* she donned men's clothing and made playful sexual advances to other women. She also sported this notion of androgyny in her public life and was one of the first women to wear pants and other male attire in public. Although her characters were usually in love with the leading man, she conveyed the distinct impression that she controlled the whys and hows of her sexuality. Her husky, accented voice held the promise of a European sophistication that was beyond the average American's experience. If gay men were confused about what to do with their sexuality, Dietrich showed them how to use it to their advantage.

Until she died and an autopsy proved her to be female, many thought Mae West was not a woman at all but a drag queen. (A 1969 cult film, *Dinah East*, obviously based upon Mae West's life, did portray her as a drag queen. The film was quickly withdrawn from release, presumably because of threats from the real West.) Her trademark was the cutting one liner, the biting comeback: "Showing contempt for this court?," she says to the judge in *My Little Chickadee*, "I'm doin' my best to hide it!" There was almost no separation between West's behavior on and off the screen. She always displayed a healthy attitude towards sex and disdain for the hypocrisy and repressiveness of conventional morality. She wrote, and was prosecuted for, one of the first plays about homosexuality to appear on Broadway: *The Drag*, in 1927. In her dress, deportment, and flagrant sexuality, she parodied what men viewed as sexually desirable in women, yet she was always in complete control of the plot. While Garbo and Dietrich were victims of the sexual/political war between the sexes, West was a double agent: dressed and holding her body to please straight men, she secretly hated them and found every opportunity to expose their sexual vanity and pomposity. "May I hold your hand?" Cary Grant asks West in *She Done Him Wrong*. "That's ok, I can hold it myself," retorts West.

Mae West's physical and verbal affect is so closely tied to gay male culture one is tempted to ask: did Mae West invent drag queens or did drag queens invent Mae West? An important element of gay culture is self-preservation: self-protective camouflage and first-strike wit. Mae West was a role model for gay men in both these attributes. She took control of as much sexuality as the culture was willing to allow her and then laughed at it. She so outraged common decency that she is usually cited as one of the prime reasons that the Hays Office, Hollywood's attempt at self-censorship, was established. Like gay people, Mae West turned sexuality into a weapon against the accepted norm.

Gay men easily identified with the independent women characters in American movies during the 30s who reflected the more dominant role women were playing in the pre-war and wartime economies. These women usually spoke their minds and were assertive in their actions no matter what the consequences. The strong woman did not necessarily end up happily, i.e., with the man, in the Hollywood films, but she was a bold presence who was a reflection of reality and a barometer of changes occurring in women's roles. These women were faced with choices about social mobility as well as sexuality. They were stars like Bette Davis, Joan Crawford, Rosalind Russell, Ida Lupino, and Katharine Hepburn.

Susan Sontag notes that camp is "markedly attenuated and strongly exaggerated." One could not think of better terms to describe Bette Davis' acting. Davis' acting is so stylized and mannered that it is hard to determine how she succeeds in creating characters: logically, they should all seem like extensions of herself. However, although Davis' mannerisms, speech, arching eyebrows, and gesturing hand, with her eternal cigarette, could make her a caricature, she plays determined, uppity women without ever losing the emotional content of the character.

The artificiality of a "star," of a new persona that has little to do with who a person really is, attracted gay men to women like Joan Crawford. By sheer will, imagination, work, and luck, a poor girl from a Pennsylvania mining town named Lucille Fay LeSueur ended up as Joan Crawford. Camouflage was possible. However, Crawford also became a drag show joke because her character was so patently unfelt and artificial. Columnist Louella Parsons once wrote: "Joan

Garland at midnight recording session, 1962

Streisand, early engagement at "Hungry i" in San Francisco

Garbo, studio portrait, 1931

Dietrich, publicity photo for *The Devil Is A Woman*

Crawford, publicity photo for *No More Ladies*, 1935

Here is Garland in all of her vulnerability. The perfect pre-Stonewall icon, she contrasts perfectly with early Barbra Streisand's sharp-edged emotional stance.

Mae West averts her eyes so that *we* know she is not going to be taken in by any man. Garbo, on the other hand, is waiting for us to project emotions onto her "actively-passive" image. Deitrich possesses a sexual self-assurance which hints that there is much more beneath the surface. Devoid of subtlety, emotion, or wit, Joan Crawford steadfastly and single-mindedly "manufactures herself."

West and Victor McLaglen in *Klondike Annie*, 1936

Crawford manufactures herself." Crawford responded: "You manufacture toys. You don't manufacture stars." She was, of course, wrong. Crawford, with the help of the studios, had indeed manufactured herself. Unfortunately, her creation was a monster without passion or wit.

The other female archetype who has a great gay appeal is "the sidekick." Throughout the 1930s and 40s many top female stars were paired off with a woman friend before they ended up getting the leading man at the end of the film. The sidekick's role was generally to act as a confidante and to give the audience a pungent analysis of the plot. Sidekicks were sarcastic, unromantic, and sensible. They were cleverly self-deprecating—"Sure I got aspirin," Joan Blondell tells Dick Powell in a 1930s comedy, "I keep it next to the bed for emergencies. Like getting up in the morning"—but could also turn this wit on men. Too smart ever to get the man, sidekicks had to settle for being funnier than everybody else. For gay men who would never walk off into the sunset with a leading man, the sidekick was a dose of real life.

It is interesting to note how Hollywood handled the male version of the wise-cracking sidekick. From the 30s through the early 50s, the sissy was a stock character. Butlers, desk clerks, store managers, and man-servants were played by actors such as Edward Everett Horton, Grady Sutton, and Franklin Pangborn. Prissified and officious, they were effeminate, and foils to the film's *real* men.[4] Woman sidekicks were never played as lesbians, just "old maids," but the non-romantic male was always implicitly gay. As these characters became more blatant, the Hays Office, in 1933, found it necessary to declare that the word "pansy" was forbidden in screen usage.

During the Second World War Hollywood reflected the new "working woman"; witty and intelligent, this new woman, like Roz Russell in *His Girl Friday*, got to keep both her man *and* her job. However, when the war was over women were supposed to leave their jobs and go back to their kitchens. The images of women began to change in films. Joan Crawford's *Mildred Pierce* reflects this: deserted by her husband because she loves her children more than him, she begins a cottage business baking pies at home. Soon she owns a chain of restaurants. But because she is a working woman and has neglected her daughter (although she has done it all for her) the ungrateful wretch tries to steal Mildred's boyfriend and then kills him. Mildred feels so guilty for being a "bad mother" that she attempts to take the murder rap herself. Luckily the police are smarter than she is and at the film's end she is reunited with her husband, presumably ready to give up her career and become the good wife again. *Mildred Pierce* posits a no-win situation that is tinged with such masochistic overtones it is easy to see why it became an instant hit (Crawford won the Oscar for it) and a camp classic. Many gay men could relate to the film's message: social structures are set up so that it is impossible to win. And the final message was, as in all good Hollywood films, that the love of a good man will save you. But *Mildred Pierce* was a transitional film in more than one way. It showed that women should go back to the home, and that female initiative could almost never lead to anything good, and it also showed that a woman of Crawford's strength—no matter how strong her maternal instincts—was a monster.

Judy Garland is at the pinnacle of the gay male pantheon of idolized women. Garland was a remarkably loved performer and it was no secret that her most dedicated fans were gay men. By the time of her death she had become so much of a gay institution that many New York City gay bars draped themselves with black crepe in mourning. More than 22,000 people paid their respects at the funeral home. Some attribute the Stonewall Riots to the distress gay people felt at Judy's death.

Judy Garland led a remarkably uncharmed life that began with constant touring on the vaudeville circuit and ended with an overdose of barbiturates. Gay men in particular were drawn to her ability to spring back into action, to make so many comebacks against such great odds. (It was rumored that the New York *Daily News* had set in headline type, for instant use, "JUDY TAKES OVERDOSE."[5]) It was her ever-endured pain, and then her ability to overcome it, that appealed to her audience.

When Garland sang, she was vulnerable. There was a hurt in her voice and an immediacy to her performance that gave the impression that it was *her* pain—not merely the hurt in the song or in the persona of the actress—that she was singing about. She *became* her songs, and made the songs themselves more powerful and commanding. She projected her vulnerability as a way to gain love and friendship. She needed her audience as much as they needed her.

A great deal of gay humor is based upon camp: irony and distancing. However, Judy Garland was revered because she was the antithesis of camp: she was utterly serious. Judy Garland was the quintessential pre-Stonewall gay icon. She made a legend out of her pain and oppression, and although she always managed to come back, she never fought back.

In the 1950s, the sauciness of the 30s and the independence of the 40s was replaced with blandness. There were still movie stars—television had hit Hollywood hard, and Hollywood struck back by parading its woman stars around public movie consciousness like religious figures. Gay men were drawn to the all-out sexual allure of Elizabeth Taylor or Marilyn Monroe, and they also suffered through the emotional crises of Lana Turner or Susan Hayward, both of whom excelled in the 50s "women's films," the message of which was that suffering was the price of glamour. The woman stars of the 50s reflected the condition of many gay men: they suffered, beautifully.

By the early 1960s Hollywood took a "one size fits all" approach to women. As long as they filled up a part of the screen with some sexuality it was enough. As Carla, the out-of-work sex symbol in Robert Patrick's *Kennedy's Children* pointed out:

> Raquel Welch...did a terribly difficult thing at a time when it just didn't pay to be a girl at all. She actually made people think about her.[6]

The war also changed the way Hollywood portrayed men. The three actors who most clearly presented this changed image were Marlon Brando, Montgomery Clift, and James Dean. It is no accident that both Dean and Clift were primarily homosexual and that Brando was a self-proclaimed bisexual. What all three brought to the screen was a vulnerability and sensitivity that had never been part of the American film actor's persona. Along with this emotionalism they brought the promise of an eroticism that was pliant and engaging; the strong, silent, rugged American male would never be the same.

In *Rebel Without a Cause*, James Dean desperately tries to find new ways of being a man; the old patterns don't fit anymore. In *Rebel*, after being involved in a rival's death in a hot-rod contest, he agonizes over what was expected of him: "What can you do when you have to be a man? It was a matter of honor. They called me a chicken. You know, chicken? I had to go." He realizes his mistake in buying the image: "You can't keep pretending you're tough, you know?" Dean even accepts the affections of the troubled Sal Mineo. Mineo is even more mixed up than Dean. When we first see him, in a jail cell, the policeman asks: "All right, Plato. Why did you shoot those puppies?" He even keeps a picture of Alan Ladd in his school locker. The homosexual subtext is clear throughout the film, even though, at the film's end, Dean gets Natalie Wood and Mineo gets shot.

While Dean, Mineo, and Wood were troubled because they came from bad homes, Brando, in *The Wild One*, was just *bad*. "What are you kids rebelling against?" someone asks him at the film's beginning. "What d'ya got?" is his classic answer. Both Brando and Dean expressed the masculine dilemma of the decade: how could men assert themselves in an increasingly restrictive society? Even when playing a brute, Brando brought a yearning and need to the part: when he screamed "STELLA" outside of Kim Hunter's tenement in *A Streecar Named Desire*, he released more emotion than film actors had released collectively from 1925-1945.

Montgomery Clift was about the same age as Brando and Dean but he played older characters: the doomed and upwardly mobile man in *A Place in the Sun* or the overly sensitive soldier in *From Here to Eternity*. He acted with his eyes when most other male stars acted by punching someone out. His body language was different from the men who came before him. He was fluid without being feminine; he had both grace and strength and did not need to swagger or stalk about. Dean, Brando, and Clift brought emotion and eroticism into film acting and paved the way for future male actors.

When Hollywood decreed that men could have emotions there was no longer any need for women in films. Older female stars like Bette Davis, Olivia DeHaviland, and Joan Crawford were jobless after the 50s unless they wanted to play aged psychos in films like *Whatever Happened to Baby Jane?*, *Hush, Hush Sweet Charlotte*,

Lady in a Cage, Straitjacket, and *Berserk.* In Hollywood films, a cowboy's best friend had been his horse, then his girl; now his best friend was his best friend.[7] Many film critics—including some feminists—viewed the 60s buddy films as an essentially homosexual phenomenon. *Village Voice* critic Andrew Sarris wrote again and again that there were no good heterosexual romances because the "homosexual" buddy film dominated the screen. In her book on men in American movies, *Big Bad Wolves,* Joan Mellon theorized that the repressed or latent homosexuals of the buddy films were the real oppressors of women. By refusing to acknowledge that heterosexual men could (and do) bond together for any number of reasons, including misogyny, these critics tried to pin the blame for women's oppression upon homosexuals (repressed or not). For the gay male audience, the buddy films sometimes touched upon adolescent fantasies of male companionship, but the films solidly represented, to both straight and gay audiences, a heterosexual view of the world.

In the 60s Hollywood also began to make films that dealt with the lives of homosexual men and women. *Boys in the Band, Sunday, Bloody Sunday, Dog Day Afternoon,* and *Fortune and Men's Eyes* all had gay men as major characters. A host of other films had gay supporting characters who were stereotyped in varying degrees, ranging from the queer as victim in *The Detective* to the happy lesbian couple in *A Perfect Couple.* As the gay liberation movement made some cultural inroads the image of gay people in films changed a bit, or, at least, people gave second thoughts to images they had always accepted in the past. The violent demonstrations that accompanied the filming and screening of *Cruising* in 1979 showed that the gay community was determined to make public statements objecting to what it found distorting and offensive in films.

Although there are more portrayals of gay people in films Hollywood hasn't yet managed to make a film that seemed accurate to a gay audience. Some alternative films—*Word is Out, Nighthawks, Taxi zum Klo, Gay USA, A Very Natural Thing*—do portray a valid gay experience but they have not received wide distribution and have been, for the most part, ignored by the general public.

The careers of both Barbra Streisand and Bette Midler reflect the influence of a gay sensibility upon the larger culture. Streisand got her start playing in gay clubs in Greenwich Village: The Lion's Head and Bon Soir. Her style of singing was startling. Departing from the mellow sound of the early 1960s, she borrowed some of the phrasing of jazz singer Anita Ellis and mixed it with an all-out, dramatic approach to the lyrics. If Garland represented the pre-Stonewall sensibility, all hurt and empathy, Streisand was a new breed of gay idol. If it was Garland's stamina that appealed to her audience, then it was Streisand's *chutzpah*. When Streisand sings "Cry Me a River," she is out for blood, not sympathy. She is as sensitive as Garland, but tougher, capable of anger and self-defense. Streisand was an outcast, a Jew who refused to hide her ethnic background. While ethnic appeal has had some success on Broadway—Fanny Brice, Eddie Cantor, Buddy Hackett—it almost never played to non-urban America. Streisand became a success not because she was acceptable, but because she refused to be acceptable. In her early records her most outstanding qualities are her bitterness and anger. Men who had grown up to Bette Davis' dramatic power and Mae West's ironic wit could easily relate to this odd girl out of Brooklyn. She was a survivor. The message of post-Stonewall gay liberation politics was for gay people to express themselves, no matter what. It is no surprise that gay men immediately connected with Barbra Streisand, and formed the same sort of relationship with her that they had had with earlier stars.

If Streisand coincided with Stonewall, Bette Midler was a product of it. Having gotten her start by playing the Continental Baths in New York, Midler gave her gay audience what they wanted. She became a female female impersonator, singing old torch songs, and inventing off-color impersonations. Cultural critic Richard Poirier has compared her to T.S. Eliot in her ability to assimilate and use past culture to re-create her own. This used to be called "camping it up": now it's "art."

Novelist Rosalyn Drexler has said that Midler has "taken camp and given it back to women." The statement is not quite accurate because camp is the ability to transform a culture you have access to. Few women have had the privilege or the power to take the prevailing culture and turn it around to their own advantage. Midler observed how gay men have used this re-creation of culture to their own advantage and for self-protection. In taking on camp for women, Midler transformed it. If men told jokes about women's bodies then Midler could top them with more, grosser jokes. "I'm sick of hearing big dick jokes," she announced during her 1982 concert tour, "so I have a big pussy joke to tell you. Nobody ever tells big pussy jokes." Sex gets Midler her biggest laughs and they are often at the expense of straight male pretensions and obsessions. While heterosexual society was still groping about in the dark to find replacements for outmoded sexual mores, gay men had been experimenting with alternative sexual arrangements for years. Midler has learned from that and has brought some of the pleasure and the freedom that gay talk, life, and camp have always promoted to a mainstream audience. She has been a major conductor of gay sensibility to the straight world.

Movies, especially Hollywood movies, have had a profound effect upon American culture. Viewing them was, and is, an experience which cuts across gender, race, class, and regional boundaries. Their plots and themes have reflected what people want to believe, but more importantly, they have been extremely influential in shaping people's notions of what life could be like.

Gay men, needing an alternative to their oppressive everyday world, would turn to film both to find a means of escape and a vision of something, someplace different. Because movies are an accessible art form, films provide a common bond as real in New York City as in Hot Coffee, Mississippi, between diverse gay men.

Deprived of the ability to "act" in real life, gay men identified with the ability to "feel" portrayed by female movie stars. The emotion might be "love" with Greta Garbo or "strength" with Bette Davis or "wit" with Eve Arden or perhaps simply "beauty" with Elizabeth Taylor. But in each case, gay men experienced the vicarious pleasure of entering a safe world where they could experience emotions and fantasies without threat.

As post-war America began to change, so did · gay men's relationship to films. With the changes in women's roles, sexual permissiveness, the breakdown of the family, and the rise in value placed on personal growth, gay men found that their "alternative lifestyle" was becoming more acceptable. Movies changed and the strict dichotomy between male/female acting/feeling was not as true as it had been. The social changes which followed the war were reflected in films. Strict gender roles were now seen as straitjackets. Gender flexibility, once associated with gay culture, was popular in mainstream film. It is ironic that at first, gay men had looked to Hollywood stereotypes for a release of their own emotions, but more recently, Hollywood has been learning from gay men. The spate of films about gender role reversals in the last few years—*Victor/Victoria, Tootsie, La Cage aux Folles, Liquid Sky, Yentl*—are all manifestations of dissatisfaction with prevailing gender arrangements. *La Cage aux Folles* (the most popular foreign film ever to play in the U.S.) demonstrated people's boredom with the male role, and the glamour of "emotional" femininity. *Tootsie* postulated that men "have to get in touch with the women in themselves to be better men," an idea that sounds suspiciously like the turn of the century theories of Edward Carpenter and Karl Ulrichs.

Movies shape culture, including gay culture. But movies are also shaped by the culture in which they exist. Just as Hollywood has responded to the changing role of women in American society, it has responded to changes in attitudes towards sex and gender. Hollywood turned to the gay sensibility to give straight audiences an alternative view of sexuality and gender. The impact of gay sensibility on American culture as seen through films is undeniable.

Theater
The Third Sex and the Fourth Wall

The *theatuh*. Perhaps nowhere else in popular culture were, and are, gay men so accepted. From the self-congratulatory expectations of 1920s Greenwich Village to the shocked, yet titillated "lady from Dubuque," *everyone* knew that the theater was a haven for homosexuals. The stereotypes abound: the high school drama coach; the foppish, vain leading man; the nelly chorus boy; the supercilious gossip columnist *cum* critic. Perhaps the most common gay image is the sheltered young boy who lives in a dream world of "going to Broadway." For years, it was Broadway that symbolized the glittering world of theater for most of America. It was Broadway where the threat and the promise of toleration for homosexuals found a sort of social truce: the theater was the circumscribed playground for "artistic types" (a euphemism that included everyone from the most flaming queen to the confused young man). For the young queen, going to Broadway was not unlike going over the rainbow to Oz: except once on Broadway, you'd never want to go back to Kansas.

110

Although common perception saw Broadway, and hence the theater in general, as a port of safety for homosexuals, the reality was quite different. Who can come out and who remains closeted raises the important issues of what and how society allows gay artists to create, how this informs the creations, and how this affects gay sensibility. An interesting measure of social tolerance is the ratio of actual homosexuality portrayed on the stage to the number of gay people involved in the theater, and the appearance of covert aspects of gay sensibility in popular plays.

Homosexual characters have always been present—if intermittently—on the American stage. As early as 1896, Henry B. Fuller published *At Saint Judas's*, a short one-act play about a groom who discovers, minutes before the wedding, that he is really in love with his best man.[1] Edward Bourdet's *The Captive* (1926) and Mae West's *The Drag* (1927) so incensed the theatergoing public that playboy Mayor Jimmy Walker demanded that producers censor themselves more strongly if they wanted to avoid an official crackdown. The plays were raided anyway and the case prompted a state law banning the depiction of homosexuality on New York stages which remained on the books until 1967. The statute was mostly a scare tactic: Mordaunt Shairp's *The Green Bay Tree* was produced in 1933, and a year later Lillian Hellman won critical and popular acclaim with her lesbian girls' school shocker, *The Children's Hour*.[2] Other plays mitigated the supposed immorality of their subject matter by underplaying it or using it as a subtext to discuss other topics. For the most part these plays, both serious and scandalous, were produced and directed for a straight audience. The exception was Mae West's *The Drag*.

In April of 1926, West, under the name Jane Mast, wrote and starred in a sensational pot boiler, provocatively titled *Sex*. The play was so successful that she decided to capitalize on the homosexual theme *The Captive* had introduced the year before and wrote *The Drag*, described in her own publicity as "a homosexual comedy" and "the male version of *The Captive*." *The Drag* had a plot that made gay mincemeat out of a turgid family melodrama: gay son of conservative father marries daughter of doctor and then falls in love with a straight man who is in love with his wife. Enter ex-lover who cannot be "cured" by doctor/father-in-law, and kills the main character. The affair is hushed up and passed off as a suicide. The nominal "family tragedy" angle of the play was quickly obscured by its sensationalism. Although the play opened with a scene between a doctor and a judge discussing the causes of homosexuality—a bit of redeeming social value that would show up in porn films as late as 1970—the play quickly moved into the world of queens and it was full of gay humor, switched pronouns, and camp comebacks that West had picked up from gay theater people. West recruited gay actors from Greenwich Village bars to audition for the play and whatever her mixed intentions, (she claimed public education, but wouldn't mind a big hit) the play presented a slice of real gay life on the stage. *The Drag* closed out of town (it had made it from Stamford, Connecticut to Bayonne, New Jersey) because of pressure placed on the producers by religious groups and the Society for the Prevention of Vice.[3]

Because she was a heterosexual woman, Mae West was able to bring gay life onto the stage with impunity. Nevertheless, *The Drag* provided evidence that the theater was filled with homosexuals, playwrights as well as actors. During the 1930s, Noel Coward flirted with his public in a way that was reminiscent of Wilde. In *Design for Living* (1933), he presented an ambiguous *menage a trois*. The play was advertised as being about "three peole who love each other very much" and one of the two men explains to the third: "I love you. You love me. You love Otto. I love Otto. Otto loves you. Otto loves me."[4] Hiding behind his dandy prose and sophisticated wit, Coward got away with it. *Design for Living* was so popular, at least in New York, (its London premiere was held up for six years because of censorship problems) that it was parodied in the 1934 revue *Life Begins at 8:40*.

> Night and day, ma cherie,
> me for you, and you and you and me.
> We're living in the smart upper sets.
> Let other lovers sing their duets.
> Duets are made for the Bourgeoisie—oh
> But only God can make a trio.[5]

The year before, in *Words and Music*, Coward had written "Mad

About the Boy," an ironic love ballad sung by several women to a young matinee idol. This apparently simple heterosexual lyric is filled with obvious "in jokes."

> Mad about the boy,
> It's simply scrumptious to be mad about the boy,
> I know that quite sincerely
> Housman really
> Wrote *The Shropshire Lad* about the boy.

> In *Can Love Destroy?*
> When he meets Garbo in a suit of corduroy,
> He gives a little frown
> And knocks her down.
> Oh dear, oh dear, I'm mad about the boy.

> Mad about the boy,
> It's pretty funny but I'm mad about the boy,
> He has a gay appeal
> That makes me feel
> There's maybe something sad about the boy.[6]

On Broadway, Cole Porter was regaling New York theatergoers with such songs as "Farming," a spoof on high society slumming in which George Raft's non-reproducing bull is described as "beautiful, but he's gay."[7]*

Although gay men may have been everywhere working and writing and directing and producing theater, there was no social permission for them to openly express their sexuality either in their lives or in their work. They resorted to hidden references, like Coward's mention of Housman.

It was during the 1940s that a more explicit homosexual identity began to emerge in the theater. In 1944, Tennessee Williams wrote *The Glass Menagerie.* A gentle, poetic, regretful play, *Menagerie*

---

* The Cole Porter estate refused permission to reprint six lines of lyrics from "Farming" because they did not want them to appear in a "risque context".

focused upon the feelings of the outsider, the plight of the sexual and emotional misfit. Its opening lines said much about what gay playwrights would be doing for the next 20 years on Broadway.

> **Tom:** Yes, I have tricks in my pocket, I have things up my sleeve. But I am the opposite of a stage magician. He gives you illusion that has the pleasant disguise of truth. I give you truth in the pleasant disguise of illusion.

The frivolousness of Porter's and Coward's 1930s was over. The antics that had characterized Depression America were rapidly losing their charm in the face of a worsening world situation. Dramas concerning the war proliferated on the stage: *The American Way*, *The Winged Victory*, *Margin for Error*, *The French Touch*, *Watch on the Rhine*, *Home of the Brave*. American history was dredged up to reinforce sagging morale in *Abe Lincoln in Illinois* and *The Patriots*. The heterosexual family was memorialized and enshrined in *I Remember Mama* and *Life With Father*. But there were also signs of moral disengagement. *Arsenic and Old Lace*, written as a melodrama and played as a comedy, showed that murder could play on Broadway. Even an arch comedy of manners like *The Philadelphia Story*, though quite traditional, displayed a juggling of the usual sexual expectations.

In the midst of this came Tennessee Williams with his pocket full of tricks. Williams' plays won popular acclaim and cleaned up on every prestigious theater award available: Tonys, Pulitzers, and a few Drama Desk Awards. To write about his own gay experience, Williams realized that he had to make it as palatable to his audience as possible. It was 15 years before audiences—and critics—discovered the "truth" beneath Williams' stage illusions, and responded with the vituperation of a lover betrayed. Homosexuality was almost never explicitly mentioned in his work, although both *Streetcar Named Desire* and *Cat on a Hot Tin Roof* have off-stage gay male characters who kill themselves. However, the subtexts of Williams' plays, their emotional content, grew out of Williams' experience as a gay man.

While other playwrights, like Robert Sherwood, Phillip Barry, Lillian Hellman, and S.N. Behrman concerned themselves with social issues, Williams dealt obsessively with matters that were not only personal and private, but explicitly sexual. Williams brought to the Broadway stage a poetic intensity and a radically new vision of human relations: intense, volatile, many times tinged with hurt or fear. While the characters in *The Philadelphia Story* or *Born Yesterday* were clearly interested in sex, they did not burn with it, as Williams' characters did. If he did nothing else, he can be credited with legitimizing sexual passion as a motivating force in contemporary drama.

Williams brought an empathy and dimension to his female characters that had little precedent on the stage. He imbued all of his characters—women and men—with a vitality that was uncommon in American drama. Most of his characters exhibit dignity and pride in being outsiders. Sometimes, their difference breaks them. More often, his characters find the strength to overcome the odds against them: to create themselves in a hostile world.

As his most famous character, Blanche DuBois' destruction caused many to see all of Williams' women as doomed. Buying a colored paper lantern to brighten up her sister's dismal apartment in *Streetcar*, Blanche exposes her fragility: "I can't stand a naked light bulb, any more than I can a rude remark or a vulgar action." "I've always depended upon the kindness of strangers" has become a cliche in gay English. But the truth is that the majority of his women characters are survivors. Williams himself even saw Blanche as a survivor. He claimed, "I am Blanche DuBois."[8] It was Williams' life as a gay man that enabled him to create a character who survives by rejecting the sordidness of this world and creating a better one of her own.

Other gay playwrights approached adult themes with a bit more decorum. From *Come Back Little Sheba* (1950) through *Picnic* (1953), *Bus Stop* (1955), and *The Dark at the Top of the Stairs* (1957), William Inge won major awards and public accolades for his presentations of Midwestern life. In contrast to Williams' passionate characters, Inge's were small people with small problems. Inge's plays were family dramas with the themes of sexual repression and frustration. His screenplay for the immensely popular *Splendor in the Grass* clearly stated that if the sex drive were inhibited, madness would result.

But even with his small town folk, Inge could stir the sexual imagination in his audience as much as Williams' Stanley Kowalski and his talk of "getting those colored lights going." In *Come Back Little Sheba*, the young Turk (whom Inge describes as having "stature and physique" and who enters wearing "faded dungarees and a T-shirt") explains javelin throwing to the middle-aged, sexually denied Lola.

> It's a big, long lance. *(Assumes a magnificent position)* You hold it like this, erect—then you let go and it goes singing through the air, and lands yards away, if you're any good at it, and sticks in the ground like an arrow. I won the State championship last year.[9]

In both Williams and Inge, the tension between sexual fulfillment and sexual fears is what moves the plots. All of their characters battle against repression; Williams' more often break through, even if they are punished in the end, and Inge's are more or less trapped in their thwarted desires. Both playwrights are emblematic of the plight of sexuality during the 1950s. The high degree of social repression made any discussion or depiction of sexuality, especially homosexuality, suspect and provocative. Williams and Inge pinpointed sexual dissatisfaction in the culture.

The theme of the disenfranchised bourgeois family in the theater goes back as far as 1936 with George Kaufmann and Moss Hart's Pulitzer Prize-winning play *You Can't Take It With You*. The unconventional Vanderhofs make fireworks in their basement, take in a displaced Russian Countess, refuse to pay their income tax, and succeed in changing the middle class notions of their future in-laws. But the Vanderhofs also perpetuated the myth of the nuclear family as the central motivating force in people's lives. Oddball as they are, their family ties are what support them. (Using the same plot, in the late 1970s, the French farce *La Cage Aux Folles* substituted old fags and drag queens for the lovable Vanderhofs.) The closeness of the gay *La Cage aux Folles* "family" made the subject matter comforting to its gay audience—it was a positive portrayal—and less threatening to the straights: "Look. They're (almost) just like us."

The dotty outcast appeared again in 1944 in Mary Chase's

Pulitzer Prize-winning *Harvey*. Here the kook, Elward P. Dowd, is an older, unmarried man who drinks a bit and lives with his sister. His only real peculiarity is that he has a very close male friend—Harvey—who is a six-foot tall, invisible white rabbit.

> Harvey and I sit in bars and we have a drink or two and play the jukebox. Soon the faces of the other people turn towards mine and smile. They are saying: "We don't know your name, Mister, but you're a lovely fellow." Harvey and I warm ourselves in all these golden moments. We have entered as strangers—soon we have friends.[10]

Most of the play centers around the problems that Elward causes for his family. He brings Harvey to public gatherings and introduces him to everyone. Elward is obviously crazy (gay) and shocks people because he will not keep quiet about it. The only place where he and Harvey are accepted as friends is in the bar where they first met. Broadway audiences could accept eccentricity as long as it was sufficiently charming and *Harvey* was a gay play which was coded enough not to threaten or challenge a straight audience.

John Van Druten was a displaced Englishman who scored huge hits with *Voice of the Turtle* (1944), a sweet boy-meets-girl war romance, and *I Remember Mama*, which detailed family life among Norwegian immigrants in San Francisco at the turn of the century (and later became a tremendous radio and television hit). Although Van Druten was gay, his audience made little connection between his private life and his work. However, two of his plays, *Bell, Book and Candle* (1950) and *I Am A Camera* (1951), provide perfect examples of obscured gay subject matter.

I Am a Camera was based upon Christopher Isherwood's *Berlin Stories*. Isherwood's homosexuality is quietly omnipresent in these novellas, but Van Druten concealed it by focusing the play on the relationship between the Isherwood character and his woman friend, Sally Bowles. The play is a portrait of a lonely gay man who befriends the frightened, yet bravely "decadent" young woman. The 1950s audience did not acknowledge the source of the displacement that brought the two together and viewed the play as a *very* "modern" romance in which boy meets girl, but they just remain friends.

If audiences were happy to accept the asexual hero of *I Am a Camera*, they were even more susceptible to the trio of gay witches and warlocks Van Druten conjured up in *Bell, Book and Candle*. Read today, the play's gay subtext is obvious. Three witches— Gillian, a beautiful, intelligent, artistic young woman, her younger, bohemian brother, and their inept Aunt Queenie—move into a fashionable New York apartment building. Even with their oddities, they know that they easily pass. As Queenie explains:

> He'd never suspect, darling. Not in a million years. No matter *what* I did. Honestly, it's amazing the way people don't. Why, they just don't believe there *are* such things. I sit in the subway sometimes, or in buses, and look at the people next to me, and I think: What would you say if I told you I were a witch? And I know they'd never believe it. They just wouldn't believe it. And I giggle and giggle to myself.[11]

When Gillian falls in love with the man upstairs (witches can't fall in love, cry, or blush) Queenie admonishes Gillian on her new feelings.

> **Queenie:**   I think you're *ashamed* of being what you are.
> **Gillian:**   Ashamed? I'm not in the least ashamed. No, it's not a question of that, but...(Suddenly) Auntie, don't you ever wish you *weren't*?
> **Queenie:**   (amazed) No.
> **Gillian:**   That you were like those people you sit next to on the bus.
> **Queenie:**   Ordinary and humdrum? No, I *was*. For years. Before I came into it.
> **Gillian:**   ...I don't *mean* humdrum. I just mean unenlightened.
> **Queenie:**   Darling, you're just depressed.
> **Gillian:**   I know. I expect it's Christmas. It's always upset me.[12]

Although Van Druten takes the analogy as far as possible—the witches frequent special clubs in the Village—the play ends with Gillian turning straight (or at least non-witch). Ultimately pro-heterosexual, *Bell, Book and Candle* exemplifies the degree to which a gay theme could infiltrate a mainstream production. If it was impossible for gay people to write openly about themselves, they would find other ways to express their experience on the stage.

Plays like *Bell, Book and Candle* and *You Can't Take It With You* tried to persuade audiences that oddballs and misfits were not dangerous and could even be more engaging than "regular" people, as long as they were safely contained within the biological family. *Auntie Mame* (1956), adapted from the Patrick Dennis novel of the year before by Robert Lawrence and Jerome Lee, was closer to *Harvey* in pitting the outcast *against* her/his family. In contrast to the quiet, dipsomaniac Dowd, Mame is a flamboyant, fun-loving, on-the-ball lover of life. "Life is a banquet" she exclaims at the end of act one, "and most poor bastards are starving to death." It is easy to see why the novel and its dramatization appealed to a gay audience. Straight audiences responded to the fun-loving-in-the-face-of-respectability aspect of the play and were not threatened by it because of the fairy tale quality of the presentation. The difference was that while they may have received a thrill thumbing their noses at the Babbitts of the world, the same response in gay audiences was deeply felt and liberating. The Dennis novel includes gay characters and a *bon vivant* attitude towards life that is more in tune with gay than straight culture. Mame is independently wealthy and can satisfy most of her whims, from redoing her townhouse in Chinese restaurant decor to buying property in "restricted" Darien, Connecticut to establishing a home for Jewish war orphans just to spite anti-semites. In *Auntie Mame* fun-loving people battle ignorant, prejudiced, middle class dolts. Called by one critic "the *Peter Pan* of the post-war era,"[13] it is an outcry against the era's expectations of grown ups. Like the Barrie play, but without Barrie's underlying sorrow, it glorifies both acting different and acting out. *Auntie Mame* is every young queen's dream to be taken away from the dreariness of everyday life and whisked off to the never-never land of bohemia. Mame experiences biological family as a source of repression and lack of freedom. Towards the end of the play, when her nephew is on the verge of making a disastrous marriage to "an Aryan from Darien," Mame invites some of her more unusual friends to meet her prospective in-laws. Nephew Patrick is

Jessica Tandy in original production of
Streetcar Named Desire.

Roz Russell, dressed by Travis
Banton, in *Auntie Mame.*

While critics insisted that
Tennessee Williams was
pawning off "unreal" women
on an unsuspecting audience,
they seemed to miss the fact that
Rosalind Russell dressed and
behaved like a drag queen in
Auntie Mame.

Discussions of which
playwrights or characters
"were" or "weren't" was blown
away when Harvey Fierstein
made his stage appearance in
Torch Song Trilogy as a *real*
drag queen. While gay
sensibility was marching onto
Broadway, it also made further
inroads into the gay
community. Doric Wilson's
The West Street Gang
premiered at The Spike, a
popular leather bar. Four years
later, his *Street Theater*—about
the Stonewall riots—played at
the Mineshaft, an even more
popular leather bar.

Harvey Fierstein in *Torch Song
Trilogy,* 1982

Doric Wilson's *Street Theater* at the Mineshaft

Fierstein, Patrick, and Wilson at Pheobes, NYC, 1979

appalled and protests that he wants "just family." "But these are our family, Patrick dear," Mame explains. And although she is doing it to ruin his engagement, she is right.

Auntie Mame may have been the last extreme in placing a hidden gay sensibility upon the Broadway stage. (It was *very* extreme; in both the play and the film Rosalind Russell in her Travis Banton outfits looked more like a drag queen than an eccentric woman.) In 1953, two theater seasons before *Auntie Mame*, Broadway was jolted by a "mature" drama entitled *Tea and Sympathy*. Now hopelessly dated and silly, the play managed simultaneously to bring up and ignore the subject of male homosexuality. It also managed to get points for being liberal and not pandering to the more base responses of the audience on the topic. Set in a boys' boarding school, Robert Anderson's *Tea and Sympathy* tells the story of Tom Lee, a sensitive young student who likes to sing, read poetry, play the female lead in school plays, and hang out with the headmaster's wife. After he is caught swimming nude with one of the male teachers, the rumors that he is a homosexual begin to proliferate. After a ghastly encounter with the town prostitute, he tries to kill himself. Scorned by just about everyone, and convinced that "he isn't a man," Tom is ultimately saved by Laura—the headmaster's wife—who tells him that he is "different." "One day you'll meet a girl, and it will be right." In a shocker of a final curtain, she goes into his room and begins to unbutton her blouse, delivering what has become a howling example of unintentional camp.

> **Laura:**   Years from now...when you talk about this...and you will...be kind. (Gently she brings the boy's hands towards her opened blouse, as the lights slowly dim out...and...THE CURTAIN FALLS)[14]

The audience gets both the titillation of thinking that Tom may be gay (he certainly seems gay) while at the same time being allowed to feel morally superior to the bigotry of all the other characters. Sympathy is elicited on the basis of Tom's *not* being gay.

Although Broadway in the 1950s was in the vanguard of maturity in American culture, (at least compared to film and the newly emerging world of television) it was hardly an avant garde mecca. Production costs had been rising steadily and it cost so much to put on new shows that trying something new became prohibitively expensive. The result was a plethora of "safe" shows. In response to this situation, off-Broadway materialized. Off-Broadway, as a cultural and theatrical force, probably began with the Circle in the Square 1952 revival of Tennessee Williams' 1948 Broadway flop *Summer and Smoke*. Staged by Jose Quintero and starring Geraldine Page, the show garnered such critical raves that audiences began flocking to the Village to see what was going on. New theaters sprang up and the already existing ones flourished. They began by presenting revivals, plays that had failed uptown, foreign plays that were not considered commercial—like the Brecht/Weill *Three Penny Opera*—and by the beginning of the 1960s had spawned enough energy and excitement to do plays which were too political and too avant garde to play uptown.

While adventurous theatergoers were served large doses of Brecht, Shaw, and revived O'Neill, they were also introduced to Genet's overtly gay *Deathwatch*, *The Balcony*, and *The Maids*. In 1958, Williams presented a double bill of one-acts, the second of which, *Suddenly Last Summer*, in less than an hour regaled the audience with pedophilia, incest, homosexuality, and cannibalism. It was a hit and won Anne Meacham an Obie Award for best actress. Besides providing an alternative to Broadway, off-Broadway also radically changed what was permissible on stage in both form and content. The Living Theater of Julian Beck and Judith Malina wedded the personal and the political in stark, unconventional theater terms. Jack Gelber brought members of his audiences closer to the actors' on-stage action than they ever wanted to be in the partly improvised *The Connection*. In 1960, Edward Albee, whose work had grown out of the off-Broadway aesthetics and structures, won Obie and Vernon Rice Awards for *The Zoo Story*, a one-act with the simplicity of Ionesco, exploring themes of violence and homosexuality.

Off-Broadway spawned a whole new way of looking at theater and provided competition and new blood for the more traditional uptown stages. Downtown, there had been a Williams revival and many of his rarely produced one-acts had found an audience.

Uptown, he had a solid hit with *The Night of the Iguana*. In the tradition of his other major works, *Iguana* was well received, but a backlash was brewing. This building anti-gay reaction needed an issue around which to catalyze. The success of Edward Albee's *Who's Afraid of Virginia Woolf?* lit the fuse.

The crypto-homo *The Zoo Story* drew notice in 1960 and Albee's absurdist attack on the family in *The American Dream* received even more attention the following year. In 1962, he broke uptown with his scathing, blackly funny dissection of marriage, academia, success, parent-child relationships, and the illusion of happiness in America with *Who's Afraid of Virginia Woolf?* Albee shocked with foul language and an outrageous mixture of blatant sexuality and dramatic conceits, but the audience loved it and the production won five Tony awards. It did not win the Pulitzer prize, in spite of the recommendation of the drama committee. Several members of the committee resigned in protest and it was generally conceded, though never publicly, that the play had come a little too close to home for the Columbia University-based Pulitzer committee. But another unspoken reason why Albee's play did not receive the prize was that critics were uneasy with the idea that three of America's leading playwrights—Albee, Williams, and Inge—were homosexuals.

The fact that there were homosexuals in the theater was no news to anyone. The private lives of single, male personalities are always suspect when they work in the theater. Tennessee Williams never tried to hide any aspect of his life. Even in the 1950s, his alcohol and drug problems were front page news. When rumors of his homosexuality seeped into print, he did nothing to deny them. In time, this just became one more public aspect of his private life. In contrast, William Inge always kept a low profile. Unlike Williams, he never paraded his personal problems. Those in the know assumed that he was a homosexual, but it was hardly ever mentioned until the critics decided to "do something" about homosexuals in the theater. Albee's reputation was always that of a single man who had no women in his life. Knowledge of his homosexuality was implicit in some of the writings about his early work. By never denying it, he tacitly agreed to its truth.

However, critics felt uncomfortable with the rise of off-Broadway and the progressive themes of the new theater. To succeed, the backlash would have to be put in terms that would shock seasoned theatergoers and frighten the average person. The argument critics made was twofold: (1) American theater was in danger of being overrun by homosexuals; and (2) homosexual writers were promoting their own sexual pathology in the guise of writing about real (heterosexual) men and women. In short, they were repeating the tried and true tactics of Joe McCarthy: homosexuals were everywhere and they were destroying the world's natural, moral order.

In November of 1961, *New York Times* drama critic Howard Taubman began the attack in the Sunday Arts and Leisure feature: "Not What It Seems: Homosexual Motif Gets Heterosexual Guise."[15] The staid critic for *The Times* was filled with concern, not invective, and accused three unnamed playwrights of purposefully portraying marriage negatively and painting women characters as destroyers and sex maniacs. The seeds were planted and as the off-Broadway and off-off-Broadway movements flourished, these criticisms became more and more hostile. The liberal *Ramparts* magazine published a vicious attack by Gene Marine in early 1967 entitled "Who's Afraid of Little Annie Fanny?"

> The point is that homosexual playwrights and homosexual directors and homosexual producers are having more and more to say about what can and can't be done in the American theater...I'm getting damned tired of all the art being campy and all the plays being queer and all the clothes being West Fourth Street and the whole bit. *Some* I don't mind, but it's getting too close to *all*, and I have the feeling that there are healthier bases for culture.

Marine didn't stop at the more common cultural institutions; in his world, nothing was safe.

> You can take almost any part of the world of culture, and there it is in bold lavender. Dance and interior design, fashions (women's *and* men's), music—especially outside the relatively virile jazz and rock fields—and music promotion, novels and poetry, little theater and magazines.[16]

The exception for the "virile" fields of rock and jazz was probably a reflection of *Ramparts'* anti-establishment cultural inclinations. Rock and jazz were considered more "progressive" than older, more established forms of culture.

The Times subsequently reconsidered the debate (with their new drama critic, the more liberal, but equally tedious, Stanley Kauffman) in more rational terms. Kauffman argued that homosexuals were forced to write about heterosexuals because they were denied the right to detail their own experiences. The problem wasn't that they presented a "badly distorted picture of American women, marriage, and society in general," although, of course, they did. Rather, their plays were "streaked with vindictiveness towards the society that...discriminates against them." The true sin of the homosexual playwright was putting style before content.

> [Camp] can be seen, I believe, as an instrument of revenge on the main body of society. Theme and subject are important historical principles in our art. The arguments to prove that they are of diminishing importance—in fact, ought never to have been important—are cover for an attack on the idea of social relevance. By adulation of sheer style, this group tends to deride the whole culture and the society that produced it, tends to reduce art to a clever game which even society cannot keep from playing.[17]

What is striking in Kauffman's essays on homosexuality in theater is not his misplaced, condescending liberalism, but rather his insight. There *is* a tradition in gay culture which emphasizes style over content, which is an attempt to "deride" mainstream culture. Kauffman called it destructive. Others have called it revolutionary.

One of the more bizarre aspects of this debate was its focus upon the works of Albee, Williams, and Inge. Even the liberal Kauffman argued that:

> ...we have all had much more than enough of the materials so often presented by the three writers in question: the viciousness towards women, the lurid violence that seems a sublimation of social hatreds, the transvestite sexual exhibitionism that has the same sneering exploitation of

its audience that every club stripper has behind her smile.[18]

Yet, a close reading of most of the works of these playwrights does not reveal these traits at all. Are Williams' portraits of Blanche DuBois, Lady Torrance, Hanna Jelks, or Alexandria Del Largo vicious? Are Inge's dissections of marital problems anything other than revealing and, in many cases, overly delicate? Even Albee's rambunctious stage behavior, exemplified in *Virginia Woolf*, ultimately points towards a constructive vision of marriage and human relationships.

None of these critics complained that Cole Porter or Noel Coward exhibited any of these traits. Certainly, Coward's *Private Lives* could as easily be read as a play about two male couples as *Who's Afraid of Virginia Woolf?* If they were looking for transvestism, Auntie Mame was a more likely suspect than Blanche DuBois. And as for attacks on the family, *Harvey*, by implication, was as subversive as the blatant, absurdist dramatics of *The American Dream*. The critics were incensed less by the idea that the playwrights were homosexuals than by the fact that they were *identifiable* to some degree by their own choice; they were "out" homosexuals who refused to play the game and remain in the closet.

American culture was in the midst of a rocky transition from the late 1950s into the new decade. Nothing was quite as it had been and people were looking to pin the blame on someone. Since it was common knowledge that "they" were involved in the arts, it was a quick jump to suppose that "they" were responsible for warping American society. Inge, Albee, and Williams wrote about family problems, about the struggle between the sexes, about the sexual dissatisfaction that most people felt. They wrote about what they saw going on around them: art imitating life. The critics began insisting, quite against their usual precepts, that life was in danger of imitating art.

The notion that an invisible group of homosexuals was conspiring to corrupt American culture and morality rests upon the assumptions that all homosexuals think alike; and that they have accumulated an amazing amount of power for a group which by its very social definition is invisible. Imagine Tennessee Williams, Cole Porter, Lorenz Hart, Marcel Proust, Jean Genet, and Liberace getting together to plot the overthrow of Western morality! As late as 1970, critic and novelist William Goldman was touting the Howard Taubman line in his book on Broadway, *The Season*. Not unlike Kinsey, he felt obligated to convince his reader with hard core "facts."

> Of the 58 productions listed in Variety's year-end survey as either "successes," "failures," "status not yet determined," or "closed during tryout or preview," at least 18, or 31% were produced by homosexuals. Of the same 58 productions at least 22, or 38% were directed by homosexuals.[19]

Then he remarks that his figuring is somewhat low because lots of homosexuals are married and it is difficult to identify who they *really* are.

Criticism a la Taubman continues in the theater even today, and has become codified in a set of phrases which lets the reader know that they are dealing with a homosexual playwright. In his 1965 review of Albee's *Tiny Alice* for the *New York Review of Books*, Philip Roth was at least direct in accusing Albee of writing "pansy prose."[20] By 1976, the queer-baiting was a bit more subtle. In a review of a new play in the *Village Voice*, (another bastion of liberalism) their drama editor managed to use nearly every cliche and innuendo this school of criticism had developed.

> ...the basic comic device seems to be to strike out randomly at everything we regard as having any solidity or value whatsoever...and reduce it to shambles—culture, family, sexual identity, the traditions and conventions of theater itself. ...it seems to me quite clear...that his anger at female sexuality is surpassed only by his fear. ...self-hatred often takes refuge in contempt for others.[21]

Off-Broadway may have been experimental, but off-off-Broadway was absolutely revolting. It is one thing to perform plays by Genet; it is quite another to write plays about homosexuals not translated from the French, and not bother pretending to be straight. Off-off-Broadway was the beginning of political gay theater as it exists today. On off-off-Broadway, theater happened in cafes, coffee houses, lofts, and anywhere people could get together to put on a show.

The first off-off-Broadway theater was Cafe Cino. Opening some time in December of 1958, Joe Cino made his one-room coffee house a gathering place for his friends in the "arts." The theater began with a reading by Doric Wilson of a few scenes from Oscar Wilde's *Salome*. Plays proliferated: by William Inge, Tennessee Williams, Oscar Wilde, Jean Genet, Lanford Wilson, Robert Patrick, Doric Wilson, William Hoffman, Tom Eyen, and Sam Shepard. Cafe Cino had no entertainment license and existed by avoiding or paying off (with money, drugs, or sex) the law.

What made Cafe Cino exciting was the feeling that anything could happen there. There were few standards: when Joe thought a play moved too slowly, he would ring a loud bell as a signal to pick up the pace, but that was it. Many of the people involved were openly gay: there was no longer any need to hide, invent disguises, or pretend to be something other than what you were. "Are you a homosexual?" a young man asks the title character in Robert Patrick's *The Haunted Host*. "I'm *the* homosexual!" is the reply. Until that point, the gay sensibility had functioned as camouflage; on off-off-Broadway, gay playwrights could express themselves openly and freely. Playwright Doric Wilson commented:

> *Is* there such a thing as a gay sensibility? Yes, there *has* to be; but as to narrow it down...I think there is very much a closet gay sensibility, and since most gays working in the arts are in the closet, there very definitely is the end result of a closet gay sensibility—its worst excesses can be seen at the Metropolitan Opera House, New York's principal gay theater. But as far as *healthy* gay sensibility in the arts, that's something new. And as gay artists are more directly honest about being gay and being gay artists, I think we will start to see gay sensibility.[22]

The Cafe Cino was that turning point in gay and theater history when the older gay sensibility gave way to the new. The transition was not easy. After all of his work and dedication, Joe Cino committed suicide in 1967 at the age of 36. His death, brought on by many personal and professional problems, (not the least of which was constant harassment from the city and police) was a tragedy which marked the beginning of gay theater.

In addition to the Cafe Cino, off-off-Broadway consisted of small theaters like The Judson, Genesis, La Mama, Chelsea Theater Center, and The Negro Ensemble Company. At first, critics saw these as a place to go gay slumming: easier than a bar. Eventually, off-off-Broadway succumbed to professionalism, in many ways becoming an adjunct to mainstream Broadway theater. It was not unusual for shows that succeeded downtown to move to a larger uptown theater, gaining both respectability and large profits. Cafe Cino closed, a result of "press, drugs, success, and failure (in about that order of importance)" according to playwright Robert Patrick. However, some other theaters carried on, bearing out the fears of the mainstream cultural critics.

The problem of what to do with an openly gay playwright was handled differently than the trashing that Williams, Albee, and Inge had received. Despite the enormous outpouring of work from off-off-Broadway playwrights, despite the fact that they had a profound influence on the New York theater scene and the art world in general, they were simply ignored. After more than 20 years in the theater, Tom Eyen finally made a name for himself with the book for *Dream Girls*, ironically one of his least imaginative works. Robert Patrick— probably the most produced playwright in the country—had to go to Europe to score a hit with his *Kennedy's Children*. Even as late as 1975, during out-of-town tryouts, drama critic Eliot Norton of the *Boston Herald* told Patrick that he "loved *Kennedy's Children*, but drop the homo."[23] Van Itallie became better known for his adaptations of Chekhov plays in the 1970s than for his successes in the early days of off-off-Broadway. Many other writers simply fell into obscurity.

Off-off-Broadway brought the movements for social change of the 1960s to mainstream theater. With its beginnings in social unrest, the new theatrical temperament evoked and provoked social and cultural change. As the whole culture became more permissive— with a deeper understanding of the personal and political in people's lives, whether it was black liberation, feminism, youth movements, leftist politics, anti-war activities, or gay liberation—off-off-Broad-way promoted and presented the changes.

Off-off-Broadway shows also presented openly gay material. In 1968, Mart Crowley's *The Boys in the Band* opened at an off-Broadway house and ran for a neat 1000 performances. Crowley's characters camped their way through more than two hours of creaking melodrama. Playwright Crowley made sure that hetero-sexual critics and audiences saw what they really believed: gay men who were unhappy and willfully cruel to one another. However, whatever its panderings to homophobia, *The Boys in the Band* created possibilities for presenting gay material on the stage. Soon after it opened, plays with gay characters began appearing off-Broadway: *And Puppy Dog's Tails, Geese, Naomi Court*, and even on Broadway: *Find Your Way Home, Butley, The Killing of Sister George, Loot* and *Entertaining Mr. Sloan*. By the early 1970s, gay characters appeared in shlock musicals like *Applause*, and by the late 1970s, *A Chorus Line* presented a fully realized gay character. In a few more years, Harvey Fierstein's adaptation of a French farce with music by Jerry (*Hello Dolly* and *Mame*) Herman would result in the huge hit, *La Cage aux Folles*. (After the gala opening of *La Cage Aux Folles*, a disgruntled queen muttered that "It's nothing more than *Mame* in drag." The obvious answer, proffered by a close-standing wag, was: "But, my dear, *Mame* was *Mame* in drag.")

The most important legacy of off-off-Broadway was that gay people began to write and produce their own shows. In the early 1970s, Doric Wilson started TOSOS, (The Other Side of Silence) the first explicitly gay theater in New York. TOSOS had its own space for a time, but closed because of lack of support. Its last production was Wilson's *The West Street Gang*, a play about queer-bashing and community organizing set in a leather bar. In a move that would have cheered Joe Cino's heart, (and Brecht's for that matter) it was performed in The Spike, a leather bar, bridging the gap between the stage and the audience. Soon after TOSOS was founded, the Glines, a theater dedicated to producing and promoting gay plays, was started. Like TOSOS, it had problems finding a permanent space and eventually became a producing company. In 1981 it presented Harvey Fierstein's *Torch Song Trilogy* (each act of which had been performed separately at La Mama) off-Broadway. The story of a drag performer who has boyfriend problems, mother problems, and adopted son problems, *Torch Song Trilogy* managed to portray a real gay experience without modifying its language, action, or message to placate straight audiences. Its view of alternative gay family life made it somewhat non-threatening to mainstream audiences, in much the same way that the film and musical versions of *La Cage aux Folles* did. *Torch Song Trilogy* did so well in its off-Broadway Glines production that it moved to an uptown theater and won two Tony Awards, one for Fierstein's acting in the title role, and another for best play. When John Glines accepted the award as the producer on national television, he publicly thanked his lover.

The road for gay theater was not entirely clear, however. Meridian Theater had formed to produce gay plays and J.H. Press, part of the Gay Presses of New York, began publishing a gay play series. These productions are all but ignored by the major media and press. Even the popularity of *Torch Song Trilogy* did not prevent some critics from making snide remarks about it. Robert Brustein, in *The Nation*, was crass enough to say that the Fierstein play had won its awards because of the AIDS sympathy vote.[24] Fierstein's next serious play after *Torch Song*, *Spookshouse* (1984) was attacked by the critics. The message was clear. Gay plays were all right on off-off-Broadway where they were relatively ignored and unobtrusive. Except for a fluke like *Torch Song*, Broadway was not a haven for gay plays or gay culture. In a way, the acceptance that *Torch Song Trilogy* received allowed Broadway to prove its open mindedness and then continue to define narrowly what would be permissible. The inherent political challenge of gay theater is too obvious for a field which is already presumed to be homosexual. One wonders whether *Torch Song* would have won its Tonys had voting not been by secret ballot.

Gay theater and gay playwrights have come a long way during the past 40 years. Occasional successes aside, it is clear that the most important and vital gay theater is going to be made and supported by gay people, and that mainstream, public acceptance is not going to appear at the second act curtain.

Opera
Mad Queens and Other Divas

The "opera queen" is a significant creator and participant in the gay sensibility. He typically spends weeks, even years arguing the fine points of Maria Callas' dramatics and Joan Sutherland's technique; he has three different recordings of Donizetti's *Lucia di Lammermoor*; he meticulously compares the Birgit Nillson *Turandot* at La Scala to the Eva Marton rendering in Prague; he admits that although Regine Crispin may have revolutionized the very *concept* of *Carmen* in 1955, the poor thing hasn't been able to get through the part since. Tempers can run so high and opinions so wild that it is hardly exaggerated to claim that "there is no position so absurd that an opera queen won't defend it."[1] This stereotype illuminates truths about the class structure of high art and its particular appeal for gay men. Understanding why gay men are so drawn to this art form offers unique insights into the politics of gay culture.

Gay men are certainly interested in other art forms: sculpture, painting, design, photography. However, these forms cannot compare with opera's gay reputation nor its role in gay culture and community. What largely distinguishes the performing arts is that they can be experienced collectively: they are social as well as artistic events. Many more people, even many more gay men, may travel through the Museum of Modern Art in any given week than attend *Tristan und Isolde* at the Metropolitan Opera, but the emotional experience of viewing a painting (even among a group of friends) is essentially a private one.

Many gay men go to the symphony; there may be an underground gay contingent at the races; and some gay men even enjoy baseball. What is it about opera that makes it different? The collective emotion unleashed at the opera is induced by the music and the drama in the story. Passions at a baseball game or a prize fight may run high but excitement is not guaranteed. Opera plays on our emotions through the deliberate manipulation of a predictable form. This predictability can allow the safe experience of emotions which we may have been taught to ignore or repress. Similarly, emotions may be elicited by listening to a symphony, and concert-going is also a social experience. But without the narrative, people may not feel moved collectively for the same reasons. In *Howard's End*, E. M. Forster describes several characters' responses to Beethoven's Fifth Symphony. Each responds uniquely, according to his or her life experiences. At the opera, people's responses are more uniform. Empathy with the performers gives permission to the audience to respond openly to the plot. People might be moved by a Mozart string quartet, but at the end of *La Boheme* or *Madame Butterfly* they are weeping.

The opera is also, in the plainest terms, a *respectable* place where gay men can meet and socialize . There is a famous story of a coterie of men who were fixtures at the Met's standing room, the backs of their trousers discreetly parted so they could experience a little extra pleasure while viewing the spectacle on stage.[2] I'm sure that the irony of mixing profane love with sacred art was not lost upon them. Although most opera queens don't have sex during performances, socializing is an important part of the experience of opera-going.

Opera also represents a triumph of form over content, a theme that comes up repeatedly in the historical development of gay sensibility. Vocal virtuosity is what gives it meaning. The content is convincing only insofar as the form is mastered. "All art is at once surface and symbol," wrote Wilde in *The Picture of Dorian Gray.* "Those who go beneath the surface do so at their peril."[3]

In opera, more than in other performing arts, performers are divorced from the characters they play. An enormous, middle-aged soprano can sing the part of the lithe, young Madame Butterfly; a hefty Wagnerian can become the temptress Salome. It is the voice, not the singer, who fills the role.

There is little realism or normality in opera. Emotions and plots are exaggerated to the point of absurdity. As Mrs. Wititterly, the hypochondriac in The Royal Shakespeare Company's production of Dickens' *Nicholas Nickleby*, exclaims: "I am always ill after the theater, my Lord. And after the opera I scarcely exist."[4] It is not just the ecstasy of emotional exhaustion which is physically satisfying. In *On Wings of Song*, gay novelist Thomas Disch depicts a future world that is so full of political and emotional repression that the only escape for the spirit is literally to leave the body while singing: song transcends the material world.

The cult of the diva has had an important place in the relationship between gay men and opera. Even stauncher than the fans of Judy Garland or Barbra Streisand are the claques of Maria Callas (*La Divina*) or Joan Sutherland (*La Stupenda*). It is interesting to note the differences between these two singers. Callas is noted for her dramatic power. She may not hit all the notes all the time, but her gift of projecting passion through virtuosity and acting ability is at once great opera and great theater. In contrast, Sutherland is noted for her technical precision. Detractors complain that there is little feeling behind her singing. However, both are important parts of the opera experience for gay men. Extreme dramatics represent a release from a sexually repressive world but the vocation of transcendent song is also crucial.

In a world that persecutes homosexuals, gay men easily identify with the love-torn, victimized heroines who populate most operas. In her aria "Vissi d'arte" Tosca sings:

I lived for art,
I lived for love,
Never did I harm a living creature!
Whatever misfortunes I encountered
I sought with secret hand to succor.
Ever in pure faith
I brought flowers to the altars,
In this hour of pain,
Why, Why, oh Lord,
Why dost thou repay me thus?

Opera is outlandish, in the most imaginative sense of the word; no one ever goes through life singing all the time. It flaunts reality. In a world that represses emotions and forbids homosexuality, opera is a victory for art and feeling over social and moral conventions.

Perhaps because gay men are defined, by the society at large, by their sexuality, much of gay male culture revolves around sex. In his essay "Finer Clay," Seymour Kleinberg argues that "gay sensibility sexualizes the world."[4] Kleinberg relates this to ways in which gay men objectify rather than empathize with women. I believe, however, that this "sexualization" has played an important and positive role in the extent to which gay men have been able to affect mainstream culture. Western culture could not ignore sexuality completely, so it tried to contain it in well delineated compartments, thereby rendering it non-threatening. It is socially acceptable to release emotion and sexual energy through opera, and by adopting this art form as their own, gay men have been able to influence the mainstream as well as gain acceptance into it.

Opera is a ghetto of culture that provides gay men with some security, but historically, because of this, it has also carried some degree of stigmatization. As early as 1701 Daniel Defoe wrote in *The True Born Englishman*: "Lust chose the torrid zone of Italy/ Where blood ferments in rapes and sodomy." He advised concerned parents not to include Italy, and especially the opera, on their sons' Grand Tours. It is unclear if it was the sight of the effeminate *castrati* or a racist suspicion of "Mediterranean" morals that prompted Defoe's remark.[5]

Maria Callas enraged, 1955

" HI BOB, YOU TWO HAVE STANDING-
ROOM-ONLY TICKETS TOO, HUH ? "

cartoon from *The Advocate*, 1972

Gays are fully aware of the opera queen stereotype. The famed "standing room story" gets a cartoon life while the idea that all gay men are wealthy is shot down.

Divas are loved for their off-stage as well as on-stage tempers. Here, Callas storms from her dressing room when served with a summons for breaking a contract. The contrast between the sacred and the profane, stately beauty and sexual passion, is neatly encompassed in these two photos. Both exhibit self-assurance as well as full emotional range.

cartoon from *Relax! This Is Only a Phase You're Going Through*

Grace Bumbry as Amneris at Covent Garden

Rosa Ponselle as Norma

The arts offer minority or outcast groups a way to attain some social acceptance and upward mobility. Jews found acceptance in the Italian Courts in the 15th century as dancing masters after they had been thrown out of Spain.[6] In Italy, it was possible for a peasant boy to gain both a reputation and social prominence if he were talented and willing to become a *castrato*. (In fact, many boys were sold into the practice; it was highly illegal to perform castration, but once done the church and the law looked the other way.) It was true then, as it is now, that in certain "artistic" circles one was judged more on talent than by conventional standards. In America the arts have always been suspected of a certain amount of deviance, social and intellectual as well as sexual. This association of "artiness" with "queerness" has often caused a homophobic backlash: straight male artists attack gay artists in order to prove their own manhood.

A mythological association has grown up about gay men, "high" culture, and the upper class. Part of the myth is sustained by prejudice, and part apparently true and reinforced by historical conditions. The fine arts have flourished under the patronage of the upper class. Renaissance patrons of the arts enabled artists and sculptors to work and gain critical and social acclaim. In America, where there was no formal aristocracy, much of high culture was nevertheless supported by the socially prominent.

For example, New York's Metropolitan Opera was built by a group of wealthy socialites in 1883 because Mrs. William H. Vanderbilt was unable to obtain an opening night box at the Academy of Music, the fashionable home of the city's opera since mid-century.[7] Although all the original investors in the project were wealthy businesspeople, they understood that there was no profit involved: "We never expected that it would pay. No opera house in the world has ever paid as an investment, and none ever will."[8] What it did not return in financial rewards it gave back in social prestige and publicity. Although the opera may have been funded by the wealthy, many of its ticket-buyers came from other classes—not only the ever-growing middle classes, who aped the rich in social activities, but also German, Italian, and other immigrants for whom opera had been a form of popular entertainment in Europe. In 1891, when the Met's presiding manager decided not to continue the tradition of presenting all of the operas in German, there was an outcry from the immigrant German press and community.[9]

In spite of this continuity between popular and high culture, somewhere in the evolution of American culture deep divisions occurred. Art forms such as opera gained the reputation of being arcane, overly refined, and inaccessible. Opera, ballet, or the symphony were connected in the public imagination with wealth.

In a context that associated the leisure of the upper classes with sexual depravity, it seemed clear that the refined possibilities of wealth must lead to something wicked. (The revelations of lesbianism, sado-masochism, and other sexual shenanigans in the 1934 Gloria Vanderbilt custody trial reinforced these ideas.[10] People came to view the upper class as tolerant of peculiar sexual behaviors quickly condemned by the working class. The fact is that the upper class excepted themselves, with prestige and money, from the social proscriptions they had invented to keep the working and middle classes in line.

This distortion has led to several forms of homophobia, most particularly the idea that gay men manipulate certain art forms to express their personal pathology. In her book *Off Balance*, Suzanne Gordon accuses gay men of distorting the image of the contemporary ballerina into an anorexic, de-sexualized, sexist vision of womanhood. This is in spite of the fact that she sees the main perpetrator of this image as George Balanchine, who was one of the most insistently heterosexual men in ballet.[11] In the opera world gay men are often accused of attempting to ruin a soprano's performance or career because they belong to another's claque.

There are two questions here. Are gay men wealthier than other people, and is this why they support high culture? How many gay men actually work in these fields and do they have any real control over what happens in them?

During the 70s, a new stereotype of gay men developed, fostered partly by the efforts of some gay men and largely by the homophobia of our culture. No longer a pathetic swish, gay men were now presented as white, middle class, urban professionals. Supposedly they had no children to support and lovers with comparable incomes. This image of gay men is as patently misleading as any popular stereotype. Invisible in it, as usual, are working class gay men and gay men of color, who may not have access to middle class job opportunities, and lesbians, who make the same 59 cents to the male dollar that straight women make. White professionals do have money to spend, but there are certainly more heterosexuals than gay people in this class. If people despise middle class gay men for spending money on opera tickets, it is not because they have the money to spend, (in America, no one is really put down for *that*) but because they are gay. The association between high culture, gay men, and money is based more on homophobia than on reality.

The question of gay men working in the arts is more complicated. There are, of course, gay people working in the arts (just as there are gay football players, newscasters, or insurance brokers). However, because of the historical development of the gay sensibility, many of the gay men who work in the arts can be open about their sexuality. As with any other field, it helps to know people, as well as to have talent, to move ahead and make a career. The negative stereotypes that have emerged about gay men attending or working in the arts have come about mainly because the arts permit and reinforce gay male visibility. If gay men, as a group, decided to attend baseball games *as* gay men, to socialize during them *as* gay men, and to center a large part of their cultural interest around baseball gossip, a whole new set of stereotypes would grow up around baseball as the national gay sport.

Because there is a real connection between social position and patronage of the arts, it *is* possible for a gay man, of whatever class background, to gain some upward mobility through interest in opera. Not only can it provide an entrance into gay social circles, it also allows an acceptable way to be gay in the larger world.

Opera has not provided other minorities with the same opportunities, and stereotypes, as it has gay men. A few famous but exceptional performers obscure how restricted opera really is. No black woman sang at the Met until 1955, when Marian Anderson, then nearing the end of her career, made her debut there in Verdi's *Un Ballo in Maschera*.[12] In the past 20 years, other black opera divas have broken through the color line: Shirley Verrett, Grace Bumbry, Jessye Norman, Leontyne Price, Leona Mitchell, and Kathleen Battle.

Although some black female singers have found success in opera almost the opposite is true for men of color. Many people, both black and white, believe that the reason for this is nothing less than sexual stereotyping and prejudice.[13] Audiences accept white actors relating sexually to black women on the opera stage, or black women who act emotional or sexual, but they will not accept such sexual or emotional behavior from black men.[14] While opera has enabled some gay men to achieve acceptability and upward mobility, it has reinforced cultural stereotypes and oppression of other minorities.

The opera offers gay men a social experience in which they can be openly gay. The sensibility of the art—especially the triumph of form over content and the permission which opera gives to the expression of sexuality and feeling—also attracts a gay male following. Because gay men were attracted to opera, and because opera itself was perceived as corresponding to certain stereotypes of gay men, it became a haven—or ghetto—in which gay men could be open about their lives. Historic associations between high culture and wealth reinforced other traditional associations between wealth and sexual non-conformity. Both before and after Stonewall opera has offered gay men a space where they could listen to the love which might sing—but dared not speak—its name.

Gay Publishing: Books and Periodicals
...and the word was made flesh...

Read any number of coming out stories and you will discover that many gay men and lesbians first identified their sexual feelings and desires after reading something about homosexuality. A passing reference, an entire book of psychoanalytic theory, or even a gay character in a novel can make all the difference to a young gay person because they give concrete form to unspoken, unacknowledged, and unexpressed feelings. Although film, television, and recordings may reach more people, it is probably print media—with its relatively cheap technology and the possibility of private consumption—which has most expanded and extended the popular thinking and images of homosexuality.

The post-Stonewall gay liberation movement has given birth to the ever-growing openly gay press. Gay content existed in literature before this, and there was some (mostly negative) writing about the social phenomenon of homosexuality, but almost none of this material was written or produced for gay people. The past thirty years have witnessed the first efforts to produce material specifically for a gay audience. Some of this early movement material, for its own safety and legal security, was presented as written for anyone "interested" in the question of sexual freedom. Other material, especially popular novels, may have been directed to a gay audience but, by and large, they were not published by gay-identified publishers.

It was the development of a lesbian and gay liberation movement which opened the floodgates and allowed the founding of print media run by and for the gay community. The gay press covered all aspects of gay life; it published newspapers, magazines, bar rags, books of fiction and non-fiction, pamphlets, and poetry broadsides. The gay identification of the producers and the market politicized the publishing endeavor. No matter what the individual publisher's politics—from radical to conservative—the collective driving force was the idea that homosexuality was a good, natural state unto itself and that there was such a thing as a "gay community" with a shared gay culture. These ideas distinguished the new gay press from all that had preceded it.

The impact of gay movement publishing reached beyond its initial purposes. After a while, mainstream publishers saw that there was a definite market for gay-oriented material—and a lucrative one at that—and they began their own gay lines of books and magazines. Novels, non-fiction, scholarly literature, coffee table books, magazines, and newspapers began appearing in bookstores and on newsstands. Because gay material was easily marketable, it had a bigger impact on commercial culture than its producers had intended. Through the commercialization of gay images, gay liberation ideas made inroads into the American popular imagination.

Perhaps the first continuously published, gay-identified magazine in the U.S. was *ONE*. First published in October of 1952 by progressive members of the Mattachine Foundation, it was followed one year later by the *Mattachine Review*, a mouthpiece for the newly formed Mattachine Society. In 1955, the Daughters of Bilitis began publication of *The Ladder* specifically for lesbians. Although the organizations themselves had small memberships, the magazines did very well for the times. By 1956, *ONE* had subscribers in every state, a fair number of newsstand sales, and readers around the world. Its readership was undoubtedly larger than the circulation figure; these magazines were passed around a lot and by 1960, *ONE's* circulation was 5000, *Mattachine Review's* 2500, and *The Ladder's* 750. These three magazines alone made enormous gains in organizing and communicating within the scattered American gay community.[1]

Both *ONE* and *Mattachine Review* found themselves caught between caution and rage. They urged calm discussions of "the homosexual" and his/her position in society. They referred to the "problem" and the "solution," using language which would not antagonize straight readers and government officials. On the other hand, they could not ignore the grave injustices being done to gay people across the country. Both magazines encouraged a sense of intellectual homosexual community. They insisted that homosexuals were just like everyone else except for their sexual orientation, and since the magazines almost never mentioned sex or sexuality, even that difference seemed negligible. At a time when the swish stereotype was all the popular imagination contained, they emphasized the opposite image of the responsible, mature, and straight-looking homosexual. *ONE* and *Mattachine Review* attempted to end gay oppression through "fitting in" respectably. Although they did promote a positive identity and tried to suggest ways for gay people to cope in a hostile world, they did not have the political support or resources to advocate a widespread, cultural basis for a self-conscious gay community. "Your magazine is aimed at people who think, not at people who feel," wrote a subscriber.[2]

ONE and *Mattachine Review* did not wish to draw much attention to the everyday gay lives of their readers. *Mattachine Review*, for example, did not accept advertising for anything other than books. Looking through old issues, you get the feeling that homosexuality is an intellectual pursuit rather than a sexual orientation. These publications were oriented towards civil liberties, and tried to convince the population at large that homosexuals should not be excluded from American life because of one little quirk. Gay people were so isolated at this time that the position taken by *Mattachine Review*, *ONE*, and *The Ladder* was probably the most practical way to take a first step towards community. Their desire to avoid a "bad image" must be understood in the context of the virulent homophobia which pervaded the entire culture. What they did not consider, however, was that for many people, no "good image" of homosexuality was possible. The main contribution of these magazines was in stressing the idea that a nationwide community of homosexuals had some unifying concerns and experiences.

It was *The Advocate* in 1967 that brought the gay subculture into print. Where *ONE* and *Mattachine Review* focused on intellectual exchange and on instances of gay oppression, *The Advocate* was a tangible symbol of a gay male presence within the culture, expressing both pride in difference and a longing to be part of the mainstream. Although it shared the legal and civil rights concerns of the homophile movement, *The Advocate* also catered to the lifestyles of its readers. Along with news and interviews, it featured advice on personal and etiquette problems, fashion hints, kitchen chat, and recipes. Reviews covered anything entertaining that might have gay appeal; performers with a gay following were given a lot of coverage. The expanding world of gay male porn was noted and appreciated.

The Advocate was an early descendant of, yet a radical departure from, *ONE* and *Mattachine Review*. It retained the schizophrenic insistence upon acceptance by a culture that could not regard gays as acceptable. Editorials and cartoons portrayed gay men again and again as as much a part of American society as anyone else. Personal and institutional homophobia was exposed in every issue. At the same time, *The Advocate's* editorial stance insisted that inclusion in American culture was a worthwhile goal. Although it is tempting to argue that *The Advocate* was a major factor in creating and disseminating gay politics nationally, it is also true that gay culture had reached a point by 1967 where it could be marketed at a profit. It had become a saleable commodity—in all of its various forms—and political differences abounded about whether gay culture would be created for the community or for a profit. The marketing of gay culture was possible only to gay people and then only after a gay movement had emerged and given the community a more visible and national presence.

ONE and *Mattachine Review* had insisted on a straight-looking, "good gay" image to counter that of the swishy queen. *The Advocate* portrayed the homosexual as a good consumer. Although *The Advocate* pushed harder for legal reforms than either *ONE* or *Mattachine Review*, it was not strictly reform-oriented. If the earlier publications had been concerned with social appearances, *The Advocate* placed the "bad gay" label on gay radicals (and lesbians), portraying them as agitators unwilling to wait patiently for reforms.

> Well, it has happened again. The gay destroyers have had another one of their "good" days, and the California Committee for Sexual Law Reform lies in shambles. The midget-minded masochists among us, it seems, cannot bear even the slightest hint of progress towards law reform and justice for Gays. It is a sad, but old story, and each time it happens, the disappointment becomes keener, the dis-illusionment greater, the despair deeper. The mature, talented segment of the gay community finds it increas-ingly easy to give up, say "What the hell," and retreat into their closets.
>
> Ironically, although the fate of the CCSLR itself is in doubt, the entity that the destroyers wanted to take over, the Whitman Radclyffe Foundation, has a good chance to survive independently...It has the potential of being what this newspaper has long advocated—a team of mature, responsible, talented experts with widespread financial backing from all strata of the gay community.
>
> But perhaps to some, helping Gays isn't as important as the fun of pulling down the pillars, the joy of parlia-mentary maneuvering, the vicarious pleasure of plotting, then the final tantrum. Now there's the real fun—the climax of it all—more fun even than sex. Remember how mom and dad always caved in at the final tantrum? Wasn't that great? Isn't it still great, boys and girls? Wipe your nose, Johnny, your mental age is showing.[3]

Gay liberation groups followed the tide of late 60s counter-culture in not demanding acceptance into the mainstream but rather widespread changes throughout society. In the 1973 editorial quoted above, *The Advocate*, uncomfortable with this shift to the left, pointed out exactly who it thought should be running things: "a team of mature, responsible, talented experts with widespread financial backing from all strata of the gay community."[4]

In 1953, the publication of *Playboy* magazine equated the idea of sexual freedom for men with what they called the "playboy lifestyle." They sold this idea, enticing readers with pictures of naked women. The famous centerfolds were less about sex than they were about money. The "playboy lifestyle" was composed essentially of consumer items.[5] "Lifestyle"—the *Playboy* sort or any sort—consisted of buying and possessing the accoutrements of upwardly mobile, middle class life. As homosexuals began to discover themselves and formulate a group identity, it was only a matter of time before they too would define a "lifestyle" useful for reinforcing personal identity and also creating a whole new market for consumption. *The Advocate* began publishing at a time when a large segment of the gay male population was eager for that consumer identity. In 1975, David Goodstein bought the paper and changed its format further: less news, more features, and ads featuring the slogan: *"The Advocate Touches Your Lifestyle."*

Before and after Stonewall, *The Advocate* was a major proponent of gay consumer culture. Sometimes the events or the objects being sold were aimed directly at the gay male community: bars, baths, porno films, and books. Sometimes *The Advocate* was after a broader audience, but aimed at gay men whom the advertisers felt were likely purchasers of Hollywood movies, recordings, fashionable furnishings, and clothes. The basis for this thinking was "liberation by accumulation"; social acceptance and mobility could be achieved by buying the correct accessories.

Besides consumer items, gay papers, especially *The Advocate*, made the bulk of their advertising income by selling sex. Classified advertising in search of sexual partners, or offering escort or massage services was standard fare. As *The Advocate* grew, and began to try for a larger audience, the sex ads were printed on pink paper and inserted as a supplement into the middle of the paper. That way readers who did not want to deal with them did not have to. Conversely, those who wanted the ads but not the paper were equally satisfied.

The position of *The Advocate*, and other gay papers, on gay sexuality was paradoxical. Where *ONE* and *Mattachine Review* had gone to extremes to deny its existence, *The Advocate*, in features and ads, clearly endorsed gay male sexuality as both a pastime and a means of selling products. What might appear at first to be a sex-positive attitude was in fact more of a marketing device. In their editorials, *The Advocate* generally took a conservative political approach. Although it promoted sexuality in certain ways, the paper's positions on such explosive sexual issues as S/M, boy love, and public sex were not progressive. A paper like Boston's *Gay Community News*, on the other hand, presented its readers with a more radical political approach. It gave extensive coverage to the "hot" issues by providing an open forum for all sides. Yet, because they did not choose to run large numbers of sexually-oriented ads, they were often perceived as conservative on sex. Part of this reputation resulted from an ad policy prohibiting "sexually exploitive" advertising (a policy which, in reality, actually prohibited very few ads). The other factor in the perception of *Gay Community News* as the paper that "took the sex out of homosexuality" was the strong presence of lesbians on the staff. Many gay male readers simply assumed that the lack of sexually explicit content, ads specifically, was a lesbian anti-sex plot. The truth was that *Gay Community News* did not get the sort of ads that *The Advocate* did; their editorial direction tended away from "gay lifestyle" and towards more news stories and analytical features. Nevertheless, the paper was presumed to be sex-negative, and women on the paper became an easy scapegoat.

As lesbians and gay men began to organize politically and form social groups, they also began their own publications. Many covered local news, much of which was missing in *The Advocate*, as well as reports from all over the country. Other papers emphasized culture, presenting a forum for the latest in gay poetry, prose, and criticism. Because of small budgets and lack of access to sophisticated printing equipment, many of these papers and magazines began as mimeographed, stapled handouts. As gay communities grew and proliferated, so did the size and scope of these publications. The purpose of *ONE* and *Mattachine Review* had been to expose and reform the grossest inequities of the system. Many post-Stonewall publications took a more radical view of homosexuality and its relationship to the general culture. They saw homophobia as only one structure among many which oppressed women, racial minorities, youth, the elderly, the poor, the disabled. It was this larger political analysis, a product of the movements which comprised the new left, which informed the direction of many new gay organizations and publications.

Because they took the position that the personal was political, (the logical outcome of the individualism which Oscar Wilde embraced) they saw their very existence as political in nature. They were creating a politicized environment in which gay activism and culture would grow. They were not looking for changes around them: they *were* the changes; they were going to make the news as well as report it. Flouting conventional journalistic ethics, the political gay press made no distinction between itself and the subjects it covered. The new gay press was at once an extension of and a technique for outreach and communication within the gay community.

The politics and cultural attitudes of the new publications dictated their relationship to the wider culture. A paper like *The Advocate* based its definition of gay community upon those aspects of gay culture most likely to win outside approval. In contrast, the small community papers advocated a sense of self-approval and a culture which operated separately from the mainstream.

Some of the smaller community papers, like New York's *Come Out*, were short-lived. Others, like Boston's *Gay Community News* and *The Philadelphia Gay News*, are still publishing today. After the first few years, the papers that lasted (a surprisingly large number, given the lack of money and experience that accompanied their birth) found themselves in a unique position. They had been founded to serve local gay communities and generally reflected those interests.

The national network of gay presses is a very complex and quirky institution. It ranges from the anarchist *Fag Rag*, which has no advertising and an editorial policy oriented towards sex radicalism, to throwaway bar rags, publications which exist mainly to promote gay bars but which may include some entertainment news or even political commentary. Mainstream publishing and com-

cartoon from *The Advocate*, 1972

Gay Community News cover, 1981

The veiled gay images used to advertise early Isherwood and Goodman novels were replaced in the 1960s by more blatant representations. *A Brother's Touch* projects a low-life decadence while the pseudo-Cocteau look of *Nocturnes for the King of Naples* lets the buyer know that this book is not only "gay"; it is also "art."

Although perceived as a sexually-oriented paper, *The Advocate* has consistently gone out of its way to inform readers that it is just like any other paper. *Gay Community News*, on the other hand, has a reputation for placing politics before sex even though it has been in the vanguard of discussing "hot" sexual issues. Their infamous cock and barbed wire cover showed that they were far from prudish.

Making Do, 1963

A Meeting by the River, 1968

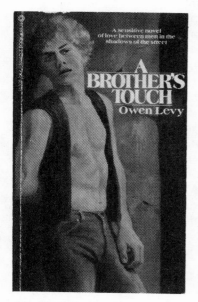

A Brother's Touch, 1981

Nocturnes for the King of Naples, 1980

mercial concerns ignore the gay press. Papers like *The Advocate* and the *Philadelphia Gay News* did manage to get some commercial advertising. While advertising of some sort was generally necessary for survival, the relationships between the gay press, the gay business community, and mainstream advertisers are complicated.

Many papers which started as community services were dedicated to presenting all aspects of the news. This approach was not always in the interest of gay-owned or gay-operated businesses. When gay papers did not cater to the needs or demands of business, they were accused of being "too political," of not caring about all members of the gay community. Bar rags often began as a way for businesses, especially bars, to self-advertise and control the editorial content of the paper.

Since the purpose of business is to make money, papers which thrived on controversy (anything from leftist politics to man-boy love) did not receive business support because business did not want to be associated with controversy. Many gay businesses threw their financial support to bar rags (or papers which featured puff features rather than news and analysis) and the more substantial and often far more radical members of the gay press pursued their interests without interference, but also without much money.

Questions that concern the gay press are by definition controversial and raise high tempers. Coverage of national issues—who is and who is not supporting a gay rights bill somewhere—can also cause problems. Gay concerns are as diverse as gay people; it is impossible to represent the opinions of an entire newspaper staff, never mind the community as a whole. When gay papers take critical positions on some aspect of the gay community, (racism at gay bars, for example, or misogyny among gay men, or anti-sex attitudes among lesbians) they are immediately charged with not being positive, with attacking one part of the community and favoring another, with "reverse discrimination," sexism, and even homophobia. Papers like *Gay Community News*, the *Body Politic*, and the *New York Native* have opened themselves to internal and community criticism because of their commitment to providing an open forum.

In the final analysis, most gay publications (bar rags excluded) have tried, and some have managed, to walk a fine line between soliciting support from the business community and remaining independent to report on news and culture as they see it. It is ironic that with all of the in-fighting, the real threat to many gay papers is a completely external one. The Canadian government tried to close down and destroy the *Body Politic* by charging the paper with obscenity after it published a story on man-boy love. Boston's *Gay Community News* was burned out of its offices by arsonists. Other gay papers around the country have encountered problems with local governments, the postal service, police, and just plain harassment. Nevertheless, the gay press continues, and sometimes even flourishes. It has functioned as a conduit for news and culture and has created, in a short period of time, the basis for a more cohesive gay community and culture.

The notion that publishers could sell books to homosexuals began years before gay liberation became a topic for *Time* and *Newsweek*. In the early 1950s, novels appeared which had homosexual characters and plots. Books like *Quatrefoil* and *Finistere* were published by mainstream publishers and featured the requisite unhappy endings. (These particular two books actually presented some positive images despite the downbeat resolutions and *Quatrefoil* was reprinted in the 1980s by Alyson Publications, an openly gay publisher.) They were aimed at a specifically gay male market. They were discussed, reviewed, and advertised in *Mattachine Review* and *ONE*. The paperback book industry had begun to prosper after WWII and by the mid-1950s, the book boom was in full swing. *ONE* and *Mattachine Review* each had their own presses and mail order companies, but mainstream publishers were also interested in selling books to gay men.[6]

Even a casual look at the book covers of gay-oriented paperback novels from the 1950s onward shows a trend towards displaying identifiable gay images. An early paperback reissue of *Finistere* under the title *The World at Twilight* features two good-looking, slight, Greenwich Village types standing in sinister green and lavender shadows. In the mid-1960s, the cover of Jess Stern's pseudo-scientific study of male homosexuality, *The Sixth Man*, also used the telltale lavender to identify one out of six figures. The cover of *The*

Problem of Homosexuality in Modern Society, a serious collection of psychological and anthropological articles, clearly identified itself with two boyish-looking men, one with his hands on the other's shoulders, emerging from a murky void. Novels from established writers like Paul Goodman, James Purdy, and Christopher Isherwood sported drawings or cover copy indicating gay content. In 1963, with the publication of John Rechy's *City of Night*, Grove Press broke an unwritten rule and placed a photo of actual Times Square hustlers on the cover. This was probably the first time that a blatantly gay image—and of male prostitutes to boot—was used to sell a book. Although *City of Night* received exceptionally good reviews, the packaging of the paper and cloth editions made it clear that Grove was mainly interested in targeting a gay audience. This was even more obvious four years later with the paperback publication of Rechy's second novel, *Numbers*. It featured a full-length, side view, nude male model on the cover. Until then, it was unusual for even soft core pornography to be so bold with its cover images. Some bookstores provided wrap-arounds to hide the cover (and make it even more titillating). Although both books sold well, other publishers did not take up Grove's lead.

Books were more profitable than magazines or newspapers. It was in this area of book publishing that many mainstream presses experimented with gay marketing. During the 1970s, a network of gay-owned and operated small presses began to evolve. Small presses had historically been more open about gay material. Small presses published Allen Ginsberg, John Wieners, Harold Norse, and other gay beat poets. Such publishers as Fag Rag Books, Gay Sunshine Press, Naiad, Out and Out Books, Good Gay Poets, Calamus, Persephone Press, Diana Press, and Sea Horse Press began publishing gay work in the 70s and 80s. The tradition of small alternative presses was perfect for gay publishers and writers because they could control the editorial content and the production process. Although distribution posed some problems, it was compensated for by the fact that these publishers knew their audience well. Through mail order, the developing network of alternative distributors, advertisements in the gay and feminist press, gay and feminist bookstores, or through gay and feminist organizations, they were able to reach their readers.

Once the small gay presses had proven that there was a good, solid market for gay-oriented books, mainstream publishers were quick to jump on the bandwagon. In 1972, Daughters Inc., a small feminist press, published Rita Mae Brown's *Rubyfruit Jungle*, a sassy, upbeat novel about coming out and surviving as a lesbian. The book did so well that the mass paperback rights were bought by Bantam Books and eventually went through more than ten printings. Other companies also promoted gay titles. St. Martin's Press brought out such varied titles as *Kevin*, a novel about man-boy love, *A Queer Kind of Death*, a reprint of a 1966 murder mystery which had become a cult item, *David at Olivet*, a historical/biblical gay novel, and *Special Teachers/Special Boys*, a book that treated the difficulties of being a gay teacher in a school for problem students. Avon also tried a "gay line" of paperback originals with specific genre appeal: mysteries, occult, and historical novels. After a few years, St. Martin's and Avon gradually decreased their "gay lines." Although some of their titles did very well, expectations of huge profits probably overreached the initial sales. Much the same phenomenon occurred with the publication of black and women's studies books in the late 1960s. Publishers, perceiving a "new" and profitable audience, were quick to flood the market with new and old material. (The publication of feminist classics, for example, all in the public domain, was cheap and profitable.)

Rubyfruit Jungle ended up being a fluke, moving as it did from a small press to a mainstream house. There are almost no other crossovers in that direction. Some gay writers have published with mainstream publishers: Andrew Holleran's *Dancer from the Dance*, Arnie Kantrowitz's *Under the Rainbow*, and Edmund White's *States of Desire* are good examples. But there are quite a few authors who, having had a book published by a large house, then relied upon the small, gay presses to bring out their other, possibly more controversial and less saleable work: Bertha Harris, Daniel Curzon, and Richard Hall.

Because large-scale publishing is premised on the mass production of bestsellers, it is not surprising that many gay titles did not live up to expectations. Small gay publishers had a political commitment to their work. With the help and support of gay writers, they worked hard to publish and distribute their titles. Money to continue publishing more books was important, but it was not always the first consideration. Another problem was that many publishers viewed the gay community, and the gay book buyer, as a market where they could make quick money. Often, they did not bother spending enough money on promotion or packaging. They did very little outreach to a non-gay market (thus cutting drastically into sales) and if the book did not do well, they removed it from the market rather than trying new approaches (the sad fate of *any* book not able to make it quickly and profitably). Finally, they did not take the limits of the gay market into account.

In many ways, the experience of the mainstream book industry is a microcosm of the experience of discovering the gay market in general. Any subculture's unique characteristics may be marketed for the group's own benefit, like *ONE* or the community-based papers that appeared in the early 1970s. The next step is wider commercialization within the community for the purposes of expanding and sustaining production. However, as soon as something is proved profitable, it is inevitably taken on by the straight mainstream culture and resold to the very people who originated it. Although this pattern is true of most minorities and their relationship to the dominant culture, it is particularly true of gay culture because gay people—especially gay men—have survived by adopting the role of cultural trendsetters. Gay men have attempted to influence culture through both invention *and* consumption.

There is a dialectic between a self-contained gay culture and the dominant culture, based upon the tension between the desire for assimilation and the desire to remain distinct and separate. Many small, community-based and overtly political papers have opted to market themselves within the gay community. Other papers—like *The Advocate* and some soft core porn magazines which perform a similar function—have tried defining gay men primarily as consumers in order to attract some crossover advertising: ads for movies or records which may hold some appeal for gay men. This advertising, however, is not what sustains the papers. There are also ads for liquor and a smattering of one-shot ads from national travel agencies. Although these magazines have promoted a "gay lifestyle" to their readers, they have not managed to make the mainstream producers of "gay lifestyle" articles (Levi-Strauss jeans, Calvin Klein sportswear, Lacoste shirts, Vuitton luggage) consider them fruitful places to advertise. The myth that assimilation is possible through upward mobility is true only up to a point. *The Advocate* would like to believe that homosexuals can achieve equality and dignity through purchasing power. This buying power, unfortunately, does not characterize all or even most gay people. Even where disposable producers of "gay lifestyle" items (Levi-Strauss jeans, Calvin Klein producing any of the desired social results.

The split between the more commercial mainstream and the small, community-minded press is essentially a split between a gay-defined culture and one that seeks approval from the straight world. Homosexuals were perceived as a potential market and were targeted by mainstream producers as a new source of sales. It would be simplistic to imply that small presses and papers do not care about money; profits are important to survival and to continuing their work. But they do lack the pure profit motive of mainstream producers. The paradox is that while they are busy creating and defining new aspects of gay culture, the more commercial interests will use them for market research, as a technique for learning what trends might prove profitable in the future. In the meantime, small presses and publishers continue to create and discover an everlasting, imaginative wealth of gay culture and sensibility.

Gay Publishing: Pornography
...and dwelt among us...

Bob had turned about on the bed, seeking out Jack's trembling flesh, now pointing out at him strongly. As he shifted into position he felt Jack reaching for him in a like manner, and soon they were engaged—one on the other—their joint actions becoming more feverish by the second. They began at the exact same time, and now they knew no holding back. Their lips crushed together, then hands sought flesh, and they were sweating, grasping, and slamming together and finally moaning until their throats burst into shrieks of shattering ecstasy. Then they lay back, breathing heavily, limp. They cuddled together, holding one another without embarrassment and it seemed obvious to Jack that he had never been so satisfied before in all his life.[1]

In the late 1950s, mass production of pornography for gay men began. This passage from *Gay Whore* (1954) is indicative of the important political function of gay pornography. In *A Room of One's Own*, Virginia Woolf talks about the importance of the sentence "Chloe liked Olivia" in a popular novel.[2] Until then, women in literature had related to each other primarily through men. Similarly, "it seemed obvious to Jack that he had never been so satisfied before in all his life" was for many people, gay men especially, a revelation and an essential statement.

There has never been any hard and fast rule for defining pornography. Generally presumed to be some depiction of sex, either in pictorial or written form, the limits of what is or is not pornographic change across culture and history. What for the Restoration was perfectly permissible, the Victorians considered highly immoral, and to us seems unexceptionable. Even the current categories of "hard core" and "soft core" are arbitrary social and semi-legal classifications. Whatever the specifics of a definition, it is impossible to separate any pornography from its social context. In a sexually repressive culture, any depiction of sexuality is unusual. In a society which has a distinct heterosexual bias, any depiction of gay male sexuality is, for gay men, a breath of fresh air.

Until ten years ago, most pornography was restricted, homosexual pornography even more so. It was difficult to obtain, and often, illegal to possess. In the late 1940s and early 1950s, a gay artist named Blade left his pornographic drawings and stories in unmarked packages in bars or secured in bus terminal lockers, passing the key from one viewer to the next to insure safety.[3] Pornography, like the sexual lives of gay men, had to be kept quiet out of fear of persecution or arrest.

In a world that denies the very existence of homosexuality and homosexual desires, gay pornography performs two vital functions. It depicts sexual desire, bringing it out of the mind and into the reality of the material world. Porn becomes a sexual object. The sexual identity of the viewer is consequently reinforced, bolstered by the fact that the viewer has been engaged by, and responded to, a sexual object.

For many gay men, pornography was one of the few ways to assess and affirm their sexual feelings and desires. Pornography, by presenting the male body or male sexuality in a glorified form—went beyond depicting and defining desire. It attempted to compensate for the generally negative and oppressive social position of gay sexuality. Because homosexuality was taboo, gay male pornography—or indeed, any writing about gay men—was considered more dangerous and was prohibited more strictly than its heterosexual counterpart.

Until just 30 years ago, the legal definition of gay pornography was so broad as to include any material on homosexuality which did not conform to specific scientific perspectives. In 1953, the Postmaster General of Los Angeles held up the distribution of the August issue of *ONE* for two weeks. A year later, he seized the October 1954 issue and demanded that *ONE* show cause that it was not "obscene, lewd, lascivious, and filthy." *ONE* brought the decision to federal district court and after a long delay, the trial began in early 1956. The defense argued that *ONE* was "serious, responsible" and that its overriding tone was "with all its imperfections and amateurism...one of sincerity."[4] Both the court and the appeals court refused to view the case as freedom of speech.

The two offending articles were "Sappho Remembered," a short story about a lesbian's coming out, and "Lord Samuel and Lord Montague," a satiric poem about aristocratic homosexuality in England. The court was very specific in its objections.

> This article is nothing more than cheap pornography calculated to promote lesbianism. It falls far short of dealing with homosexuality from a scientific, historic, or critical point of view...The poem is dirty, vulgar, and offensive to the moral senses. An article may be vulgar, offensive, and indecent even though not regarded as such by a particular group...because their own social or moral standards are far below those of the general community... Social standards are fixed by and for the great majority and not by and for a hardened or weakened minority.[5]

The language of the court makes it quite clear that the basic issue was the power of the "great majority" over the "hardened or weakened minority." Despite the noises about "social standards," the real battle was about freedom of speech, access to information, and most importantly, freedom of the imagination. Existing social standards precluded any depiction, graphic or written, of homosexual love or relationships. The opinions of openly gay people did not count because they had, by their very nature, "social or moral standards... far below those of the general community." Thus defined, *any* homosexual writing was *ipso facto* pornographic.

Although *ONE* lost its original case, it appealed to the Supreme Court and on January 3, 1958, the court ruled that the issue of *ONE* in question was not obscene, and that it was a matter of free speech. The legal battle had been won.

> Thus for the first time in American publishing history, a decision *binding on every court and every public agency in the country* now stands: a decision affirming in effect that it is in no way improper to describe a love affair between two homosexuals, that humorous and satirical light-hearted handling of homosexuality by no means constitutes obscenity.[6]

The court ruling set a legal precedent for the production and distribution of male homosexual pornography. The heterosexual porn industry was also growing by leaps and bounds. Films, magazines, and novels proliferated over the next two decades, although the *Playboy* type of newsstand magazines were probably getting most of the attention. Legislating the restriction of sexually explicit material became a hot topic for the next 25 years. In 1957, the Supreme Court ruled in the Roth case that "obscenity" was not protected by the Constitution. For the next 12 years, there was endless discussion over what exactly constituted obscenity. In 1969, in Stanley v. Georgia, they declared that the individual had a constitutional right to own or view such material. For all the hair-splitting of the Supreme Court's definition, the ability to purchase sexually explicit material in any given store in any given community boiled down to who was in city hall and whether the police had been paid off. The confusion about the precision of legal statutes and language led to generally more permissive attitudes towards such material.[7] Publications like *Penthouse*, *Oui*, and *Hustler* used sexual pictures as come-ons. What they were actually selling was a "lifestyle." They used high-tone fiction and current events reporting as a cloak of respectability. The truth was they existed more for the ad content than for their features *or* their sexual material. In the early 1970s, similar gay lifestyle magazines appeared. *Mandate, In Touch, Blueboy, Honcho* and *Numbers* featured male nudes, sexually explicit stories, and pieces on travel and middle class living. Like *Playboy*, they featured advertising and sales pitches for items that went with this class status. While their sale on newsstands represented a major step forward in tolerance of homosexuality by the American public, (based partly upon the inroads which gay liberation had made into the public consciousness) the real key to success was cooperation with the prevailing climate of consumer capitalism. Pornography—by whatever definition or sexual persuasion—reflected major cultural and economic changes. Not only was producing and marketing sexuality profitable, but the use of explicit sexuality to sell other products caused a major shift in the consumer mentality.

In the mid-1970s, feminists began to question and reevaluate the place that pornography had appropriated in American culture. Some theorists claimed that pornography was not just *symptomatic* of sexism and misogyny, but was a primary *cause* of women's oppression. Robin Morgan summed up this position by stating that "pornography is the theory; rape is the practice."[8] Most feminist objections to pornography centered around the fact that women were objectified and thus dehumanized by pornography, increasing their vulnerability to rape, battering, and sexual abuse. Some feminists attacked all pornography with the argument that "where there is any attempt to separate the sexual experience from the total person, that first act of objectification is perversion."[9]

Some writers, convinced of the universal truth of heterosexual dynamics, attacked gay male pornography for the same reasons they attacked heterosexual pornography. Kathleen Barry stated that "homosexual pornography...acts out the same dominant and subordinate roles as heterosexual pornography."[10] And Gloria Steinem has stated that gay male porn "may imitate this [heterosexual] violence by putting a man in the 'feminine' role of the victim."[11]

This analysis of pornography, and its misapplication to the gay male experience, raises interesting questions about the differences between heterosexuality and homosexuality and about the nature of gay male porn. When Robin Morgan stated that heterosexual pornography is propaganda for rape, she postulated a dynamic in which the viewer, through his desire, becomes a predator, and the image, a victim. In fact, the relationship between homosexual men and gay male pornography is completely different.

While it is true that the viewer, sexually aroused, lusts after the object, it is equally true that he may also want to *be* that object. This element of identification *with* as well as desire *for* the sexual object distinguishes gay and straight porn. This is perfectly illustrated in the 1976 porn film *Heavy Equipment*. In an old magic book, a meek young clerk finds a formula which will transform his physical appearance. Looking through porn magazines, he finds a picture he likes, mixes his elixir, and, reciting the incantations, becomes the magazine image. The fact that identification exists simultaneously with objectification transforms the power relationships which some have presumed to be inherent in the viewing of sexual images.[12]

Although pornography today is easily available, arguments against it are as widespread as the product itself. Religious, legal, right-wing, left-wing and even gay liberation fights have raged over the meaning, effect, and worth of pornography. The power of sexual images is strong, generating high feelings on all sides. These debates often go beyond pornography to examine the sexual images prevalent in many aspects of our culture: advertising, television, the record industry, theater. The dissemination of sexual images in the mainstream media—especially the male image over the last 15 years—is closely connected with the emergence and growth of the gay liberation movement.

Gay male pornography is twice forbidden. It is clear from the lower court's decision in the *ONE* case that the very depiction of homosexuality in anything other than a negative context was at one time considered dangerous and subversive. In our culture, *all* sexual images are suspect. Heterosexual pornography is tolerated because it is thought to reinforce "normal" sexual and power arrangements within the culture. Homosexual pornography, however, does not fall into this category and is generally considered threatening. Gloria Steinem's heterosexual analysis of gay male pornography is misguided, and Kathleen Barry's assertion that homosexual pornography "appeals not only to gay but to straight men"[13] is unsubstantiated. Homosexuality itself is such a threat to the prevailing social/sexual power structure that its pornographic representation terrifies people. Homosexuality and pornography are both unacceptable forms of behavior and expression; they are twice as potent when linked together.

It is because the power and force of the sexual image is so heady, so potent, that there is such fear of it. One of the most common complaints against homosexual pornography (or any homosexual writing or imagery for that matter) is that it will "cause" people, especially young people, to become homosexual. In a sense this is true. Pornography is powerful because it represents sexual desire. In a culture which is determined to keep all sexuality—and especially non-reproductive sexuality—under tight control, the depiction of sexuality is a real threat. The women's movement has always fought for women to control reproductive sexuality. The issue of total sexual freedom was not addressed fully at first, but gay liberation has had the effect of making it an integral debate within feminism. In a society that desperately pretends that homosexuality does not exist, gay pornography tells the truth. It also represents an enticing yet dangerous promise. There is a direct correlation between the social repression of an object or idea and the power that object may carry.

Another powerful, threatening characteristic of pornography is that it blurs the lines between fantasy and reality. While there are definite rules which govern our sexual behavior, imagination is not understood and not controllable; it is also boundless. Because the sexual imagination can and does respond to all sorts of stimuli, it is not possible to protect and shelter it. Sexual images, however, because they are both blatant and suggestive, play a large role in sparking the imagination. Pornography may present us with images, ideas, or feelings we have never experienced before, or it may ignite dormant feelings and desires which needed affirmation.

Gay pornography often features men who are unusually good looking, or examples of a sexually desirable "type": musclebuilder, preppy, leatherman, or jock. These are glorifications of the male figure. However, sometimes, the models fall into the ordinary realm of good looks, instilling in the viewer a sort of boy-next-door feeling.

The variety of "types" in gay male porn is indicative of the impulse to eroticize as many images of men as possible. While certain magazines may feature a certain style—*Drummer* capitalizes on the older, mature, hirsute man, while *In Touch* is more interested in the smooth-skinned, late adolescent—a wide variety of pornographic gay images are being produced and appreciated.

This reality/fantasy split in pornography is best seen in films. There is a long standing porn tradition that all sex scenes end with a "money" or "cum shot." The male lead must ejaculate in full view of the audience. (Although *de rigueur* in heterosexual films, this is even more important in all-male films.) The point is to prove to the audience that they have not been cheated. They have seen actual sex—and sexual pleasure—on the screen. While most people accept movies as strictly "made up," the "proof" of reality within a fantasy is peculiar to porn films. It would certainly be considered odd for audiences to want to know that an actor was really shot as part of a movie.[14]

Susan Sontag has written that photographs—because they can be created to suit a certain aesthetic as well as convey a seemingly exact approximation of reality—can be either art or evidence. But because a photographer consciously shapes reality to fit his/her vision, they are rarely both. Pornographic films seem to fall somewhere in between the two. Some of the more adventurous gay male filmmakers like Wakefield Poole and especially Peter de Rome have done away with the "cum shot" and attempted to make thoroughly erotic films without the usual trappings of the genre. However, whatever artistic merits some pornography may have, its function as "evidence" is an important part of the gay experience.

The drawings and photos of the mid-1950s *Physique* magazines were presented and marketed as aesthetic material. The advent of mass-marketed hard core pornography eliminated the pretense of "art" and the photos stood as clear "evidence" that homosexual acts did indeed occur. Photographs have always seemed more real than other forms of visual representation: they must be true since the camera never lies. The social, cultural, and sexual impact of a picture of two men fucking cannot be underestimated.

Looking through early photographic porn now, the men seem

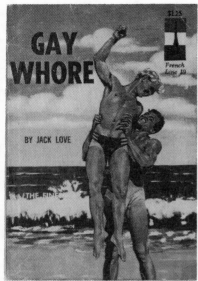

Gay Whore, 1967

Physique Pictorial, 1956

The gay male image from the 1950s to the 1980s: swish to butch. The slim-hipped, boyish blonds on the cover of *Gay Whore* found their idealized counterparts in the muscled models of *Physique Pictorial*. This was the first rebellion against, and accomodation within the stereotype. In the late 1970s, the look was still slim and blond, but the image was gay-identified and totally masculine in a post-Stonewall world. Youth was often reinforced by juxtaposition with older images. As gay men broke with previous stereotypes, the older, bearded gay look became popular. Members of the baby boom generation were growing up and looking for images that reflected their own lives and sexual desires. The older, mature man—in business drag no less—came into his own in the 1980s. Even with all the trappings of traditional masculinity, this image is presumed to be openly and positively gay.

Richard Locke and Robert Adams in Artie Bressan's *Forbidden Letters*, 1980

Physique Pictorial, 1956

Richard Locke, Fred Halsted, Mike Morris, and Jared Benson in *El Paso Wrecking Corp.*, directed by Joe Gage, 1979

extremely unattractive by current porn standards. They almost contradict Susan Sontag's maxim: "Nobody ever discovered ugliness through photographs. But many through photographs have discovered beauty...what moves people to take photographs is finding something beautiful."[15] The "beauty" of the early photographs was perhaps not slick, but it was the beauty of gay male sexuality. By 1970, a distinct market for gay male pornography had been discovered and both fly-by-night and professional studios and publishers flourished. Large scale operations like Brentwood, Target, Colt, and Arena packaged and sold 8½ by 11 photobooks with quality reproductions, good paper, and clean color. But these books represented more than the discovery of a new market and the deregulation of pornography. They were a response to the acceptance of the eroticization of the male body and the gradually changing self-perception and self-acceptance of gay men.

Mainstream culture disdains sexual desirability. Before the 1970s it was (weak) women for heterosexual men and for heterosexual women it was (strong) men. For homosexuals of either gender—that was a problem: there weren't supposed to be any homosexuals. In porn, or in the mainstream novels that dealt with homosexuality before Stonewall, there is a clear pattern. The typical gay men desired "straight trade": hustlers or young boys. Anyone but another gay man. (Of course real gay men did have lovers, sex with other gay men, and gay male friends—but there was little literary recognition of this reality.)

In the 50s, the predominant stereotype of a gay man was the limp-wristed swish. He was mocked by the general culture and even early homophile publications like *ONE* or *Mattachine Review* were unwilling to claim him. Most of the sexual iconography from this early period was an attempt to break away from, or modify, sexual stereotypes of gay men. If the gay stereotype was the 90 pound weakling of the Charles Atlas body-building ads, the "real" men had to be muscular and well built. Homosexual attraction to muscle magazines like *Iron Man* or *Strength and Health* was partially the simple appeal of uncovered male bodies. But these publications were also appropriate sexual objects for gay men because they were clearly *unlike* the standard gay stereotype. When gay-oriented muscle

magazines first appeared—*Vim* and *Physique Pictorial*—the images
were slightly different. The men were muscular but they were also
slightly effeminate; they had the slim waists and shoulders which
were generally associated with the image of the queen, but they also
sported huge arm, pectoral, and thigh muscles.

In pornographic films and photos from the early 1970s, these
trends are still evident. Without social permission for self-love or
self-esteem, gay men were attracted to—and bought—images unlike
gay stereotypes. In a replay of the social and cultural aesthetics of
John Addington Symonds or Baron von Gloeden, a great deal of gay
male pornography worshipped youth. The images in this porn were
of clean cut, all-American high school or college types. Even when
the models were obviously older—in their 20s or even early 30s—they
still retained their boyish manner. Part of this was a reaction to the
stereotype of homosexuals as dirty old men. Youth is also equated
with innocence and is therefore not stereotypically gay.

As pornography and other sexual images proliferated in the
1970s and 80s, the number of different "types" and images in gay
porn also increased. The advent of soft-core magazines like *In
Touch*, *Mandate*, *Blueboy*, and *Honcho*, beginning in 1974, brought
the material to the newsstands and also reflected changing tastes in
attractiveness. The idea that the sexually desirable object had to be
the "other" was diminishing. The straight-looking counterpart to
the swish stereotype was now replaced with very masculine looking
models who were also obviously gay. Over time, "types" were created
which reflected gay men's self-images as well as their relationship to
mainstream culture. For example, gay "clones" sported slim, but
well-built bodies, short masculine haircuts, tight jeans, work boots,
tee shirts, and a denim or leather jacket. The clone made his way into
the mainstream and could be found selling assorted artifacts—jeans
or boots, for example—to a straight market. It became difficult, in
certain parts of certain cities, to tell gay men from real construction
workers, or straight men dressing like gay men from gay men
dressing like straight construction workers.

The average age of the models in gay pornography has risen over
the last ten years. The slim hairless images of youth have gradually
been replaced with more fleshy bodies. Clean shaven models gave

way to bearded, hirsute men, whose demeanor and attitude spelt
maturity and experience rather than innocence. Even the all-
American look gave way to more ethnic models. Part of the reason for
the growing differences in age was the fact that a huge number of
baby boom men were now between 28 and 45, forming the largest
group of gay producers and consumers in the country. Many of them
came out after Stonewall. One of the most profound effects of the gay
movement upon the lives and loves of gay men is that it gave them the
social permission to like and to love themselves. The burden of being
homosexual was lifted. Rather than furtively seeking the "other,"
gay men were finally able to enjoy their own sexuality, their own
sexual images, and their own "types."

Although pornography may be a reflection of gay men's self-
images and desires it is also an industry, which like any industry
functions by selling many things to many people. Since the mid-
1970s, gay male pornography has become a very profitable business—not as profitable as heterosexual porn, but a well-established,
money-making concern nevertheless. As a commodity, pornography
is exploited.

Hard core pornography, gay or straight, is usually sold *as*
pornography. That is, depictions of sexual activity are sold as such:
hard core porn sells sex. Soft core porn uses sex to sell other products.
In *Playboy* (and its heterosexual imitators) as well as *Blueboy*,
Playguy, *Mandate* and *In Touch*, the sexual pictures are a come-on, a
sales pitch to get people to buy the magazine. Once people buy the
magazine, they can be exposed to the ads that fill in the spaces
between the nude pictures. The real motivation behind the gay
soft-core porn magazines is not sexual stimulation, but enticement to
buy. The slick photography, glossy covers, good reproduction
techniques, and occasionally interesting articles are paid for by mass
distribution and large advertising income.

Many gay business people believe that the success of these
magazines is an indication of the acceptance of homosexuality in
American culture. In a sense they are right. Over the past 30 years
there has been a growing acceptance of more open sexuality. What
made *Blueboy* or *Mandate* palatable to the public at large was not
that they were presenting positive gay images, but that they fit in

perfectly with American consumerist values. As a "lifestyle," gay was ok.

There is probably no way for these magazines to escape the connections between sexuality and consumerism: they don't try to since they are turning a profit. It is not a sin to sell ads in order to be able to publish gay material, but the entire purpose of the gay soft core publications is to promote gay consumerism. Even *Drummer*, which began in the early 1970s as a magazine for gay men interested in S/M and leather, and eschewed much commercialism, within a few years was promoting a Mr. Leather contest (sponsored by leather bars throughout the country) and running long feature articles on gay life in Houston or Chicago, carefully mentioning all the leather shops.

There is nothing unusual about magazines existing to sell a product or a lifestyle. *The New Yorker* gets its readers to look at expensive liquor, clothing, and furniture ads by presenting top-drawer fiction, intelligent reviews, and funny cartoons. But the gay soft core magazines are exploiting the positive gay identity created by the gay movement. In many people's minds—gay as well as straight—there is little difference between being gay and having a "gay lifestyle."

What is the effect that these magazines and their message have had upon gay and straight culture? They have made images of gay male sexuality available to a large number of people, an especially important thing for gay men who may be insecure in their identities. They have also promoted a notion of a gay sensibility, and a gay community—albeit one based on consumerism—both to the straight and the gay worlds. They have insisted, by their very presence, that gay people exist and are not going away.

Gay life has always allowed and promoted fantasy because homosexuality itself is such a forbidden fantasy. Because it breaks taboos about sexuality and gender it allows and encourages sexual experimentation. It promoted the eroticization of the male, which has had a profound effect upon popular culture. It celebrates sexual experimentation and endorses sexual freedom; this too has been felt in the mainstream. Even the flexibility of gender roles, embodied in such films as *Tootsie*, *Yentl*, and *La Cage aux Folles*, has moved out of gay culture to influence ideas and actions in the straight world. To a very large degree, gay male culture has contributed to the increased sexualization of mainstream culture, some of this in conjunction with the feminist vision of freeing women from repressive gender and sexual roles. It has contributed to a re-evaluation of the prevailing ideologies about sexuality, gender, beauty, and art. Gays have been assimilated through economic and cultural upward mobility. Soft core gay porn magazines reflect this by combining class and culture and presenting them in a way that will not conflict with prevailing cultural attitudes.

American life, of which consumerism is an essential part, depends on the repression of sexuality. Production of any product is dependent upon the purchasers feeling that they are not satisfied with what they have. Repressed sexuality guarantees that one will never be satisfied. Therefore, it is not surprising that good pornography—open, honest representations of sexuality—is hard to come by. The commercial variety is produced to match prevailing marketability standards rather than explore sexuality and the human sexual imagination.

Gay Publishing: Advertising
...and was marketed...

By the 70s, there was an overall impulse in America to discover and be more tolerant towards behavior which had been labeled deviant: communal living, recreational drug use, homosexuality. Emphasis was placed on the search for the self and the overriding social structure was changing accordingly.

New ideas—gay liberation, youth culture, feminism—do not exist on an intellectual plane alone. To remain in the public imagination, they must be popularized by the consumer aspects of our culture. Here they are depicted as part of everyday life. The recording and fashion industries were quick to commercialize youth and drug cultures. Rock and folk music quickly changed from expressions of collective feeling into industries. Magazines like *High Times* and *Rolling Stone*, movies like *The Trip*, *You Are What You Eat*, and *Woodstock*, wearing apparel such as head bands, embroidered shirts, tie-dyed clothing, and beaded jewelry were all commercializations of popular subcultures.

176

The commercialization of a subculture is one way to promote the assimilation of that culture into the mainstream. The mass production of objects and trends associated with a subculture represents concretely that subculture's success in a world which has traditionally been hostile to it. The effect of the creation of consumer items is that they make money. Money is one well-established way to move up in our culture. This is especially true in a capitalist economy which depends on conspicuous consumption. Since the discovery of "lifestyle," many consumer items are valued not for their intrinsic worth but for their symbolic meaning. *Playboy* touted the idea that expensive cars, stereo equipment, and clothes were necessary parts of the *"Playboy* lifestyle." Post-feminist women have been targeted as buyers of everything from Virginia Slims cigarettes ("You've Come a Long Way, Baby") to Stay-Free maxipads ("for the active woman") to Harvey's Bristol Cream ("it's downright upright" to be sexually assertive). The symbolic use of consumer items as a means of reinforcing social identity, as well as a measure of acceptance within a rigidly structured class society, has helped gay people assimilate, while altering radically many of the gay movement's basic assumptions.

Much of the impact that gay sensibility has had on popular culture is suggestive; gay men have influenced rather than dictated taste. Also, unlike blacks, women, or youth, homosexuals do not exist as an easily visible minority. Many trends which have had the gay sensibility as their origin have not been perceived as such. In many cases, both taste makers and consumers are unwilling to identify the origins of fashions and attitudes. Because gay men traditionally have survived by acting as trendsetters, they have been both consumers and producers.

The myth of the gay consumer is one serious misconception about the relationship between gay sensibility and popular culture. The homosexual, in the popular imagination, is a white, middle class, male, professional, urban dweller with what is considered good taste and a lot of discretionary income. This image has been promoted for a variety of reasons by heterosexuals, and has also been used by many gay men to heighten their own respectability and insure their own acceptance in society. The reality of gay identity, however, is quite different. Homosexual desire and behavior cuts across all class, ethnic, and racial lines. Although it is nearly impossible to collect accurate statistics because homophobia prevents most gay men and lesbians from openly identifying themselves, there are probably similar proportions of gay people in all classes and racial and ethnic communities.[1] Individual subcultures have a variety of attitudes (from restrictive to progressive) about homosexuality, but there is probably little variation in the actual numbers of gay people within them. Gay people grow up and reside in such geographically disparate places as Nome, Alaska and Wheeling, West Virginia, but many gay people actively seek the security, social networks, and cultural activities of well organized gay communities in urban areas. Homosexuals are also economically diverse. As women, lesbians still earn 59 cents for each dollar earned by men.[2] Gay men who are members of oppressed racial or ethnic groups are oppressed economically, both because they are gay and because of their ethnicity. It is true, however, that single white male homosexuals (and remember that there are many gay people who have families) often do not have dependents, and therefore do have money to spend.

The idea that gay people (especially men) are wealthier and more consumption-oriented than other people is false. Yet this idea is often promoted by the gay press itself as well as others involved in marketing items to the gay community. In its early days, *Christopher Street* attempted to lure advertisers with the slogan "What people do in the privacy of their homes is their business—big business." West American Advertising made a hard sell to prospective clients.

> Gay money. Twenty-five thousand dollars. That's how much your average gay worker earns a year. Multiply that by twenty million gay consumers, and you've got an affluent and very powerful market. Gay dollars are just as green as anyone else's. And West American Advertising will help you make sure that they stack up in the right place.[3]

In 1980, *The Advocate* did a readership survey which showed that their 1100 respondents were mainly professional men from urban

areas, between 20 and 40, with an average income of $30,000.[4] Some
market researchers refer to this select group as the "upscale tip of the
iceberg." Since there are close associations in the public's mind
between personal freedom and economic independence, images of
upwardly mobile, financially comfortable gay men are comforting to
gay men who have made it as well as to gay men who want to make it,
hoping for some relief from daily homophobia. This "liberation by
acquisition" philosophy is embodied not only in advertising but in
the plots of many gay novels. Gay books published in the 70s like *The
Lure, Dancer from the Dance, Tory's* and the short fiction collection
Aphrodisiac are peppered with brand names and tales of expensive
vacations. They create the impression that gay male life in the 1970s
and 1980s is one long consumer orgy.

Not only is the assumption that being gay enables men to afford
high living false in economic terms, but the idea that money and
consumption lead to a decrease in personally experienced homophobia and an increase in personally experienced acceptance is also
false. The well-off as well as the poor get queer-bashed when leaving
gay bars. Money and fine clothes do little to soften the hearts of those
who hate queers. It is true that money often provides an entree into
certain segments of society, but this should not be confused with
social tolerance.

Gay papers and magazines have always managed to secure
advertising from local and gay-oriented businesses. The local gay
bookstore or gay-owned restaurant often advertises in the local gay
paper. However, many businesses which are gay-owned or have a gay
clientele will not advertise because they do not want to be labeled as
gay. A national business like the Club Baths, which has thirty-five
locations around the country, advertises in national and local gay
publications because it depends entirely on a gay clientele. Some
major industries, especially publishing and film, will advertise in a
national gay publication if they feel they have a gay product. St.
Martin's Press and Avon Books have advertised their gay books in
national and local gay periodicals. Because their books probably
appeal mainly to gay people, this advertising insured sales. Hollywood studios have a more complex advertising philosophy. Because
their products must reach a huge audience, they promote gay-interest

pictures to gay and straight people alike. With films like *Tootsie*, *Making Love*, *Victor/Victoria*, and *La Cage aux Folles*, their campaigns in gay papers differed from their regular approach. The trick was to inform the gay audience that the film had "special interest" without alienating heterosexuals. With *Making Love*, Universal used two different advertising graphics. The lover's triangle which moved the plot was pictured differently for gay than for straight papers: in the gay media, the two men were touching and the woman was isolated at the triangle's apex. Because advertising can make or break a film in the first week of release, it is of utmost importance for Hollywood to target the market as carefully as possible. A movie which has some gay interest cannot appear *too* gay and run the risk of losing its straight audience. The studios have always been aware of this. In 1967, Universal's *The Wild Rovers* inadvertently began with a campaign deemed too gay, and it caused a major industry flap.[5]

Possibly because they do not want to be stigmatized as "gay," some companies which manufacture items popular among gay men (Levi-Strauss, Calvin Klein, Lacoste) do not advertise at all in the gay press. There are ads in gay papers for Seagram's Boodles Gin or Absolut Vodka, and R.I.D. (a delousing medication) has found that advertising in gay papers can be successful. But these cases have not created a trend which other companies have followed. The advertising that these companies do in mainstream publications, on billboards, and in other media already reaches gay consumers; companies feel little need for special outreach. When questioned about their subtle homoerotic advertising, a spokesperson for Calvin Klein stated:

> We did not *try* to appeal to gays. We try to appeal, period. If there's an awareness in that community of health and grooming, then they'll respond to the ads. You really want to reach a bigger market than just gays, but you don't want to alienate them.[6]

The gay community, and gay publications, cannot depend on mainstream businesses to support them with advertising, no matter what the consumer profile of the gay buyer is made out to be. The most to be hoped for is an effort by business not to alienate gay people. The influence of gay sensibility upon mainstream advertising is clearly not based upon an economic exchange since most advertisers are unwilling to spend much money to reach gay people.

The gay sensibility, as we have seen, has had a tremendous influence on many aspects of popular culture. Both the women's and men's fashion industries reflect gay male sensibility. Disco crossed over to the mainstream from black and gay culture. Much of the music began with black singers and entertainers. Gay bars and discos popularized it, proved that it was profitable, which brought it into the mainstream. New York clubs like Studio 54 or Twelve West were as well known for their gay ambiance as for their superstar patrons. After the success of Bette Midler at the Continental Baths, other female vocalists such as Karen Akers or Jane Olivor used their status as gay cult figures to move into the mainstream. Gay support for supper clubs like Reno Sweeney's, Michael's Pub, and Snafu fueled the comebacks of such entertainers as Barbara Cook, Alberta Hunter, Sylvia Syms, and Julie Wilson.

Gay men themselves have promoted the idea of gay sensibility as sophisticated and stylish. While this has sometimes reinforced oppressive stereotypes, it has historically been a method of psychological and social self-protection. Inventing and promoting this image had other effects as well. Having always been told that they were different, gay men consciously set about to make themselves different, or at least distinctive. During the times of Oscar Wilde, cultural communication depended upon the written word, the correct social circles, and personal appearances. It has become considerably more complicated with modern class structures, electronic media, and the reality that culture itself has become a highly profitable commodity.

Popular culture often originates in urban centers and is then sold to other parts of the country. While advertising demographers survey the entire country to see what will and will not sell, it is in the large cities that companies try to start and measure new trends. For example, the early word on Streisand's 1983 film *Yentl* was that the film was too "ethnic" (i.e. Jewish) for popular distribution. The studio opened the film two weeks early in New York and Los Angeles

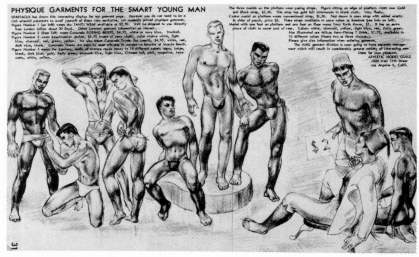

Physique Pictorial, 1956

Hollywood has always had trouble appealing to everyone. This 1971 poster for *The Wild Rovers* predated notions of a "gay market." As it was, the poster was a bit too obvious in its "buddy" imagery and was quickly withdrawn once *Variety* took notice. When Hollywood's public relations experts put their minds to "gay marketing" the best they could come up with was a "separate but equal" approach. *Making Love* was a rehash of the standard love triangle/other woman story. Only this time it was another *man*. Ads in the mainstream press presented the usual triangular visuals. Ads in the gay press introduced "the other man" shirtless so there would be no mistaking what the film was really about.

Always courting respectability, *The Advocate* portrayed all non-conformists as destructive children. This cartoon accompanied an editorial which called for gay liberation to be run by "responsible, talented experts with widespread financial backing from all strata of the gay community."

Although *ONE* and *Mattachine Review* generally eschewed advertising and explicit images of gay life, it is clear from this ad that their alternative, the muscle magazines, knew both their readers and in what they were interested.

Making Love (uncloseted), 1982

Making Love (closeted), 1982

The Wild Rovers poster, 1971

cartoon from *The Advocate*, 1973

in the hope that the large Jewish and gay audiences would create box office records, thus convincing mid-country distributors to book the film. The plan worked: although *Yentl* was not a runaway hit, it recouped its original investment within a few weeks of release.

Specific items like disco music and certain clothes may cross over from the gay subculture to the mainstream, but it is the gay sensibility as a whole which has had the largest effect on popular culture. If there is an essence in gay sensibility, it is the broadening and extension of sexuality. Because homosexuality and sex are confused in the popular imagination, it is not surprising that gay people have become sexual trendsetters.

Gay men's deviation from traditional gender roles has spilled over into such areas as rock music, encouraging androgyny and drag. As early as the mid-1960s, The Rolling Stones, already somewhat androgynous, appeared in drag on the cover of a 45 rpm. The Rolling Stones, although English, took many of their cultural cues from American culture. Their music was drawn largely from American black R&B. Their early working class hoodlum image slowly evolved into a more open, hippie look which coincided with the growing audience for rock music. The hippie look, with its androgynous overtones, dovetailed closely with a popular, traditional gay male look. In the musical *Hair*, (a real indicator not of alternative culture itself but of the popular perception of that culture) the character of Woof announces that he is not homosexual, but that he would not throw Mick Jagger out of bed. The Rolling Stones used drag, as they did their other poses, as a rebellious, anti-conformist statement. A few years later, amid flying rumors of his polymorphously perverse sexual lifestyle, David Bowie performed concerts as his alter ego Ziggy Stardust, a persona which he developed by combining rock and roll, the fringe drag world of Andy Warhol's underground, and the traditional gay sensibility. Other groups played around with gender dislocations and non-traditional gender images throughout the 1970s. Some performers called their outfits "costumes" rather than drag, and in 1983 David Bowie denied that he had ever performed in drag, claiming that his avowed bisexuality of a decade before was nothing more than a promotion gimmick. Even Elton John, who did say that he was bisexual, married in 1984, apparently in an effort to get better press and stop his plummeting sales. But if the older rock stars and their fans did not want to veer off the accepted gender course very far, a whole new generation of stars and fans were taking their place.

Boy George, an English import who performs in complete drag, told a 1984 Grammy Award audience (on national television): "Thanks America. You've got style and taste and you know a good drag queen when you see one." Although Boy George, and his group Culture Club, have some roots in the punk clubs of Britain, their music is a smooth amalgamation of American pop. Michael Jackson, the youngest of the popular Jackson Five, who hit it big on his own, sports an androgynous look which is as carefully constructed as his music. Both Jackson and Boy George appeal to a young audience— pre-teen in some cases—that seems to take their appearances for granted, a sharp contrast to the Jagger and Bowie rebellions 15 years earlier. Jackson's press releases insist that he is a devout Jehovah's Witness. Boy George, depending on which magazine is interviewing him, has said that he is bisexual, non-straight, asexual, or just too busy to have sex. "I am just like everyone else in that I like sex, food, and love. I just don't believe in male or female: I'm not particularly masculine, and I'm certainly not feminine. But I don't think it matters."[7]

Both Jackson and Boy George have totally separated gender from sexual expectations. They are accepted, in non-traditional roles, because they are non-sexual, non-threatening. The power of Bowie's and Jagger's androgyny was in its underlying sexual confusion and rebellion. Jackson and Boy George have taken the trappings of drag and effeminacy from their traditional gay contexts and made them palatable and evidently loveable to the straight world by removing the sexuality. The androgyne as rebel is no longer marketable, but the drag queen as an everyday person is perfectly ok.

In the rock world, entertainers are inseparable from advertising. The Rolling Stones' and Boy George's images *are* their ads. Because sex is the foundation of much advertising philosophy, and because gay men are often connected with sex, many gay images have found their way into the popular culture as techniques to sell things. Because gay men are seen as affluent, sexual, and extraordinary taste advancers, they are a perfect sales and marketing vehicle. Of course the images cannot be too blatant, because blatant homosexuality does not have mass appeal, but the exotic implications of hidden homosexuality have huge sales potential.

Although homosexuality and homosexual behavior have been uniformly attacked and derided by Western society because of their promise of freedom from the bonds of gender, they have managed nevertheless to present an attractive, if forbidden, alternative to people. This is especially true of the trappings of gay sensibility rather than homosexuality itself. The creation of a "gay lifestyle" was a perfect way to channel these mainstream cultural fantasies.

In the mid-1970s, a trend developed of using homoerotic images in mass advertising. The products thus advertised ranged from cigarettes to western gear, from liquor to expensive clothes. The ads presented a male image considerably different from the standard ad images. Images of men in ads had previously been calculated to make the buyer feel he needed this product in order to fit in. In contrast, the new male image was focused on being different. There were two distinct strains, each having a unique sexual appeal, each with firm roots in the traditions of gay sensibility. The first was the rugged look. Tough, virile, athletic, yet sensitive, these new men were the latest incarnation of the American frontiersman. Definitely New World, they were dependent upon no person or social convention. They appeared alone. The Marlboro Man embodies the heroic male image found in the poetry of Walt Whitman and the novels of Herman Melville.

The second image was more European. The models in Calvin Klein ads are good examples. They have finely chiseled features, dapper and daring clothes—loose and flowing evening wear, tight sports clothes—and a knowing, sophisticated glance. The outdoor look of the rugged American is replaced with a precise poise and a mannered grace. Like Oscar Wilde or Noel Coward, they are decadent, effete although not obnoxious, decidedly upscale.

Both of these images sold an escape from the ordinary. For the middle class American consumer, they represented alternatives. They offered a compromise for the advertising world because they enticed mainstream buyers without turning off homosexuals. Gay people perceived the gay images, and thus the ads spoke to them. In the trade, mainstream ads which carry a gay subtext are called "gay window" ads.

For the time being, it looks as though major industries and advertisers are not going to place ads in or openly support the gay press, even though they are interested in gay money. They are, however, willing to use gay subtexts and subliminal messages to sell products to heterosexuals and gays alike. As long as gay male sexuality is considered extraordinary, inviting as well as taboo, gay images will have this kind of appeal. Some gay men have been happy to be placed in the position of trendsetters and taste purveyors because it has accorded them a measure of social status and conformity. Ironically, when gay sensibility is used as a sales pitch, the strategy is that gay images imply distinction and non-conformity, granting straight consumers a longed-for place outside of the humdrum mainstream.

Part III

The Theory of the Pleasure Class

People have always engaged in homosexual behavior, despite the fact that because of it they have been regularly persecuted, occasionally tolerated, but rarely accepted. At the end of the 19th century, a distinct homosexual identity emerged in Western culture, and along with that identity, a distinct culture and sensibility. This sensibility was a product of homosexuality and the ways society had treated it.

This gay sensibility and culture evolved over time during the past 100 years. Like any subcultural impulse, it responded and adapted to the world around it. Most modern writing about homosexuality, historical and theoretical, has focused on the persistent persecution homosexuals and homosexuality have suffered in the name of religion, the state, and medical science. Uncovering this oppressive history has provoked a gay culture of strength and resistance, but its reactive stance can also obscure the intrinsic merits and pleasures of homosexuality as well as the decisive effect which gay culture has had upon the world in which we live.

The gay sensibility has shaped 20th century aesthetics and culture. From earliest times, condemnations of homosexuality focused not on culture, psychology, or emotion, but on *sex*. This historical categorization of homosexuality as a totally sexual experience continues today. Homosexuality is considered to represent a pure, unencumbered form of sexuality. Not engendering new life, divorced from the social and economic structures of heterosexual marriage, and apparently employing sexuality as the primary form of self-definition, homosexuality represents sex incarnate. In short, homosexuals are obsessed with sex. This obsession, along with the impulse to personal freedom that makes sexual activity possible, is at the center of the gay sensibility.

Western civilization has been characterized from its beginning by deep-seated erotophobia. This fear and hatred of sexuality informs and poisons our basic ideas about sex, gender, and race upon which we base our assumptions about power, politics, and equality. Erotophobia has been the dynamic responsible for endless religious persecution, for pervasive misogyny, for the strait-jacketed gender roles which bind men as well as women, and for the destructive equation of sexuality with power. Erotophobia fosters arrangements which prevent true sexual freedom and equality for all people.

Heterosexuality can be rationalized because of its (re)productive potential and economic function, which support the existing social order: patriarchy and capitalism. Same-sex desire exists in and of itself, thus posing a deep threat to the Western culture and ideology premised on subjugating sexuality and sexual pleasure. Religious, state, and scientific forces have reinforced this repression, attempting to limit people to all but the narrowest forms of heterosexual behavior. Despite all of these prohibitions, in the history of humankind, probably not one desire or practice has been eliminated from humans' sexual repertoire.

Although homosexuality has always existed, it never functioned in a vacuum; it has always interacted with and been part of the process of social change. The second half of the 19th century provides an illustration of this political dynamic. The industrial revolution produced profound changes in economy and society. The traditional class structure of Britain, and other industrializing countries, was shifting dramatically. A new and influential middle class had money and time to spend on what was, for the most part, previously considered upper class culture. This connection between leisure time and the consumption of culture surfaced again after the second World War. Both historical periods were moments of action and reaction for gay culture and sensibility. Along with the 19th century growth of the middle class came the idea that society was made up of individual human beings; private, personal identity became as important, perhaps even more important, than social identity. This led to the belief that there was an intrinsic value in human emotional life and actions. These ideas were the first cracks to appear in what was usually considered an age of intense repression and conformity.[1]

The promotion of the individual was also a strike against the utilitarianism which had been previously applied to most of art as well as life. If the individual existed independently, then so could art. The growth of aesthetics as a popular movement was inseparable from all the other social changes which were taking place. With a new middle class that had the time and money to patronize art, there was a market for consumable culture and a need to create a theory that would simultaneously justify the art and reinforce the connection between it and consumption. The "art for art's sake" theories of Walter Pater and John Ruskin were a clear response to this need.[2] They embodied the triumph of the personal. The aesthetic theories articulated by Oscar Wilde are quintessentially expressed in his political writings. *The Soul of Man Under Socialism* argues potently for "individualism" as a motivating force in both politics and culture. Wilde, in fact, makes very little distinction between the two and this book was probably the origin of the idea that culture is innately political, as well as personal.

The last factor which set the stage for the emergence of a gay sensibility was the increasingly strong effect which science, in the form of medicine, was having upon both popular and intellectual imaginations. People no longer relied upon religion for all their explanations; instead they turned to science. Darwin's *The Origin of Species*, and other scientific works, were having a gradual effect upon epistemological methods. Consequently, sexuality was being viewed in a new light. The writings of Havelock Ellis, Kraft-Ebbing, Edward Carpenter, and John Addington Symonds all argued for a more rational, scientific, and non-judgmental view of all forms of sexuality. Homosexuals, who had until then not had the social permission to speak of or act upon their feelings, suddenly found a new freedom. It would take Freud, in the beginning of the 20th century, to add a psychological dimension to the new scientific and social construct of objectivity.

The origins of the modern gay sensibility are in the rise of the post-industrial middle class and its use of aestheticism to attain social mobility. It would be absurd to imply that all of the men in this newly emerging middle class were homosexuals. However, the shift from Victorian utilitarianism to "art for art's sake" encouraged the use of the imagination. In art there was a movement away from naturalism and towards the expressive. The works of Edward Burne-Jones and Aubrey Beardsley demonstrate this movement and expose its obvious sexual implications. To the repressed Victorian mind, freedom of imagination meant freeing sexuality.

Having lived under the oppressive emotional and material circumstances that affected the entire culture, gay men found themselves in a unique position. The role of outsider gave them a critical distance with which they could view the culture in which they lived. This distance allowed them the possibility of creating a culture which was outside of the mainstream, which could be innovative, yet critical of existing social and cultural standards. Because so much of their cultural creation was imaginative and different, gay men were in the forefront of new cultural tastes and trends.

The new aesthetic also promoted the idea of the beautiful. Greek statuary had first incited the sexuality of Edward Carpenter and John Addington Symonds. As the notion of "art for art's sake" gained in popularity, so did the idea that "beauty" could exist purely for the sake of the pleasure it gave people. The notion that something could be created for "pleasure" alone was a shocking contrast to the Victorian ethic as well as to traditional Western cultural self-denial.

Gay men in Victorian England prized the classical tradition of male friendship. For one thing, it was a safe way for men to express emotions. Because it involved an equal relationship between two men, (social and sexual equals) it posed no threat to the sexual or gender status quo. Fascination with male friendship was both a cover for forbidden sexuality and a manifestation of male bonding. While straight men have bonded in order to accumulate power, they generally form uneasy alliances with one another: at the top of the social hierarchy they vie for control. Gay men have generally come together to protect themselves from a hostile culture. In both cases, however, bonding reinforces the power accorded to maleness, even though gay male bonding is often based upon mutual respect and caring rather than upon power struggles. Gradually, people became less naive about the psychology of friendship and more aware of the sexual component of everyday life. As a result, male friendships were increasingly viewed as at least latently sexual.

Victorian aestheticism was a flight away from the harsh, material realities of industrialization. Cities became overcrowded, their factories filled the skies with polluting smoke, and their streets were lined with unsanitary tenement apartments. The aesthetic theorists tried to create something of beauty in the midst of this squalor and poverty. If this failed, they used their imaginations to flee. Ancient Greece, the Italian Renaissance, or the mythical world of the Middle Ages represented historical alternatives full of imagination and beauty. For the male homosexual, they also represented a refuge from the dangerous real world where sexual imagination could not be exercised in peace and safety. The flight itself could take any number of forms. For many homosexual men, the flight from Victorian England was not only away from oppression, but also in search of beauty, sexual comfort, and security.

In addition to being one of the most important forces shaping Western culture, the gay sensibility has also been one of the most progressive, liberating, and visionary. The association of homosexuality with the sexual, and the cry of "sex obsession" have been used to attack homosexuals and anything connected with them. But it is precisely this quality, this "obsession with sex," which is at the basis of the liberation offered by the gay sensibility. Gay men have constantly argued in favor of an open sexual imagination, sought to present images of beauty to a culture which has demanded only the most utilitarian necessities, and portrayed alternative worlds as a release from an oppressive reality. Because gay men are producers, consumers, and promoters of culture, their influence has, in certain historical periods, been noticed and usually condemned. Yet the influence they have exercised upon culture was in the interest of all people, and was often gratefully accepted and absorbed. Freeing sexuality and eroticism is an impulse everyone feels on some level, no matter how much they consciously support the existing system. Whenever the threat of that impulse seemed too great, repression occurred.

Victorians were perfectly happy to accept Oscar Wilde until his message became too clear. From the very beginnings of modern gay sensibility, people suspected that promoting "art for art's sake" was really a high-tone cover-up for promoting sexual pleasure. When Wilde wrote to Douglas, "it is a marvel that those red rose-leaf lips of yours should have been made no less for the music of song than for the madness of kissing," he tried explaining it to the court in artistic and literary terms. Although it fit conveniently into his aesthetic theories, everyone understood the passage's sexual intent. After the second World War in America, there was also a backlash against homosexuals and the gay sensibility. The country was attempting to restabilize itself and to re-establish the rigidity of economic, sexual, and gender roles which the war had thrown askew. The sexualizing and non-gender-defined influence of homosexuals was considered very threatening.

In Victorian England or the contemporary U.S., homosexuality and gay sensibility are viewed as examples of decadence and non-productive desire and experience. Pleasure has never ultimately been appreciated or integrated by Western culture; rather than being seen as a legitimate end in itself, it was always yoked with punishment or duty. Unrestrained sexual passion, culturally connected to the arts, (a passion of a different sort) was in conflict with the existing power structure. Defending homosexuality and gay culture is thought by many to be a defense of unadulterated pleasure. From the writings of the Greek philosophers through the Middle Ages and the present, there has been little philosophical interest in pleasure as an end unto itself. The repressed social majority, viewing homosexuality and everything connected with it as unrestrainable pleasure, called it a sin, a crime, or a disease.

For over 100 years, gay people have been creating and promoting culture which has been assimilated into the mainstream. This was a way for gay men to achieve some form of upward mobility within the existing social structure. It was also a way for mainstream culture to diffuse the threat of gay culture. There was an advantage to both sides in this process which was tacitly recognized, but rarely discussed openly. Mainstream culture borrowed from the gay sensibility but never acknowledged the source.

The post-Stonewall gay liberation movement insisted upon the relevance of gay culture to the political aims of the movement, and began to spell out explicitly the covert influence of gay sensibility over the years. The movement's combination of politics and culture was something really new on the American political and social scene. Taking their cue from earlier liberation movements—especially black liberation and the second wave of feminism—gay activists began the work of understanding gay oppression. They denied and rejected the religious, legal, and medical stigmas which had plagued homosexuals for centuries. Like other oppressed groups, they insisted upon being completely accepted by society.

As gay liberation grew, different strategies and factions emerged. Some women and men focused upon the civil rights aspects of the struggle, working to reform laws and secure legal rights for lesbians and gay men. Their impact upon society was limited, not only by the existing social standards under which they were trying to operate, but also by the rigidity of legal and governmental systems themselves. Others believed that securing rights under the existing system would never change the system itself, nor ever question the precepts upon which it is based.

Another branch of the lesbian and gay movement remained closer in spirit to the political philosophies of the first post-Stonewall gay liberation groups. Eschewing a simple stand on civil liberties, these men and women named heterosexism an oppression, connected in theory and practice to the oppressions of other peoples. Taking their cues from the sexual political analysis of feminism and the cultural analysis of the black liberation movement, they attempted a synthesis which understood homosexuals as a distinct social and cultural group whose oppression stemmed from the same hierarchical, patriarchal, and anti-sexual precepts which ruled the rest of the world.

Focusing primarily upon sexuality and gender definitions, gay liberationists called for the elimination of prohibitions against different forms of sexual behavior which challenged restrictive gender roles. They were less concerned with passing anti-discrimination laws than with creating a society and culture which would celebrate sexual expression. While gay rights activists worked in the sphere of legal reform, gay liberationists intended to effect profound social change.

The dichotomy between reform and revolution has been present in all progressive movements. While the benefits of progressive reforms are tangible and have the potential to change people's lives and consciousness, I believe there are reasons, theoretical and historical, why reformism is short-sighted and quite possibly doomed to failure. Erotophobia is such a tenacious strain of Western culture that it affects every aspect of our lives. It informs our attitudes towards women, children, race, class, and towards sexuality in general. It has perpetuated strict sexual and gender roles which in turn support and reinforce the erotophobia which fostered them. Homosexuality, with its blatant disregard for sexual assignments, flies in the face of this system. Homosexuality represents an antithesis of Western cultural teaching about sex and gender and is by definition the rejection of erotophobic values. Because the fear and hatred of sex is so intrinsic to Western culture, it would be almost impossible for homosexuality to attain any real acceptance within that culture. What may happen, and what has happened in the past, is that society bends the rules a bit, tolerating *some* homosexual activity under *some* circumstances for *some* people. The idea is containment and regulation.

In the long run, gay liberation's most lasting and effective changes will come through cultural rather than electoral or legal channels. Although all homosexuals are disenfranchised from the mainstream, the legislative approach to gay liberation runs the risk of giving social power only to those homosexuals deemed "acceptable," i.e. straight-looking and straight-behaving. Cultural change, in contrast, has the potential to radicalize and transform basic social structures, consequently attacking the very foundations of all systems of oppression.

Historically, profound social change has occurred along with cultural change. Gay men, since they have been a major cultural force during the past 100 years, are in a good position to enact social change. Until the Stonewall riots, gay men influenced culture covertly. For some, this became an act of social mobility, gaining them a certain amount of acceptance and credibility. For homosexuals as a group, it made the world a more tolerable place; their subculture was beginning to surface in the majority culture, reducing gay isolation and negation. But all the cultural change wrought by these people—and in the past 100 years, there has been an enormous amount—did not have as strong an effect as it might have because it was not always recognized as overtly homosexual. To be overtly homosexual, in a culture which denigrates and hates homosexuality, is to be political.

The Stonewall riots provided the opportunity for a broad-based movement for gay liberation. This movement, and the sensibility which grew with it, was a product of the experiences and politics of both gay men and lesbians. In a male-dominated society, much of gay culture has been defined and shaped by men. Feminism has shown that women can and have created and influenced culture. A movement dedicated to gay *and* lesbian liberation meant that women and men could form a new culture which would bear the unique imprint of a non-sexist gay sensibility.

The gay movement today is split between the reformist and the cultural/sexual liberationist positions. The reformists feel that the liberationists are unwilling to make concessions to mainstream society in the interests of acceptability. They criticize gay activists who flaunt their separateness, maintain a distinct sexual identity, and refuse to adhere to usual sexual or gender arrangements, claiming that they ruin gay people's chance for acceptance within the system. Most gay people fall between these two positions: they want legal reforms but also need the cultural affirmation for their lives offered by gay liberation.

The gay liberation movement has set up a complex network of organizations, publications, support systems, and cultural outreach which has established an autonomous, strong, and positively gay-identified culture which is taken seriously within gay communities and by mainstream society. Creating this culture has been an overt and political action.

The impact this has had and will have upon mainstream culture cannot be underestimated. Twenty-five years ago, progressive writers Seymour Krim and Dave McReynolds (the latter came out later as a gay man) authored a dialogue in the *Village Voice*. Krim was concerned about the new militancy he was witnessing among homosexuals; McReynolds responded.

> First, homosexuals *as a group* aren't going to lead any revolt because the last thing they want is to get involved in any real struggle. They just want to be left alone to live in their presently established, dainty fashion.

After dismissing homosexuality as a form of adolescent rebellion, like growing a beard or smoking pot, McReynolds again denied any chance of a social movement.

> I do not see, therefore, any capacity to revolt in "gay society." It is a destructive subculture...It is a subculture in which sex is substituted for real personal relations. As a subculture it produces nothing of value. The negro subculture has been and remains tremendously vital—because they desperately want to be accepted into the larger framework. They did not voluntarily separate themselves from American society as a whole...Out of the negro struggle we saw the birth of jazz...But what has the homosexual society produced *as a society?*...In every case where a homosexual...tries to produce art based on his subculture, it is fragile, brittle, and cold beyond words.[3]

McReynolds deftly subverted any idea of a gay movement by discounting the two qualities which are the bulwarks of gay sensibility. The sex isn't really sex and the culture is empty. And the reason why is the choice homosexuals make to place themselves outside of the mainstream. He claims that gay people have made themselves into pariahs, which prevents them from ever being functional and productive. The question of lesbian, or even women's culture, seems to be outside McReynolds' thinking. For him, it would probably be moot if lesbians, like their male counterparts, have placed themselves outside of the mainstream. Culture, in his terms, is produced by and for men, for the purpose of reinforcing cultural norms.

McReynolds was certainly wrong about the possibility of gay political organizing. Within 15 years, the gay rebellion has had a tremendous impact upon American society. Not only have gay men and lesbians secured a place for themselves and the movement in the public imagination, and demonstrated great influence upon mainstream culture, but they have also created a growing culture of their own.

Just as the sensibility of some homosexual men has been assimilated into the mainstream over the years, the overtly political, post-Stonewall gay culture is also being taken up by the dominant culture. Evaluating this dynamic is not so much a question of judging it good or bad, because the attempt to absorb any outside group is inevitable. Rather, the question to ask is about the effect of assimilation. Many gay people assume that assimilation means acceptance. The fact that paperback novels with gay themes are published, that record companies advertise disco records in *The Advocate*, that *Newsweek* runs articles on gay life in San Francisco, can indicate to some that homosexuality is becoming part of the "American way." In actuality, these are just signs that the dominant culture tries to absorb any group or idea it finds threatening, and that a capitalist economy is flexible enough to transform many unlikely things into money. The process of assimilation and absorption takes cultural artifacts and strips them of their political meaning, generally eliminating or minimizing the role that gay culture and sensibility have played in exploring and pushing the boundaries of sexuality.

It is ironic that the gay liberation movement is in many ways taken more seriously by the conservative right than by the progressive left. As an inevitable result of the social movements of the 1960s, gay liberation learned many of its political lessons from the old and the new left. It acquired its theories about the need for civil rights from the movement for black civil rights, and it took from feminism the consciousness of a close connection between the personal and the political.

Unfortunately, many people in the anti-war movement, the civil rights movement, and the women's movement (to name just a few) did not see the relationship between gay liberation and their own struggles. From its inception at Stonewall, gay liberation struggled for acceptance and understanding in mainstream America and among progressive movements. Although progressives have made many valid criticisms of gay liberation, (just as there have been valid criticisms of all movements for social change) most resistance from progressives rests on the collective inability to deal with the two bases upon which gay culture and gay liberation are built: sex and culture.

The American left shares the same erotophobia which grips the rest of the culture. Sexuality, sexual pleasure—all pleasure—plays an almost non-existent role in leftist thinking and organizing. The American left has a history and tradition of denial and self-sacrifice. Leftists have organized around political issues such as labor, voting, community organizing, and civil rights. Rarely have they addressed issues of popular culture and almost never have they attempted to deal with the issue of sexuality. Even though there have always been writers treating sexuality seriously, (notably Emma Goldman, Victoria Woodhull, Stephen Pearl Andrews, and Josiah Warren) they have generally been anarchists or social utopians. The left as a whole dismissed their ideas. The gay liberation movement presented a real problem for the left because, although there was clearly a case to be made for the oppression of gay people, there was no existing theoretical framework which could incorporate this specific oppression. Gay people faced much hostility to homosexuality on the left, as well as the left's indifference to sexuality and culture.

Many leftists did not view gay liberation as a legitimate civil rights movement. They argued that black people, for example, could not escape the effects of racism, while homosexuals could always "pass" if they chose. Others went even further, claiming that homosexuals deserved whatever harassment they received for choosing a perverted sexuality. This range of attitudes reflected the traditional view of sexual behavior as a personal, private decision not falling into the realm of the political.

The Stonewall riots produced not only a movement which demanded complete civil rights for gay people, but also a social network which spread the once clandestine word of gay culture. No longer dependent upon a secretive underground or the assimilation of gay sensibility into mainstream culture, gay people built their own cultural resources. Publishing houses, record companies, theater groups, community-based newspapers and magazines all meant the distribution of gay culture was in the hands of gay people. For the first time, the gay community gained control over its portrayal and self-image. This power was an important element in the coalescing of a political and cultural community which functioned autonomously, without interference from the outside.

This autonomy was not much different from the community organizing that had taken place among other oppressed minorities. Nevertheless, the growth of gay culture, especially under the auspices of gay liberation groups, was not taken seriously. Gay culture was attacked for being "narcissistic" and "self-indulgent"; it was attacked in psychological terms for being "arrested development" or an "unresolved oedipal fixation"; it was attacked in political terms for being non-productive. The left, and many reformist groups, refused to acknowledge and appreciate the fact that gay culture, and to a large degree gay liberation, made its most important contributions through cultural channels. Just as it has resisted taking on sexuality as a political question, the American left has also avoided dealing with the politics of culture.

One consequence of this is that the gay liberation movement has often perceived the left as no less homophobic than the rest of American culture. The image of the gay man as overly-sexed, inappropriately gender-identified, and concerned only with frivolity equally characterized the views held by the left and the general public. (Lesbians, as usual, were ignored.) The fear of homosexuality, a gut reaction not covered by the niceties of political and psychological jargon, pervades American culture and has infiltrated even the most radical enclaves. This fear is based upon the threat which gay people pose to gender arrangements by not adhering to the "correct" sexual desires and by not acting in accordance with "appropriate" gender roles. Since the left has been male-dominated, it is not surprising that it would be threatened by the emergence of an assertive gay movement and politic which demanded recognition from the left. "Sex," as British gay writer Quentin Crisp has said, does have a way of "rearing its ugly head," and the left has recently tried to take on the challenge of sexual issues. Some of these attempts were half-hearted and thus nothing great came of them. It would, however, be both deterministic and fatalistic to conclude that homophobia and erotophobia are intrinsic to the left. By seeing how little distance we have come, we can see how far we must go.

Gay liberation is a progressive movement, which has, by and large, supported other progressive movements, and which has demanded, by definition, that the left broaden its definition of "political." While feminism has treated questions of women's sexuality, (and to a large degree the meaning and significance of lesbian sexuality) its main focus has been within a specific hetero-sexual context. Gay liberation has insisted that the very structure of sexual desire itself be examined. (This has not been without struggle. Many lesbians had to push for discussion of lesbian sexuality as an important issue within a mixed-gender gay community.) Because homosexuality cuts across lines of class and race, the gay community has had to approach these divisions non-traditionally and creatively. Gay liberation, by politicizing sexuality, cut through many obstacles which often presented themselves to a political critique, such as "ranking of oppressions" among race, gender, and class. While some members of the gay community are not oppressed by their gender, race, or class, *all* are oppressed by the orientation of their sexual desire. While there has been criticism, much of it justified, pin-pointing racism, sexism, and class bias within the gay movement, the movement has usually attempted to rise to the situation. The 1979 National Gay March on Washington, through the institution of racial and sexual quotas for local representatives and through offering financial assistance to those who had to travel long distances, was relatively successful in its outreach to lesbians and to minority gay people. The ties that bind people who live an outlaw sexuality have provided an impetus to work on overcoming internal divisions.

Although the gay movement must learn to challenge racism,

sexism, and class oppression, other movements must challenge homophobia. When it offers support to other struggles, such as the fight against U.S. intervention in Central America, it is met with embarrassed acceptance at best, outright rejection at worst.

The oppression of gay people in post-revolutionary Cuba is a good example of a conflict between gay liberation and the left. Some gay liberationists could not totally support the new Cuban government because of its treatment of homosexuals, which included placing some in camps, prisons, and psychiatric institutions. Some leftists insisted that the gay movement refused to understand the particular historical role which institutionalized homosexuality had played in Cuba and accused gay people of "cultural imperialism." Although this conflict has had no real resolution, it instigated a dialogue which has had some impact on the left's and gay activists' thinking about these issues.[4]

The relationship between gay liberation and the women's movement has been somewhat different. Early gay liberationists learned much from feminist theorists about the nature of sexual oppression, gender roles, and the ways in which male-dominated social structures use sexual repression as a political tool. Feminist theorists hit at the root of sexist ideology by exploding the myths of correct sexual or gender behavior. Because many of the same structures which oppressed women also oppressed homosexuals, feminist theory informed the development of theories of gay oppression. However, because the gay movement included both men and women, sexism came up again and again as gay men were forced to come to terms with their position as *men* within the culture. Gay liberation turned to feminism for creative ways of developing politics, uncovering history, and constructing future visions.

Books such as *Sexual Politics* by Kate Millett, *The Dialectic of Sex* by Shulamith Firestone, and *Lesbian Nation* by Jill Johnston focused upon the roles of sexuality and gender in the culture. Groups like Radicalesbians and Redstockings issued manifestos about the interactions between women's sexuality and prevailing cultural norms. Articles appeared in feminist newspapers and magazines about everything from "The Myth of the Vaginal Orgasm"[5] to the pros and cons of celibacy to the joys of lesbian sexuality. Millett was especially good at dissecting the politics of culture; others followed with lively discussions of how sex and gender could be examined, created, and re-envisioned.

Many of these early writings on sexuality and gender were vital for feminists and for the women and men working in gay liberation. However, there was a point at which many mainstream feminist writers parted company with the goals and politics of gay liberation. Betty Friedan, who wrote the groundbreaking and popular *The Feminine Mystique*, attempted to purge the National Organization for Women of lesbians—whom she called the "lavender menace"—in the early 70s. As late as 1973, she wrote in *The New York Times* that radical feminists and lesbians were CIA infiltrators in the feminist movement.[6] Other heterosexual women had great trouble working with lesbians within the women's movement. Leah Fritz, in her historical appraisal of the early women's movement titled *Dreamers and Dealers*, blames the straight/lesbian split in the movement upon the lesbians.[7] It was also becoming commonplace to equate gay men with the worst kind of misogyny. Male sexuality was often considered disgusting and intrinsically oppressive to women, and gay men were unrepentantly sexual.

Because they felt that drag parodied women's oppression, rather than traditional gender roles, some feminists were harsh and unrelenting in their criticism of it: "We know what's at work when whites wear blackface; the same thing is at work when men wear drag."[8] Other women went so far as to compare drag queens with wife beaters.[9] If drag was threatening, transsexualism was even more so. Janice Raymond, a professor of women's studies and medical ethics, wrote in 1979: "All transsexuals rape women's bodies by reducing the real female form to an artifact...[and] violate women's sexuality and spirit, as well."[10] Some feminists saw the gay male influence on culture as even more dangerous than their actions.

> How many of us will try to explain away...men who deliberately *re*-emphasize gender roles, and who parody female oppression and suffering as "Camp"?...the emphasis on genital sexuality, objectification, promiscuity, emotional non-involvement...was the *male style*, and that we as

women, placed greater trust in love, sensuality, humor, tenderness, commitment.[11]

The sexual permissiveness advocated by gay liberationists seemed to be a seductive threat to sisterhood.

> Further, no one seemed to question whether this contro-
> versy [lesbian S/M] was linked to recent re-identification
> with male homosexuals (among whom such practice was
> more openly affirmed by a larger number for a longer
> time)—a possible by-product of the new "bonding" within
> the "gay community," a way of gaining male approval
> from many homosexual "brothers."[12]

One strain of feminist thinking moved along the theoretical line of distinguishing women from men. Women, it was argued, were unique because they had the capacity for giving birth. With that came the attendant, innate capacity for nurturing and sensitivity. Susan Griffin, in *Women and Nature*, and Carolyn Merchant, in *The Death of Nature*, were primary theorists of women as nurturers. Adrienne Rich wrote in 1976:

> In...four years...I have seen the issue of motherhood grow
> from a question almost incidental in feminist analysis to a
> theme which now seems to possess the collective con-
> sciousness of thoughtful women...[13]

This consciousness of women as nurturers and mothers gave rise to a movement within feminism which promoted women's unique spirituality and which focused upon the healing and caring charac-teristics which some claimed were inherent in women.

Because women, historically, suffered because of and through their sexuality, the role of sex was generally played down and replaced, in theory, by the maternal instinct. Sex, consequently, was understood as essentially a masculine activity, usually rather nega-tive. The other reason that some feminists developed conservative positions on sexuality and gender had more to do with the embattled position of feminism in America. Initially thought to be totally crackpot, women's liberationists faced constant threats posed by conservative elements in the culture. Some frightened feminists thought facing off that threat meant toning down the discussion of sexuality. Women as mothers was a much less threatening image than women as independent and autonomous sexual actors. From a defensive posture, the aspects of gay culture and gay liberation that dealt with issues such as pornography, S/M and intergenerational sex looked like trouble. They did not fit in easily with a feminist theory that emphasized caring and support, motherhood, and sisterhood.

Many of these strains in feminist thinking merged, in the late 1970s, with a more pervasive pro-family sentiment on the left. Liberal intellectuals like Christopher Lasch (in *Haven in a Heartless World*) praised the family. *Time* and *Newsweek* heralded the return of the family. Popular novels like *The World According to Garp* stated flatly that family life was an emotional necessity. *Ms.* magazine insisted repeatedly that it was possible to be a good feminist and have a traditional family too. Much of this liberal and/or feminist response expressed the deep fear elicited by challenges to traditional sexual and gender roles which had, ironically, been introduced by feminists in the first place. It was also a response to the rise of the new right, a cohesive, conservative movement which had singlemindedly focused upon family and sexual issues.

Perhaps the main reason why the right managed to get so much mileage out of its pro-family rhetoric is that the family in history and tradition has been linked with security, safety, nurturance, and love. That it has actually come through with any of this is open to great debate. Many experience the institution of heterosexual, patriarchal family as oppressive, restrictive, and damaging. Whatever people's experiences of their own family lives, it was easy to use the spectre of homosexuality to frighten them by implying that gay liberation would do away, not only with the actual institution of the family, but also with all of the warmth and goodness which people associated with the *idea* of the family.

By promoting the family as the solution to social chaos, (rather than its cause, as the early gay liberationists and feminists had proposed) the right put its finger on the pulse of many people's fears. Phyllis Schlafly claimed that the passage of the ERA would destroy the family. Anita Bryant covered the same ground in her homophobic "Save the Children" campaign, making clear that it was not really "working mothers" but unregulated (homo)sexuality which was the true threat to the family.

The pro-family stance was offered by feminists and leftists as an attempt to meet the attack from the right halfway. By claiming to be pro-family, they tried to undercut the fear perpetrated by anti-sexual conservatives and reclaim the family as progressive turf. Such a stance implicitly denied and rejected the goals of gay liberation. Despite the complex realities of family in the lives of gay people, the gay sensibility *is* inherently anti-family. Homosexuality challenges traditional heterosexual, nuclear family structures. Open-ended sexual options, gender role flexibility, and permission for non-monogamous and purely sexual relationships do not support the family structure.

Gay people, who have been excluded from the usual notion of family, have created alternative communities and family networks among themselves. These consist not only of the monogamous gay male or lesbian couple who have lived together for 30 years, but also of people who have found love and support in their friendships with one another, in working together on a community project, in meeting together at a favorite bar over a period of time, or even in coming together for a pleasurable sexual interlude for a few hours. Gay liberation has created a climate in which gay men and women find the security and love which was once only the province of the family, with one another.

In the past few years there has been a renewal of interest among feminists in sexuality and the family. Ellen Willis has written:

> Just as any real sexual revolution must be feminist, a genuinely radical feminism must include a critique of sexual repression and the family structure that perpetuates it.[14]

Women have begun writing and talking more about their sexual experiences and about their relationship to "deviant" forms of sexuality. The *Heresies* collective published a special issue of their magazine in 1981 on sexuality in which women voiced many different opinions on such topics as sexual roles, pornography, and sexual desire. This sharp departure from mainstream feminist writing during the previous ten years was due, to a large degree, to the impact which lesbian and gay liberation had had upon the social and sexual climate of political culture.

Although gay liberation has had a definite impact upon feminist thinking, and some impact upon the way in which the left has looked at sexuality and culture, it has faced its greatest challenge in the right. Where the left has refused to take the ideas of gay liberation seriously, the right seems to have appreciated the power and the intrinsic radicalism of the gay sensibility. Additionally, it was partly because the left had no sound analysis of sexuality that the right picked that very subject with which to attack. From the ERA through abortion through the proposed Family Protection Act and numerous attacks upon sex education and attempts to censor sexual materials, the right systematically attempted to destroy the credibility and the reputation of the left by attacking it on sexual grounds.

It may be stretching the truth to say that the right has a solid political analysis of sexuality, but it certainly has a definite point of view: sexuality (i.e. heterosexuality) is only acceptable when in the service of marriage, family, and reproduction; pleasure, especially in and of itself, is totally antithetical to these structures. The position of the right is an extreme manifestation of the erotophobia of Western culture in general. Because homosexuality, as an activity, a lifestyle, a culture, a sensibility, or a political movement counters erotophobia, it is singled out by the right for very harsh treatment. Homosexuality is equated with unadulterated pleasure which is equated with destructive sexuality which is the first step in the downfall of civilization.

Perhaps the cheapest charge leveled against gay liberation and the gay community in general is that of decadence. The decadence charge is usually leveled by people who refuse to see the issue of sexuality as important. (Sex is a private, bedroom activity, and nothing to shout about in the streets.) It is also proffered by those who believe gay people, especially gay men, are irresponsible and immature, since mature sexuality requires procreation and support of the economic structures of heterosexual family life.

The root of this stereotype is located in the fact that our culture is extremely production-oriented. Effort (usually called work) must produce results. Art does not exist in and of itself, but to produce some (usually moral) effect. Sex does not exist for pleasure, but to produce children. The production model affects all aspects of our lives. Its source can be found in religion, capitalism, family structure, and established gender roles. Because gay men have aspired to material comfort and emotional acceptance and have used upward mobility as a strategy for escaping oppression, they have become associated with the upper class in people's minds. Gay men are seen as idle, unproductive dabblers. This stereotype is further complicated by the fact that in the past 20 years the commercialization of the "gay lifestyle" has projected this very image. The popular stereotype of the urban gay man and the *"Advocate* lifestyle" are identical. The difference is that the stereotype supposedly applies to all gay people, but the truth is that only a very small percentage of gay men actually conform to it.

Although homosexuality has hardly been welcomed with open arms by the political left, there is no comparison to the tremendous harassment it has received from the new right. Since the Stonewall riots, there has been a slow increase in acceptance of homosexuality and gay culture by the mainstream. This tolerance was brought about through social change. But with growing power also came the threat of backlash. By focusing on "decadence" and the unavoidable sexual issues raised by gay liberation, the right presented gays to the American public as threats to national morality and destroyers of traditional values.

The attack on sexuality by the right was, and is, an attack on all progressive movements. Without support from these movements, gay liberation stands at particular risk. Homosexuals have become a special target for the right. Not until the mid-1980s, however, did the right find its most perfect attack upon homosexuals: the AIDS epidemic.

Most early studies of AIDS hypothesized that the Acquired Immune Deficiency Syndrome was a communicable disease. It was appearing in large numbers of gay men, and it was immediately assumed that the syndrome could be sexually transmitted. Because of the strong link in the public imagination between sexuality, sin, and disease, AIDS was soon understood as a "homosexual disease." In fact, its original media designation was GRID: Gay Related Immune Deficiency. Even after that changed the mainstream press continued labeling it the "gay cancer" or the "gay plague." The popular image of the homosexual—especially the urban male homosexual—facilitated this quick transformation of lifestyle into disease. The equation was sex equals sin equals death. If homosexuals insisted on living their degenerate lives, even demanding legal protections, then they would, eventually, suffer and die.

After almost a year of this sensationalism in the mainstream press, the protests of gay women and men, along with some progress in understanding the syndrome, brought some changes in reporting. Even as the press had been sensitized to AIDS the right wing seized upon it to further its anti-sex, anti-homosexual campaigns. Time and again, the right preyed upon the profound homophobia of our culture:

> The homosexual plague *is* sending people to their graves—including the general populace. This year the number of AIDS victims contracting the disease for "unknown reasons" has increased more than five times over 1982.
>
> But AIDS is not the only disease that homosexuals are contracting or spreading. During the past decade...San Francisco's homosexuals have had a 100 percent increase in infectious hepatitis A, a 300 percent increase in infectious hepatitis B, and a 2,500 percent increase in amoebic colon infections.[15]

Many of the figures in the above Moral Majority report are simply false. Even when it gets the statistics correct, new right literature never discusses wider social issues: preventive medicine, better health care, more sex education. What the right is quick to point out is that homosexuals are having a deadly effect on American life:

> Quite clearly, the "private act between consenting adults" is having a devastating effect on an unconsenting public.

> Unfortunately, real love in the homosexual community
> is elusive. In its place, anonymity, promiscuity, and
> perversion are often substituted.
>
> Obviously, the homosexual's pitiful search for mean-
> ing, love and fulfillment usually results in more degra-
> dation, humiliation, and further rejection.[16]

Making homosexuality synonymous with sin and death fits
perfectly into the thinking of the right. It could be used as a scare
tactic for AIDS and also to reinforce the scapegoating which the right
had always addressed to the gay movement. After they invaded
Poland in 1939, Nazi officials posted signs and flashed on movie
screens the equation Jews equal Lice equal Typhus, fueling Polish
anti-Semitism.[17] The Moral Majority's AIDS propaganda is no
different except for the details of the equation: Gays equal Sex equal
AIDS. The massive amount of anti-homosexual propaganda put out
by the right also resembles Nazi anti-Semitic campaigns in other
ways. The image of gays as non-productive, socially destructive
parasites who have connived more economic advantages than
honest, hard working people, is similar to the ideas circulated by the
Nazis about the Jews. By blaming the Jews for all social ills, the Nazi
government was able to rally the populace against a targeted internal
enemy while doing nothing to benefit the people. Through its sex
and pleasure baiting, the right is attempting to scapegoat American
homosexuals in a similar manner.

Some reformist gay groups have responded by playing down the
sexual identity of gay people. They have presented a sanitized image
of gay men and women to the general public. The message "we are
just like you" is an attempt to allay fears of difference. But this
approach is really hopeless. It does no one any good to pretend that
all homosexuals live in monogamous, non-sexual situations and
that they support traditional sexual and gender roles. All progressive
movements must band together, not only to support the goals of gay
liberation, but to incorporate new notions of sexuality and gender
into radical political analyses. Until the left and all progressive
groups reach a better understanding of the roles that sexuality and
gender play in our everyday lives, our politics, our fantasies, and our
unconscious, all people will be open to attack by the right on these
very topics.

But it is not only to fight the right that this must happen. No matter how many progressive changes take place, and how much better people's material lives become, no one will be free until there is a true sexual revolution. Such a revolution must be based upon destroying not only the old notions of sex and gender, but one which opens and frees everyone's imaginations; one which will allow for the endless possibilities which our sexual diversity affords; one which supports not only civil rights but which also endorses and encourages pleasure as a basic right.

Our culture makes strong distinctions between politics and culture: how we live our lives vs. what we enjoy. This has occurred partly because we have allowed sexuality to be compartmentalized and privatized. We have denied the fact that our most fundamental experience of pleasure is essentially sexual in nature. The pleasure of a concert, a painting, a play, a movie, all relate in some way to our sexuality. Things we feel, see, hear, and touch enter our consciousness through the physical senses but they become part of our lives and beings through what they mean to us. Our experience of the material world in all of its forms and manifestations is profoundly sensual.

Our culture puts a lot of energy into separating people's feelings from their ideas and their lives. We have denied the connections between our minds and our bodies in the realms of work, politics, culture, and sometimes even in the realm of sexual activity itself. When that denial has ceased, when those connections are made, people's politics, feelings, experiences, and lives will be whole and their capability for expanding their lives will be increased. Audre Lorde has written:

> Our erotic knowledge empowers us, becomes a lens through which we scrutinize all aspects of our existence...[18]

Understanding and expanding our erotic potential is essential for not only our growth, but for our survival.

Gay liberation goes to the heart of all these separations. It offers a life-affirming vision of sexuality, gender, and personal freedom that is not only a radical critique of the state of the culture, but also a signpost to the way out, the road to change. The vision that gay liberation has to offer goes beyond freedom from sexual repression, escape from the tyranny of gender roles, or movement towards connecting culture and politics. At its most basic, it offers the possibility of freedom of pleasure, for its own sake. Until we accept the role which pleasure must play in all aspects of our lives, we will never be free.

Notes

Please refer to the bibliography for complete citations.

Part I: The Making of Gay Sensibility

1. *The Gay Militants* by Donn Teal contains a wealth of information, documents, and source material from the earliest days of the gay liberation movement. Although completely footnoted, the book is not indexed.
2. Jonathan Katz's *Gay American History* and *Gay/Lesbian Almanac* are good source books for the role and influence of gay people in American culture. John D'Emilio's *Sexual Politics, Sexual Communities* is a detailed study of the early homophile movements leading up to the Stonewall Riots.
3. *Time*, 94:56-67, October 31, 1969.
4. "The Boys on the Beach," by Midge Decter, in *Commentary*, 70:30-48, September 1980.
5. "Notes from a Journal," by Paul Goodman, in *Nature Heals*, p. 246.
6. Both *Homosexuality and the Western Christian Tradition* by Derrick Bailey and *Christianity, Social Tolerance and Homosexuality* by John Boswell give thorough, if controversial, analyses of the relationship between homosexual behavior and early Christianity. While admitting the negative impact of the Christian religion upon social and sexual attitudes, both Bailey and Boswell argue, unconvincingly, that there were also positive aspects of that relationship.
7. Jeffrey Weeks argues, convincingly, in *Coming Out* for the emergence of a solid homosexual identity—as opposed to behavior—during the 19th century.
8. Sontag, *Against Interpretation*, p. 290.
9. *ibid.* p. 290.
10. *ibid.* p. 276.
11. Kaplan, *Walt Whitman*, p. 21.
12. *ibid.* p. 20.

13. *ibid.* p. 13.

14. Although he writes from a fairly stong Freudian and heterosexual bias, Leslie Fiedler's *Love and Death in the American Novel* is probably the best source book about sexuality in early American literature. His *The Inadvertent Epic* deals more thoroughly with aspects of race and sex in American fiction. *What Was Literature?* is a quirky but fascinating examination of class distinctions between high and low culture with a good part of the book focused upon sexuality and gender. Jonathan Katz's "Melville's Secret Sex Text," an analysis of *Redburn*, is an informative and in-depth attempt to place Melville in this tradition (*The Village Voice Literary Supplement*, April 1982).

15. Brian Reade's *Sexual Heretics* is a good anthology of male homosexual writings from the last half of the 19th century. *Love in Earnest* by Timothy d'Archy Smith is a fine analysis, with copious examples, of Uranian poetry in England from 1889 to 1930. Reade focuses upon a variety of themes while d'Archy examines relationships between older and younger men.

16. Martin, *The Homosexual Tradition in American Poetry*, p. 21.

17. All of the quotations from Whitman's "Song of Myself" are taken from *The Portable Whitman*, edited by Mark Van Doren.

18. Many of Whitman's notions of sexuality are found in the writings of gay liberationists today. An especially vivid and challenging example is Charley Shively's "Cocksucking as an Act of Revolution" series which has appeared in *Fag Rag* from the first to the current issue. A complete collection of the essays will be appearing shortly from Calamus Press under the above title.

19. "A Straight Man's Guide to Walt Whitman," by Charley Shively, a review of Justin Kaplan's *Walt Whitman* in *Gay Community News*, Vol. 8, No. 29, February 1981 book supplement.

20. Ann Douglas, in *The Feminization of American Culture*, discusses the evolution of these masculinist ideals within the context of a radically changing culture. Her chapter on Herman Melville is particularly insightful.

21. Martin, *The Homosexual Tradition in American Poetry*, p. 230, n. 93.

22. Whitman, *Democratic Vistas*, in *The Portable Whitman*, p. 369.

23. Whitman, "When I heard at the close of the day," in *The Portable Whitman*, p. 196.

24. Whitman, "Song of Myself," in *The Portable Whitman*, p. 95.

25. Plato, *Symposium*, p. 47.

26. *The Omega Workshops* by Judith Collins gives a brief but comprehensive history of many of these ideas and details how they affected the artistic theories of many people connected with the Bloomsbury Group.

27. *Sex, Politics and Society* by Jeffrey Weeks and *Socialism and the New Life: The Personal and Sexual Politics of Edward Carpenter and Havelock Ellis* both address the question of the middle class suffrage movement and its differences with the more radical socialist feminist movements.

28. Carpenter, *Iolaus*, pp. 37-39.

29. The questions of sexuality and same-sex bonding among women are discussed in Lillian Faderman's *Surpassing the Love of Men*, Nancy Cott's *The Bonds of Womanhood*, and "The Female World of Love and Ritual" in *A Heritage of Her Own* edited by Nancy Cott and Elizabeth H. Pleck. Research on male friendship and sexuality has been done by Martin Duberman.

30. Coote, *The Penguin Book of Homosexual Verse*, p. 228.

31. *ibid.* p. 228.

32. Katz, *Gay American History*, p. 341.

33. *ibid.* p. 342.

34. *ibid.* pp. 348-349.

35. *ibid.* pp. 349-350.

36. Kaplan, *Walt Whitman*, p. 45.

37. Grosskurth, *The Woeful Victorian*, p. 273.

38. Katz, *Gay American History*, p. 351.

39. quoted in Weeks, *Coming Out*, p. 53 from *Walt Whitman* by John Addington Symonds.

40. In *Imagining America*, Peter Conrad describes the reactions of English travellers to America and the differences between their expectations and reality.

41. Grosskurth, *The Woeful Victorian*, p. 217.

42. Coote, *The Penguin Book of Homosexual Verse*, p. 218.

43. Katz, *Gay American History*, p. 346.

44. Weeks, *Coming Out*, p. 54.
45. *ibid.* p. 54.
46. Katz, *Gay American History*, p. 352.
47. Symonds, *Male Love*, p. 87.
48. *ibid.* p. 88.
49. *ibid.* p. 101.
50. Katz, *Gay American History*, p. 356.
51. Robinson, *The Modernization of Sex*, pp. 2-3.
52. By stirring up the public with exaggerated and sensational yellow journalism, Labouchere created a climate of anti-sexual hysteria which totally obscured any real issues. It was under this reign of terror that he sponsored the anti-homosexual laws which remained on the books for almost 80 years. This same tactic, of using real *heterosexual* abuses to rationalize passing anti-gay legislation, especially in cases of inter-generational sexual activity, is still used by politicians and the media today.
53. Hyde, *The Cleveland Street Scandal*, p. 17.
54. Williams, *Culture and Society 1780-1950*, p. xiv.
55. Brophy, *Prancing Novelist*, p. 6.
56. Woolf, *A Room of One's Own*, p. 102.
57. Isherwood, *Christopher and His Kind*, p. 12.
58. Mitzel in *Fag Rag*, No. 20, p. 12.
59. "Notes on Camp" by Susan Sontag in *Against Interpretation*, pp. 275-277.
60. *ibid.* p. 277.
61. *The Oxford English Dictionary*, p. 3796.
62. Mitzel in *Fag Rag* No. 20, p. 12.
63. Anderson, *Eros*, p. 332.
64. Reade, *Sexual Heretics*, p. 362.
65. *ibid.* pp. 360-362.
66. *ibid.* pp. 63-67.
67. *ibid.* p. 425.
68. Jenkyns, *The Victorians and The Ancient Greeks*, p. 286.
69. Rowbotham, *Socialism and the New Life*, p. 88.
70. quoted in Reade, *Sexual Heretics*, p. 428.
71. quoted in *ibid.* pp. 106-107, from "Eudiades."

72. Barrie, *The Plays*, p. 33.
73. *ibid.* p. 94.
74. Moers, *The Dandy*, pp. 16-20.
75. Wilde, *The Soul of Man Under Socialism*, pp. 229, 240, 271.
76. Croft-Cooke, *The Unrecorded Life of Oscar Wilde*, p. 118.
77. Hyde, *Famous Trials: Oscar Wilde*, p. 18.
78. *ibid.* p. 17.
79. Brophy, *Prancing Novelist*, p. 83.
80. from *Concerning the Eccentricities of Cardinal Pirelli*, by Ronald Firbank, in *The Complete Firbank*, p. 671.
81. from *The Flower Beneath the Foot*, by Ronald Firbank in *The Complete Firbank*, p. 499.
82. from *Vainglory*, by Ronald Firbank in *The Complete Firbank*, p. 213.
83. Lear has been relegated to the excusable realm of a "children's writer" (i.e. not to be taken seriously). There are several biographies, but no serious studies of his life or writings. The fact that he was an accomplished landscape artist and naturalist is generally unknown. Pioneering work has been done on Lear's life and his gay sensibility by San Francisco historian Alan Berube.
84. Like Lear, Saki (H.H. Munro) has been dismissed by literary critics as a minor writer. *Saki: The Life of Hector Hugh Munro* is the first authoritative biography. A. J. Langguth deals with Munro's sexuality in a forthright and honest manner, using it to explicate not only Saki's writing but the part it played in the social and literary world of the time.
85. Green, *Dreams of Adventure, Deeds of Empire*, p. 222.
86. Woolf, *A Room of One's Own*, p. 102.
87. King, *E.M. Forster and His World*, p. 57.
88. "Edward Carpenter and the Double Structure of *Maurice*" by Martin, in *Literary Visions of Homosexuality*, edited by Stuart Kellog, pp. 35-46.
89. Green, *Children of the Sun*, p. 143.
90. Coward, *Three Plays*, p. 227.
91. Coward, *Diaries*, p. 103.
92. Isherwood, *Down There on a Visit*, p. 14.
93. Martin, *The Homosexual Tradition in American Poetry*, pp. 90-114.

94. *Imre: A Memorandum*, published in Italy in 1906 by Xavier Mayne, (a pseudonym for Edward Prime Stevenson) an American, is a novel which sheds light on turn-of-the-century gay relationships. *The Female Impersonators* and *Autobiography of an Androgyne* by Earl Lind are fascinating accounts of both popular and scientific thinking about sex and gender. They also describe underground urban sexual networks during the early 20th century.
95. Much of the writing on Van Vechten's life avoids speaking of his sexuality. Bruce Kellner's *Carl Van Vechten and the Irreverent Decades*, for example, is a good study of his work but does not deal with sexuality. *Bessie*, the biography of blues singer Bessie Smith by Chris Albertson, does mention Van Vechten and deals in passing with his homosexuality as well as the sexuality of many of the people involved with the growth of black music and culture.
96. Lewis, *When Harlem Was in Vogue*, p. 157.
97. " 'Taint Nobody's Bizness' " by Eric Garber in Smith, *Black Men/White Men*, p. 11.
98. Chris Albertson on the album cover of *Straight and Gay*, Stash records.
99. Fox, *Showtime at the Apollo*, p. 181.
100. *When Harlem Was in Vogue* by David Levering Lewis is a detailed study of the Harlem Renaissance and its interaction with white culture. Lewis, however, is very hesitant to say much about the role of homosexuality in people's lives, and while he never quite lies, he avoids the topic as much as possible.
101. "Capitalism and Gay Identity" by John D'Emilio in *Powers of Desire*, edited by Ann Snitow *et al*, pp. 100-116.
102. "Coming Out Under Fire" by Alan Berube in *Mother Jones*, Vol. VII, No. 11, p. 23.
103. Adair, *Word Is Out*, pp. 60-61.
104. Louis Hyde, in *Rat and the Devil*, has collected the letters of Matthiessen and his lover Russell Cheney. The letters give a good picture of their relationship, but only by implication describe the broader context in which both men lived as homosexuals.
105. Tobin, *The Gay Crusaders*, p. 94.
106. Ehrenreich, *The Hearts of Men*, p. 24.
107. John D'Emilio's *Sexual Politics, Sexual Communities* is an

excellent history and analysis of the pre-Stonewall gay/homophile movements.

108. *ONE*, July 1959, p. 55.

109. *Mattachine Review*, January/February 1955.

110. *ONE*, June 1958, p. 29.

111. Ehrenreich, *The Hearts of Men*, p. 49.

112. *Seeing Is Believing* by Peter Biskind is a fine analysis of the changes in American culture as seen through 1950s films. *Running Time* by Nora Sayre is also very good; her analysis is specifically political, and she makes connections between images of deviant (especially homo) sexuality, and the communist threat.

113. "Out of the Closets, Into the Streets" by Allen Young in *Out of the Closets*, edited by Jay and Young, p. 22.

114. "A Gay Manifesto" by Carl Wittman in *Out of the Closets*, edited by Jay and Young, p. 330.

Movies: Hollywood Homo-Sense

1. "At the Movies With George Mansour" by Mitzel and Michael Bronski, in *Gay Community News*, May 19, 1979, Vol. 6, No. 42, pp. 7-8.

2. Patrick, Robert, *Kennedy's Children*, p. 19.

3. "Notes on Camp" by Susan Sontag in *Against Interpretation*, p. 279.

4. In *The Celluloid Closet*, Vito Russo has unearthed a huge, hidden, gay film history. Perhaps the most common coded gay male characters were presented as "sissies," the implication being that they were dislocated in gender as well as in sexuality.

5. Goldman, *The Season*, p. 4.

6. Patrick, Robert, *Kennedy's Children*, p. 60.

7. Molly Haskell's *From Reverence to Rape* and Margery Rosen's *Popcorn Venus* are excellent, popular analyses of the changing role of women in film. Joan Mellen's *Big Bad Wolves* is an attempt to analyze the changing images of men in the American film, but is terribly flawed by homophobia and a reluctance to break away from the most sexist gender identifications. Both Donald Spoto's *Camer-*

ado and Michael Malone's *Heroes of Eros: Male Sexuality in the Movies* are fine accounts of male iconography and the changing social contexts in America. If a bit short on theory, they are all well written and full of illustrations.

Theater: The Third Sex and the Fourth Wall

1. Helbing, *Directory of Gay Plays*, p. 12.
2. In *Scotch Verdict*, Lillian Faderman explicates the real life version of Hellman's play. It is interesting to note the differences between the actual and the dramatized stories. Faderman's book dwells upon the position of women and its significance in the court room. The changes which Hellman made for *The Children's Hour* reflect prejudices that were as strong in 1933 as they were in 1811, the time of the original incident.
3. Eells and Musgrove, *Mae West*, p. 67.
4. Coward, *Three Plays*, p. 21
5. Lahr, *Coward the Playwright*, p. 73.
6. Coward, *The Lyrics of Noel Coward*, p. 129.
7. Porter, *The Complete Lyrics of Cole Porter*, p. 214.
8. Londre, *Tennessee Williams*, p. 3.
9. Inge, in Gassner, *Best Plays Third Series*, p. 257.
10. *Harvey* by Mary Chase, in Gassner, *Supplementary Plays*.
11. Van Druten, in Gassner, *Best Plays Third Series*, p. 597.
12. *ibid*. p. 598.
13. Mordden, *The American Theater*, p. 220.
14. Anderson, in Gassner, *Best Plays Fourth Series* p. 313.
15. "Not What It Seems: Homosexual Motif Gets Het Guise" by Howard Taubman in *The New York Times*, November 5, 1961, sec. 2, p. 1.
16. "Who's Afraid of Little Annie Fanny?" by Gene Marine in *Ramparts* 5: 27-30, February 1967.
17. Kauffmann, *Persons of the Drama*, p. 294.
18. *ibid*. p. 293.
19. Goldman, *The Season*, p. 237.
20. "The Play That Dare Not Speak Its Name" by Philip Roth in *New York Review of Books*, 4: 4, February 25, 1965.

21. Wetzsteon, in the *Village Voice*, May 17, 1976, p. 87.
22. Wilson, Doric, in *The Advocate*, No. 264.
23. Personal interview.
24. Brustein, R., in *The Nation*, Vol. 189, No. 2, p. 3573, July 11, 1983.

Opera: Mad Queens and Other Divas

1. "Opera Queens: The Season Cometh" by Ivan Martinson in *Christopher Street*, issue 76, Vol. 7, No. 4, p. 58.
2. As one might expect, there is no documented proof of this in written histories of the Metropolitan Opera. Whatever it may lack in "objective" truth, however, the story is a widely accepted piece of gay history as evidenced by *The Advocate* cartoon reproduced here.
3. Opera seems to have a natural affinity for the aesthetics of Wilde. In *The Artist as Critic*, he wrote: "All art is immoral. For emotion for the sake of emotion is the aim of art, and emotion for the sake of action is the aim of life."
4. Kleinberg, *Alienated Affections*, p. 39.
5. "Coming Out to Opera" by Michael Bronski in *Gay Community News*, Vol. 9, No. 20, December 5, 1981, music supplement, p. 1.
6. Reyna, *A Concise History of the Ballet*, p. 26.
7. Kolodin, *The Metropolitan Opera*, p. 3.
8. *ibid.* p. 5.
9. *ibid.* p. 9.
10. Goldsmith, *Little Gloria...Happy at Last*, see chapters concerning the trial.
11. This cultural schizophrenia has become quite common since feminism has given more social permission to criticize men and male influence upon culture. Although heterosexual men are in many cases at fault, blame is often placed upon gay men because they are considered "unnatural" and suspicious to begin with. The dynamic involves investing gay men with a kind of power and control which they simply do not have in reality, and this in turn is a prelude to placing more blame.
12. "A Bravo for Opera's Black Voices" by Harold Schoenberg in *The New York Times Magazine*, January 17, 1982, p. 26.

13. *ibid.* p. 80.

14. Popular myths surrounding black male sexuality are as strong in the "high arts" as they are anywhere. Black male sexuality is perceived as threatening and animalistic even within the stylized form of opera. Ballet has been even more restrictive, the popular notion being that "modern dance" and more "athletic" forms of movement are better suited for people of color.

Gay Publishing : Books and Periodicals

1. John D'Emilio's *Sexual Politics, Sexual Communities* is, again, the best source on the early homophile movement and its publications.

2. *ONE*, June 1958, p. 29.

3. "The Destroyers Strike!" was an editorial in *The Advocate*, February 28, 1973, No. 106.

4. *ibid.*

5. Ehrenreich, *The Hearts of Men*, p. 49.

6. Mainstream novels with gay male themes and characters were becoming more popular at this time. Interestingly, there was a mass outpouring of pulp paperback novels which dealt with lesbians. Many of these were pure trash, but some (especially those written by Ann Bannon and Ann Aldrich) were well written and sympathetic accounts. There was no comparable publishing of gay male pulps probably because there was no perceived "gay market" for the books. The lesbian pulps were intended for straight men even though many lesbians read and continue to read them.

Gay Publishing: Pornograpny

1. Love, *Gay Whore*, p. 117-8.

2. Woolf, Virginia, *A Room of One's Own*, p. 102.

3. Blade, *The Barn*, afterword.

4. *ONE*, March 1957, p. 9.

5. *ONE*, March 1957, pp. 16-17.

6. *ONE*, March 1956, p. 6.

7. *Report of Commission on Obscenity*, pp. 354-379.
8. Morgan, *Going Too Far*, p. 169.
9. Barry, *Female Sexual Slavery*, p. 226.
10. *ibid.* p. 175.
11. "The Difference Between Pornography and Erotica" by Gloria Steinem in *Ms.*, November 1978, p. 53.
12. "Is the Gaze Male?" by E. Ann Kaplan in Snitow ed., *Powers of Desire*, pp. 309-27.
13. Barry, *Female Sexual Slavery*, p. 175.
14. The mass appeal, and revulsion towards, the alleged "snuff" film of the late 1970s was partly due to the fact that this dichotomy was supposedly broken down. Because so much attention was focussed upon whether a woman was *actually* killed during the making of the movie, few people commented that marketing the film as if this were true was also offensive.
15. Sontag, *On Photography*, p. 85.

Gay Publishing: Advertising

1. Kinsey, *Sexual Behavior in the Human Male*, pp. 610, 659
2. When less traditional forms of women's clothing, such as pants-suits, came into fashion, critics claimed that this more "masculine" look was "dykey." The charge was used only to slur and there was no implication that lesbians were influencing women's fashions. This was just another case of lesbian invisibility: admitting a lesbian influence would have meant admitting lesbian existence.
3. "What Does Soft Core Pornography Really Mean to Gay Men?" by Michael Bronski in *Gay Community News*, Vol. 5, No. 29, p. 6.
4. "Tapping the Homosexual Market" by Karen Stabiner in *The New York Times Magazine*, May 2, 1982, p. 34.
5. "On Second Thought..." in *The Advocate*", No. 65, August 4-17, 1971. p. 1.
6. "Tapping the Homosexual Market" by Karen Stabiner in *The New York Times Magazine*, May 2, 1982, p. 82.
7. Hardy, *Boy Crazy*, p. 54.

Part III: The Theory of the Pleasure Class

1. Victorian sexuality was not as repressed as is commonly believed. Steven Marcus' *The Other Victorians* gives a good analysis of how and why sexuality and pornography flourished under repressive ideology. *The Worm in the Bud* by Ronald Pearsall details the habits and mores of Victorian sexuality with particular emphasis upon the attendent negative impact it had upon both the private and social selves. Peter Gay's *The Education of the Senses* (the first in a projected series entitled *The Bourgeois Experience: Victoria to Freud*) attempts to re-examine and reconstruct a healthy and sex-positive image of sexuality during this period. While not entirely successful, the book does encourage a new discourse on sexuality and the Victorian sensibility.

2. The connections between "individualism" and "art" can also be seen in the gradual acceptance of creativity as an expression of the self: the individual making a personal statement in the face of social anonymity. The now-cliched phrase "this is how I *really* feel" to describe a just-finished painting or poem would have been without a context until these aesthetic theories were well-entrenched in the culture.

3. *Mattachine Review*, May 1959. p. 10.

4. The debate on gay people and the Cuban revolution is covered extensively in the "Cuba: Gay as the Sun" chapter of *Out of the Closets* by Young and Jay. The discussion is updated and extended in Young's *Gays Under the Cuban Revolution*.

5. "The Myth of the Vaginal Orgasm" by Anne Koedt in *Voices from Women's Liberation*, ed. by Leslie Tanner.

6. Morgan, *Going Too Far*, p. 176.

7. Fritz, *Dreamers and Dealers*, pp. 83-111.

8. Morgan, *Going Too Far*, p. 180.

9. "Speaking Out" by Karen Lindsey in *Gay Community News*, Vol. 4, No. 21, November 20, 1976, p. 5.

10. Raymond, *The Transsexual Empire*, p. 104.

11. Morgan, *Going Too Far*, p. 181.

12. *ibid.* p. 235. John Stoltenberg takes this notion of women's relationship to S/M even further in his essay, "Sadomasochism: Eroticized Violence, Eroticized Powerlessness," in *Against Sado-*

masochism edited by Linden *et al.* He argues that women do not have the power to consent to sadomasochistic encounters because "a woman's compliance or acquiescence in sadomasochism is...entirely delusional and utterly meaningless. In no sense does she share in the man's privileged capacity to act." Besides being the latest man to tell women what they can and cannot do, Stoltenberg also blames the current discussion of S/M on gay men whose actions and thinking he describes as "tantamount to spitting in the face of women..."

13. Rich, *Of Woman Born*, p. 282.

14. Willis, *Beginning to See the Light*, p. 167.

15. "AIDS: The Gay Plague," a special pamphlet from *The Moral Majority Report*, 1984.

16. *ibid.*

17. Polanski, *Roman*, p. 28.

18. "Uses of the Erotic: The Erotic as Power" by Audre Lorde in *Take Back the Night*, edited by Laura Lederer, p. 298.

Bibliography

Adair, Nancy, and Adair, Casey. *Word is Out: Stories of Some of Our Lives*. New York: Delta Special/Dell, 1978.

Albertson, Chris. *Bessie*. New York: Stein and Day, 1972.

Altman, Dennis. *The Homosexualization of America, The Americanization of the Homosexual*. New York: St. Martin's Press, 1981.

Anderson, Patrick and Sutherland, Alistair (eds.). *Eros: An Anthology of Male Friendship*. New York: The Citadel Press, 1963.

Austin, Roger. *Playing the Game*. Indianapolis, IN: The Bobbs-Merrill Company, Inc., 1976.

Bailey, Derrick Sherwin. *Homosexuality and the Western Christian Tradition*. Hamden, CT: Archon Books, 1975.

Barrie, J.M. *The Plays*. New York: Charles Scribner and Sons, 1928.

Barry, Kathleen. *Female Sexual Slavery*. Englewood Cliffs, NJ: Prentice Hall, Inc., 1979.

Birkin, Andrew. *J. M. Barrie and the Lost Boys: The Love Story That Gave Birth to Peter Pan*. New York: Clarkson N. Potter, 1979.

Biskind, Peter. *Seeing is Believing: How Hollywood Taught Us to Stop Worrying and Love the Fifties*. New York: Pantheon Books, 1983.

Blade. *The Barn 1948 and Other Dirty Pictures*. New York: Stompers and the Leslie-Lohman Gallery, 1980.

Boswell, John. *Christianity, Social Tolerance and Homosexuality*. Chicago: University of Chicago Press, 1980.

Brophy, Brigid. *Mozart the Dramatist*. New York: Harcourt, Brace and World, 1964.

_____*Prancing Novelist: In Praise of Ronald Firbank*. New York: Barnes and Noble, 1973.

Carpenter, Edward (ed.). *Iolaus: An Anthology of Friendship*. New York: Pagan Press, 1982.

Collins, Judith. *The Omega Workshops*. Chicago: University of Chicago Press, 1984.

Conrad, Peter. *Imagining America*. New York: Oxford University Press, 1980.

Coote, Stephen (ed.). *The Penguin Book of Homosexual Verse*. New York: Penguin Books, 1983.

Cott, Nancy. *The Bonds of Womanhood*. New Haven, CT: Yale University Press, 1977.

_____ and Pleck, Elizabeth H. (eds.). *A Heritage of Her Own*. New York: Simon and Schuster, 1979.

Coward, Noel. *The Lyrics of Noel Coward*. Woodstock, NY: The Overlook Press, 1978.

_____ *Plays: Three*. London: Methuen, 1965.

_____. *Three Plays by Noel Coward*. New York: Dell Publishing, 1965.

Croft-Cooke, Rubert. *The Unrecorded Life of Oscar Wilde*. New York: David McKay Company, Inc. 1972.

D'Archy Smith, Timothy. *Love in Earnest: Some Notes on the Lives and Writings of English "Uranian" Poets from 1889 to 1930*. London: Routledge and Kegan Paul, 1970.

D'Emilio, John. *Sexual Politics, Sexual Communities: The Making of a Homosexual Minority in the United States 1940-1970*. Chicago: University of Chicago Press, 1983.

Douglas, Ann. *The Feminization of American Culture*. New York: Alfred Knopf, 1977.

Dworkin, Andrea. *Pornography: Men Possessing Women*. New York: Perigree Books/G.P. Putnam and Sons, 1980.

Eels, George and Musgrove, Stanley. *Mae West*. New York, William Morrow, 1982.

Ehrenreich, Barbara. *The Hearts of Men: American Dreams and the Flight from Commitment.* Garden City, NY: Anchor Press/Doubleday, 1983.

Eisenstein, Zillah. *Feminism and Sexual Equality.* New York: Monthly Review Press, 1984.

Ellis, Havelock. *Psychology of Sex: A Manual for Students.* New York: Harcourt Brace Jovanovich, 1978.

Faderman, Lillian. *Scotch Verdict.* New York: Quill, 1983.

_____. *Surpassing the Love of Men.* New York: William Morrow and Company, 1981.

Fiedler, Leslie. *The Inadvertent Epic.* New York: Touchstone/Simon and Schuster, 1979.

_____. *What Was Literature?* New York: Simon and Schuster, 1982.

Fierstein, Harvey. *Torch Song Trilogy.* New York: The Gay Presses of New York, 1980.

Firestone, Shulamith. *The Dialectic of Sex.* New York: Bantam Books, 1971.

Firbank, Ronald. *The Complete Ronald Firbank.* London: Gerald Duckworth and Company, Ltd., 1961.

Fox, Ted. *Showtime at the Apollo.* New York: Holt, Rinehart and Winston, 1983.

Fritz, Leah. *Dreamers and Dealers: An Intimate Appraisal of the Women's Movement.* Boston, MA: Beacon Press, 1979.

Gassner, John (ed.). *Best American Plays, Third Series, 1945-1951.* New York: Crown Publishers, 1952.

_____. *Best American Plays, Fourth Series, 1951-1957.* New York, Crown Publishers, 1958.

_____. *Best American Plays: 1918-1958 Supplementary Volume.* New York: Crown Publishers, 1959.

Gay, Peter. *Education of the Senses*. New York: Oxford University Press, 1984.

_____ *Love and Death in the American Novel*. New York: Dell, 1960.

Goldman, William. *The Season*. New York: Bantam Books, 1970.

Goldsmith, Barbara. *Little Gloria...Happy at Last*. New York: Alfred Knopf, 1980.

Goodman, Paul. *Nature Heals: Psychological Essays*. edited by Taylor Stoehr. New York: Free Life Editions, 1977

Green, Martin. *Children of the Sun*. New York: Basic Books, 1976.

_____ *Dreams of Adventure, Deeds of Empire*. New York: Basic Books, 1979.

Grosskurth, Phyllis. *Havelock Ellis*. New York: Alfred A. Knopf, 1980.

_____ *The Woeful Victorian: A Biography of John Addington Symonds*. New York: Holt Rinehart and Winston, 1964.

Hardy, Karen. *Boy Crazy: An Intimate Look at Today's Rising Young Stars*. New York: Plume Books, New American Library, 1984.

Haskell, Molly. *From Reverence to Rape: The Treatment of Women in the Movies*. New York: Holt, Rinehart and Winston, 1974.

Helbing, Terry (ed.). *Directory of Gay Plays*. New York: JH Press, 1980.

Hyde, H. Montgomery. *The Cleveland Street Scandal*. New York: Coward, McCann and Geoghegan, 1976.

_____ *Famous Trials: Oscar Wilde*. Baltimore, MD: Penguin Books, 1962.

Hyde, Louis (ed.). *Rat and the Devil: Journal Letters of F. O. Matthiessen and Russell Cheney*. Hamden, CT: Archon Books, 1978.

Isherwood, Christopher, *Christopher and His Kind 1929-1939*. New York: Farrar, Straus and Giroux, 1976.

_____ *Down There on a Visit*. New York: Simon and Schuster, 1962.

Jay, Karla and Young, Allen. *Out of the Closets: Voices of Gay Liberation*. New York: World Publishing, 1972.

Jenkyns, Richard. *The Victorians and Ancient Greece*. Cambridge, MA: Harvard University Press, 1980.

Johnston, Jill. *Lesbian Nation: The Feminist Solution*. New York: Simon and Schuster, 1973.

Kaplan, Justin. *Walt Whitman: A Life*. New York: Simon and Schuster, 1980.

Katz, Jonathan. *Gay American History: Lesbians and Gay Men in the U.S.A.* New York: Thomas Y. Crowell Company, 1976.

_____ *Gay/Lesbian Almanac: A New Documentary*. New York: Harper and Row, 1983.

Kauffmann, Stanley. *Persons of the Drama: Theater Criticism and Comment*. New York: Harper and Row, 1976.

Kellner, Bruce. *Carl Van Vechten and the Irreverent Decade*. Norman, OK: University of Oklahoma Press, 1968.

Kellog, Stuart (ed.). *Literary Visions of Homosexuality*, No. 6 of book series, *Research on Homosexuality*. New York: Haworth Press, 1983.

King, Francis. *E.M. Forster and His World*. New York: Charles Scribner's Sons, 1978.

Kinsey, Alfred *et al. Sexual Behavior in the Human Male*. Philadelphia, PA: W. B. Saunders Company, 1948.

Kleinberg, Seymour. *Alienated Affections: Being Gay in America*. New York: St. Martin's Press, 1980.

Kolodin, Irving. *The Metropolitan Opera*. New York: Alfred Knopf, 1966.

Lahr, John. *Coward the Playwright*. London: Methuen, 1982.

Langguth, A.J. *Saki: A Life of Hector Hugh Munro.* New York: Simon and Schuster, 1981.

Lauritsen, John and Thorstad, David. *The Early Homosexual Rights Movement, 1864-1935.* New York: Times Change Press, 1974.

Lederer, Laura (ed.). *Take Back The Night: Women On Pornography.* New York: William Morrow and Company, Inc. 1980.

Lewis, David Levering, *When Harlem Was in Vogue.* New York, Vintage Books, 1982.

Lind, Earl. *Autobiography of an Androgyne.* New York: Arno Press, 1975.

_____ *The Female Impersonators.* New York: Arno Press, 1975.

Linden, Robin Ruth *et al. Against Sadomasochism.* Palo Alto, CA: Frog in the Well, 1982.

Londre, Felicia Hardison. *Tennessee Williams.* New York: Frederick Ungar Publishers, 1979.

Love, Jack. *Gay Whore.* San Diego: P.E.C. French Line Novel, 1967.

Malone, Michael. *Heros of Eros: Male Sexuality in the Movies.* New York: E. P. Dutton, 1979.

Marcus, Steven. *The Other Victorians: A Study of Sexuality and Pornography in Mid-Nineteenth Century England.* New York: Basic Books, 1966.

Martin, Robert K. *The Homosexual Tradition in American Poetry.* Austin, TX: University of Texas Press, 1979.

Mayne, Xavier. *Imre: a Memorandum.* New York: Arno Press, 1975.

Mellon, Joan. *Big Bad Wolves: Masculinity in the American Film* New York: Pantheon Books, 1977.

Merchant, Carolyn. *The Death of Nature.* New York: Harper and Row, 1980.

Millett, Kate. *Sexual Politics.* New York: Avon Books, 1969.

Moers, Ellen. *The Dandy: Brummell to Beerbohm*. New York: The Viking Press, 1960.

Mordden, Ethan. *The American Theater*. New York: Oxford University Press, 1981.

——————— *Better Foot Forward*. New York: Viking, 1976.

Morgan, Robin. *Going Too Far*. New York: Random House, 1976.

Patrick, Robert. *Kennedy's Children*. New York: Random House, 1976.

Payn, Graham and Morley, Sheridan (eds.). *The Noel Coward Diaries*. Boston, MA: Little, Brown and Comany, 1982.

Pearsell, Ronald. *The Worm in the Bud: The World of Victorian Sexuality*. New York: Penguin Books, 1969.

Plato. *The Symposium*. Baltimore, MD: Penguin Books, 1951.

Polanski, Roman. *Roman*. New York: William Morrow and Company, Inc., 1984.

Porter, Cole. *The Complete Lyrics of Cole Porter*. New York: Alfred A. Knopf, 1983.

Raymond, Janice G. *The Transsexual Empire: The Making of the She-Male*. Boston, MA: Beacon Press, 1979.

Reade, Brian. *Sexual Heretics: Male Homosexuality in English Literature from 1850 to 1900*. New York: Coward McCann, 1970.

The Report of the Commission on Obscenity and Pornography. New York: Bantam Books, 1970.

Reyna, Ferdinando. *A Concise History of the Ballet*. Translated by Pat Wardroper. New York: Grosset and Dunlap, 1964.

Rich, Adrienne. *Of Woman Born*. New York: W.W. Norton and Co., 1976.

Robinson, Paul. *The Modernization of Sex*. New York: Harper and Row, 1975.

Rosen, Marjorie. *Popcorn Venus: Women, Movies and the American Dream.* New York: Coward, McCann and Geoghegan, 1973.

Rowbotham, Sheila and Weeks, Jeffrey. *Socialism and the New Life: The Personal and Sexual Politics of Edward Carpenter and Havelock Ellis.* London: Pluto Press, 1977.

Russo, Vito. *The Celluloid Closet: Homosexuality in the Movies.* New York: Harper and Row, 1981.

Samois (eds.). *Coming to Power: Writings and Graphics on Lesbian S/M.* San Francisco, CA: Samois Collective, 1981.

Sayre, Nora. *Running Time: Films of the Cold War.* New York: Dial Press, 1982.

Smith, Michael (ed.). *Black Men/White Men.* San Francisco, CA: Gay Sunshine Press, 1983.

Snitow, Ann *et al.* (eds.) *Powers of Desire: The Politics of Sexuality.* New York: Monthly Review Press, 1983.

Sontag, Susan. *Against Interpretation.* New York: Delta Books, Dell Publishing, 1967.

_____ *On Photography.* New York: Farrar, Straus and Giroux, 1977.

Spoto, Donald. *Camerado: Hollywood and the American Man.* New York: Plume, New American Library, 1978.

Stone, Lawrence. *The Family, Sex and Marriage In England 1500-1800.* New York: Harper and Row, 1977.

Symonds, John Addington. *Male Love: A Problem in Greek Ethics and Other Writings.* Edited by John Lauritsen. New York: Pagan Press, 1983.

Tanner, Leslie (ed.). *Voices From Women's Liberation.* New York: New American Library, 1970.

Taylor, Barbara. *Eve and the New Jerusalem.* New York: Pantheon, 1983.

Teal, Donn. *The Gay Militants*. New York: Stein and Day, 1971.

Tobin, Kay and Wicker, Randy (eds.). *The Gay Crusaders*. New York: Paperback Library, Coronet Communications, 1972.

Weeks, Jeffrey. *Coming Out: Homosexual Politics in Britain from the Nineteenth Century to the Present*. London: Quartet books, 1977.

_____ *Sex, Politics and Society: The Regulation of Sexuality since 1800*. New York: Longman, 1981.

Whitman, Walt. *The Portable Walt Whitman*. edited by Mark Van Doren. New York: The Viking Press, 1973.

Wilde, Oscar. *The Artist as Critic: Critical Writings of Oscar Wilde*. Chicago: University of Chicago Press, 1969.

_____ *The Soul of Man Under Socialism and Other Essays*. New York: Harper and Row, 1970.

Williams, Raymond. *Culture and Society 1780-1950*. New York: Anchor Books, Doubleday and Company, 1959.

Williams, Tennessee. *Memoirs*. Garden City, NY: Doubleday Books, 1975.

Willis, Ellen. *Beginning to See the Light*. New York: Alfred A. Knopf, 1981.

Woolf, Virginia. *A Room of One's Own*. New York: Harcourt, Brace and World, Inc., 1957.

Young, Allen. *Gays Under the Cuban Revolution*. San Francisco, CA: Grey Fox, 1981.

Index

illustration and photo sources
(in order of appearance)

Richard Locke and Robert Adams in *Forbidden Letters*, used by permission of Artie Bressan
Garland at midnight recording session, from Bettmann Film Archives
Streishand, early engagement at "hungry i," by Craig Simpson
Garbo, studio portrait, by Clarence Sinclair Bull, used by permission of Alfred Knopf
Dietrich, publicity photo for *The Devil Is A Woman*, by William Walling Jr., used by permission of Alfred Knopf
Crawford, publicity photo for *No More Ladies*, by George Hurrell, used by permission of Alfred Knopf
West and Victor McLaglen in *Klondike Annie*, special collections, Doheny Library, University of Southern California
Roz Russell, dressed by Travis Banton, in *Auntie Mame*, © Warner Brothers, Inc.
Harvey Fierstein in *Torch Song Trilogy*, by Peter Cunningham
Doric Wilson's *Street Theater*, by R.A. White
Fierstein, Patrick, and Wilson at Pheobes, by Adam Craig
cartoon from *The Advocate*, 1972, used by permission of *The Advocate*
cartoon from *Relax! This Is Only a Phase You're Going Through* (St. Martin's Press), by Chuck Ortleb and Rick Fiala, used by permission of Chuck Ortleb
cartoon from *The Advocate*, 1972, used by permission of *The Advocate*
Gay Community News cover, 1981, used by permission of *Gay Community News*
Richard Locke, Fred Halsted, Mike Morris, and Jared Benson in *El Paso Wrecking Corp.*, directed by Joe Gage, 1979, by Richard Lyle
Richard Locke and Robert Adams in *Forbidden Letters*, used by permission of Artie Bressan
cartoon from *The Advocate*, 1973, used by permission of *The Advocate*

cover collage:
Billy Holliday, from the Carl Van Vechten photo collection, Yale
mastheads from *The Advocate*, *Gay Community News*, and *Fag Rag* used by permission
"Two Men" by Tom of Finland
Judy Garland, from the Underwood News Photo Archives

Grateful acknowledgement is also made to Overlook Press for permission to quote lyrics from Noel Coward's "Mad About the Boy."